The Time Was At Hand

An exposition of the major prophetic revelations found in the Bible, particularly those in the New Testament.

Things which must shortly come to pass . . .
for THE TIME IS AT HAND (Revelation 1:1, 3).

Things which must shortly be done . . .
for THE TIME IS AT HAND (Revelation 22:6, 10).

Robert Finley

PRESS

The Time Was At Hand

Printed in the United States of America

ISBN 9781600349690

All Bible quotations are from the King James Version of 1611, except for occasional personal translations by the author.

www.xulonpress.com

With deep appreciation to Cynthia, my loving and faithful wife, who devoted long hours during nights and weekends transcribing my manuscripts. Her enthusiastic endorsement of the need for and contents of each chapter supplied abundant inspiration and encouragement.

CONTENTS

.

Chapter 1

What this Book is all About

The Book of Revelation begins and ends with the phrase, THE TIME IS AT HAND. We must necessarily conclude, therefore, that the contents of the book deal primarily with events that were about to take place at that time.

In the Four Gospels of the New Testament, our Lord Jesus Christ is repeatedly quoted as saying that Jerusalem was going to be destroyed and that He was going to unleash retributive justice upon those who condemned Him to death.

On Palm Sunday, **When He was come near He beheld the city, and wept over it, saying, The days are coming when your enemies shall dig a trench about you, and encircle you, and shut you in on every side, and lay you even with the ground, and your children within you; and they shall not leave within you one stone upon another because you knew not the time of your visitation** (Luke 19:41-44). In the Apocalypse, our Lord revealed to the Apostle John that **the time was at hand** for His earlier prophecies to be fulfilled.

Why were the murdered Messiah's prophecies about the coming **days of vengeance** [when] **there shall be great distress in the land and wrath upon this people** (Luke 21:22-23) postponed for thirty-six years? In this book, I give the answer as it is revealed in Revelation. And explain that THE TIME WAS AT HAND for the fulfillment of those fateful words: **When ye shall see Jerusalem**

compassed with armies, know that the desolation thereof is nigh (Luke 21:20).

So this volume is essentially an exposition and interpretation of certain portions of the New Testament which contain prophecies concerning events that would occur in the future. I believe that most of those events were fulfilled in that generation, climaxed by three-and-a-half years of civil war in Palestine from 66 to 70 A.D., and the destruction of Jerusalem by Roman legions. These things were repeatedly foretold by our Lord Jesus Christ as the time of His crucifixion drew near.

Although prophecies in the New Testament are concerned primarily with events that would take place IN THAT GENERATION (40 years), they are not limited to that period. As I shall explain, many passages foretell events that would occur throughout the 2000 years that followed, climaxed by the second coming of our exalted Redeemer.

More than 90% of the prophecies found in the Old Testament had been fulfilled by the time the promised Messiah was identified by John the Baptizer, who was the last of the Old Testament prophets. And the other 10% were fulfilled by the time our Saviour was crucified and risen again. So that final 10% had to do primarily with the Messiah's life and ministry, as well as His death and burial, followed by His resurrection, coronation and exaltation as **King of all kings and Lord of all lords**.

So, likewise, at least 90% of the prophecies found in the New Testament have already been fulfilled. In future chapters I explain how that although most New Testament prophecies had their fulfillment in that generation, there are others which foretell the **falling away** of the churches, which began in the fourth century, the coming of **the Antichrist** in the seventh century, and other historic events to be climaxed by the **glorious appearing of our great God and Saviour, Jesus Christ.**

This book has been written with the conviction that the Old Testament and the New Testament are a unique and distinct revelation from Almighty God to the people of our planet. I quote it with confidence and authority, believing it to be the very Word of the Living God.

For this reason, I have put quotations from the Scriptures in bold face type to emphasize the source of the teaching or information being presented. Also, from time to time I have capitalized words or phrases for added emphasis.

The only English translation being quoted directly is the *Authorized Version* which was first published in 1611. Since it was authorized by James I in 1604, it is commonly called the *King James Version* (KJV). Although in some instances the language may seem archaic to modern readers, I prefer it because the translators attempted to make a word-for-word translation of the original Hebrew and Greek texts, even if they did not understand the meaning of it. Modern translators have usually tried to determine the meaning and then put into English what they think it is. In so doing, they often miss what the Scriptures are actually saying.

In 1962 my good friend and former co-worker (with InterVarsity Christian Fellowship), Ken Taylor, gave me a carton of his newly published *Living Letters* and asked me to try to help him find buyers for them. He also asked me to give him my opinion of his "paraphrase" translation. After reading it my response was to quote a nursery rhyme:

> *There was a little girl who had a little curl*
> *Right in the middle of her forehead;*
> *And when she was good she was very, very good,*
> *But when she was bad she was horrid.*

That's how I would summarize Kenneth Taylor's *Living Bible*. Most of it is very, very good, but a few portions fail to communicate the true meaning.

The same could be said of every other modern translation. If the translator has correctly perceived the meaning of the text, his English equivalent may be quite good. But all too often those who have produced new English translations within the past century have made serious errors because they have not correctly perceived what was originally communicated.

No translation of the Bible is perfect, not even the KJV. All have been made by fallible human beings. So I have taken the liberty of occasionally inserting my own translation of some words. Wherever my quotations of Bible verses deviate from the KJV, it means that I have substituted my own alternative translation for clarity. I took courses in Greek at the University of Virginia for three years (1941-44) and began reading the New Testament in the original Greek almost daily in 1943. I have continued to read it regularly for more than sixty-five years. For assistance with some words I often use *Thayer's Greek-English Lexicon of the New Testament* which was completed by J. H. Thayer of Cambridge, Massachusetts, in 1885 and published by Harper & Brothers in 1886. I have also made frequent use of *Alford's Greek Testament* in four volumes with a total of 2823 pages. My copy, which I have owned for more than fifty years, was published in London by Gilbert & Rivington in 1863.

As to Greek texts, I prefer the *Textus Receptus* (Received Text) which was used by Martin Luther for the first translation into German as well as the translators of the KJV. A later edition of the *Received Text* was edited by F. H. A. Scrivener and published by Cambridge University Press in 1894.

For many years I have also owned Greek New Testaments using other texts as well, such as those edited by Westcott & Hort (1881) and Eberhard Nestle (1904). I often use a revision of Nestle's text done by G. D. Kilpatrick, Erwin Nestle and other scholars in 1958. For final verification of the authenticity of the original Greek, I have found the *Majority Text* to be very useful. Edited by Zane C. Hodges and Arthur L. Farstad, my copy is the Second Edition published in 1985 by Thomas Nelson, Inc. Where slight variations occur in available manuscripts, editors of the *Majority Text* have done an excellent job in seeking to determine which is most likely to be the original.

For understanding the Old Testament, I have found *The Septuagint* translation into Greek to be a valuable adjunct. Made by seventy (actually seventy-two) Hebrew scholars in Alexandria, Egypt, beginning around 285 B.C., it provides helpful insights into the meaning of Hebrew expressions in the Old Testament. However, like all other translations, it is not perfect and must be read with the understanding that it also was done by fallible humans.

One trap which I have avoided is that of ascribing late dates to the books of the New Testament. When I was a graduate student at the University of Chicago, I noticed how my liberal professors were determined to teach that the New Testament books were all written near the end of the First Century, or even later. It was obvious to me that they were doing so deliberately in order to discredit the authorship of books as ascribed in their titles.

Take Matthew for example. They wanted me to believe that it was a compilation of stories which had been collected by church leaders and edited around the year 100. I didn't buy it. Matthew the Apostle is not mentioned in Acts beyond the first chapter. I believe the reason is that he devoted himself to writing down in the Hebrew language a record of our Lord's ministry, and then making copies for distribution. It would have taken up all of his time for several years. In any case, I am confident that the first Hebrew manuscript of Matthew's Gospel was completed no later than the year 32 A.D.

By ascribing a later date my liberal professors used their theories to deliberately undermine the credibility of the contents of the book. It was a ploy similar to that of my undergraduate professors of biology and geology at the University of Virginia. They would deliberately ascribe, without evidence, early dates to fossil remains in order to bolster their arguments for the theory of evolution.

My liberal professors at the University of Chicago would say that the first Epistle of Peter was probably written around 80 or 90 A.D. by someone other than Peter. But the opening verses, addressed to **the strangers scattered abroad**, are a clear indication that Peter wrote (dictated to a scribe) it around 32 A.D. It was sent to the many Hebrew believers from foreign lands who had been with Peter in Jerusalem until **there was a great persecution against the church which was at Jerusalem, and they were all scattered abroad except the apostles** (Acts 8:1).

The contents of the Book of Revelation clearly demonstrate

that it was written in the year 65 or 66 A.D. But copies were not widely distributed at that time. Writing materials and parchment scrolls must have been difficult to obtain on the sparsely settled island of Patmos. So when some of the church fathers saw copies for the first time about forty years later, they may have presumed that it had been written near the time they first saw it.

Sadly, some evangelical scholars have fallen for the late date authorship which liberals have promoted. I heard two of them on *The John Ankerberg Show* arguing against the early authorship of Revelation which had been claimed by Hank Hanegraaff in *The Apocalypse Code.* One of their arguments focused on Revelation 2:4 where our Lord expressed displeasure with believers at Ephesus for having **left their first love.** They were saying that the church at Ephesus wasn't started until after 50 A.D., so there wouldn't have been enough time for their love to cool.

If those dear brothers had studied the *Acts of the Apostles* they would have read how pilgrims from Asia had turned to Christ in Jerusalem on the day of Pentecost, and then were **scattered abroad** (Acts 8:1-4) back to their homes in Asia. Soon thereafter Peter sent a letter of encouragement to those who were scattered, including believers in Asia (I Peter 1:1). The **seven churches in Asia** mentioned in Revelation were undoubtedly started by those returning pilgrims no later than 32 A.D. The Apostle Paul wanted to visit them a few years later but he was **forbidden by the Holy Spirit** (Acts 16:6) because God wanted him to go to Macedonia where no churches had been planted up until that time. However, around the year 45 Paul did visit the saints at Ephesus and left Aquila and Priscilla there to minister in the church (Acts 18:18-19). Apollos had already come to Ephesus by that time (Acts 18:24-28), and was further instructed in the faith by Aquila and Priscilla.

So when our Lord told John that the believers in Ephesus had **left their first love,** He was undoubtedly speaking of the second generation which had grown up during the years since the first assembly of believers had gathered there around 32 A.D.

As I will explain later, I am convinced that internal evidence indicates how the Apocalypse must have been written no later than 65 or 66 A.D. because it speaks of things that were about to take place at that time.

I make no apology for doing my own translation of the Scriptures. Many of the best were done by individuals, including those of John Wycliffe, William Tyndale, Martin Luther and, yes, even Ken Taylor (when he gets it right). I sincerely hope that I may always get it right, and pray that God will forgive me if I get it wrong.

I also pray that those who read the Scriptures quoted in this book will receive what they say without prejudice. Many receive what they like and reject what does not please them. **God is love** may be liked by some who are offended by **God is angry with the wicked every day** (Psalm 7:11). Some will accept **The Lord is merciful and gracious, longsuffering and forgiving** (Exodus 34:6-7) but reject **The wrath of God is revealed from heaven against all ungodliness and unrighteousness of men** (Romans 1:18).

About fifty years ago I was invited to teach one session of a missions class at Wesley Theological Seminary in Washington. As background, I described the difference between God's people under the Old Covenant and under the New. Whereas we are now sent into all the world **as lambs in the midst of wolves** to bear witness for Christ, during the Old Testament period God gave the Israelites a less difficult environment. To avoid being corrupted by neighbors, He told them to drive out the Canaanites and occupy their land. As I said that, a student interrupted me, saying, "That's not my God, then." He wanted God to conform to his own preconceptions regarding the presumed "rights" of the Canaanites.

Most of the prophetic teachings of the Bible concern the ancient Israelites, and some rather harsh things are said about them, along with other comments that are more favorable. If we quote the negative sayings, some overly sensitive souls may be offended, perceiving that in some way we are casting a bad image of those whom in our day we fondly call "The Jewish People." But I can see no reasonable way that such an association can be construed. We will never understand prophetic Bible teachings unless we listen to what they say regarding the Hebrews of that period, none of which, in my opinion, have any relevance to the Jewish people of our day.

This book is intended primarily, but not entirely, for Christians who already have some knowledge of Bible prophecy as taught by evangelicals. Millions have read the promotions of political Zionism popularized in 1970 by Hal Lindsey in *The Late Great Planet Earth*. I enjoyed talking with him about its contents soon after it was first published. His response was that regardless of whether he was right or wrong, many persons had accepted Christ as a result of reading his book. I heartily agreed that was a good thing.

Even more millions have read the works of Tim LaHaye and Jerry Jenkins, known as the *Left Behind* series, published by Tyndale House beginning in 1995. As I said above, Ken Taylor, the founder of Tyndale House, and I were good friends sixty years ago, although we seldom talked about Bible prophecy. I say this to point out how important it is for Christians who are at different stages of growth and knowledge to respect one another and not let our disagreements embitter the sweetness of our fellowship in Christ.

I have included a great deal of repetition in this book, but it is intentional, not an oversight. The book is designed for use in seminaries, Christian colleges, Bible institutes, home study groups, Sunday school classes and other situations where individual chapters can be used as separate units for study and discussion. So it is essential that certain Bible verses, historical references and my commentary be repeated in various chapters, or even within a given chapter, to complete each one separately to deal with a specific subject. Therefore, as I said, these repetitions are intentional, not oversights.

I have avoided footnotes for a reason. I anticipate that this book will be translated into several major languages for use in Bible schools and seminaries throughout the world, so for maximum simplicity I prefer that there be no footnotes. In our day the verification of information is more widely available than in previous times. The development of Google and other internet search engines makes it possible for the reader to have information from all the world's libraries at his fingertips.

Another consideration regarding footnotes has to do with the availability of information regarding certain historical references. From childhood I have been blessed with having a photographic memory. Even at my present age I can clearly recall things I read many years ago, and hardly a day goes by but what I read still more. I never read fiction, but devour history books with relish.

For example, about twenty-five years ago the library of a church of which I was pastor had an excellent book on the history of religions. I vividly recall reading in that book an excellent account of how most of the Hebrew population of Palestine converted to Islam in the Seventh Century. As I began work on THE TIME WAS AT HAND, I wanted to quote some things I had read in that history book. But someone had removed (borrowed?) it from the church library and it could not be found. So I cannot quote it directly, but do repeat some things it said. Incidentally, if the one who "borrowed" that book happens to read this, I hope he or she will let me know where it is now. It has about 250 pages, is medium sized with a hard red cover and was published about a century ago. Thank you.

My point is that in this book I have included a great deal of historical information which has been stored in my memory during 65 years of continual reading and research. But to document the specific sources of all that information would be impossible.

Many of the persons mentioned in this book have long since departed this life, but I have avoided using the term "the late." One reason is because I hope the book will be in use for many years after even more of us have gone to be **with the Lord**.

My intended audience will likely be familiar with specialized terms, such as "the tribulation period," and "the rapture of the church." However, if the subject of prophecy is new to you, and you come to a term with which you are not familiar, keep reading and you will eventually find it explained. Most of these concepts are already familiar to Christians who attend churches that emphasize, as I do, the premillennial second coming of our Lord Jesus Christ.

15

In a later chapter I will show that there is no mention, hint or suggestion anywhere in the New Testament that events in the land of Palestine (most of which is now called the state of Israel) have anything to do with our Lord's return. Those who so teach derive all their Scripture references from the Old Testament. And most of the verses they use had their fulfillment before the first coming of the Messiah, as I will explain later.

So is this another one of those "date-setting" volumes like many others which have all proved to be wrong, going back for many centuries?

Actually, no. Just the opposite.

In Revelation 1:3 and 22:10 we are told that **the time is at hand** for some of the events predicted there. Bible teachers who project those events into the future are in serious error. Most (but not all) of the Apocalypse is about events which AT THAT TIME **must shortly come to pass** (Revelation 1:1, 22:6).

I have chosen **THE TIME WAS AT HAND** as the title for this volume because in the first and final chapters of Revelation we are told that the time had arrived THEN for events being revealed to John. So keep reading, and when in later chapters I explain some of Revelation to you, I think you will see it as clear as a bell.

Chapter 2

Why this Book is Needed

Really?

Another book needed on Bible prophecy, with hundreds in print already?

That's just it. Most of those "other books" are leading evangelical Christians astray from some of the most basic teachings of the New Testament. This book aims to win them back.

Worse yet, some of those "other books" are promoting political activism that is contributing to an increase in persecution and suffering for our fellow believers in many parts of Asia and Africa. And have caused evangelical missionaries to be put out of many countries where few churches exist.

Powerful political lobbies have been organized by evangelicals in efforts to push the U.S. Government toward fulfillment of their interpretations of Bible prophecy. Prominent evangelical leaders have publicly urged the U.S. Congress and President to send armed forces to attack other countries. And to use billions of dollars extracted from American taxpayers to finance socialistic programs and imperialistic ambitions of another country.

Other billions have been collected by churches and evangelical organizations to assist and promote political causes which they perceive to be a fulfillment of prophecy. And a large measure of these dollars have been illegally claimed as "tax-deductible."

Erroneous interpretations of biblical prophecy have stirred up hatred toward particular religious and ethnic groups in many countries, and the victims of that hatred have retaliated in kind, bringing untold suffering upon Christian minorities in those places. Whereas native Christian missionaries were formerly welcomed and appreciated for their compassion and ministries of mercy, now they are resented and persecuted because of their identification with American evangelicals who promote controversial political agendas as being the fulfillment of prophecy.

And while 50 years ago there was a great enthusiasm for world evangelism and foreign missions among American evangelicals, millions have now been distracted, and have rather turned their attention to dubious political causes which hinder the work of Christ instead of helping it.

Still, a flood of prophecy promotion continues to be poured forth within the churches, in radio and TV broadcasts, through the internet, and in print media from ten thousand sources.

So, I say, it's time for me to add my voice to the very few among evangelical Christians who dare to express a dissenting view to this never-ending chorus of political propaganda which has permeated our churches during the past half-century.

Erroneous teachings linked to prophecy have also hurt the spiritual life of millions of evangelical Christians. In a manner similar to that which misled new believers mentioned in Paul's Epistle to the Galatians, thousands of Bible teachers have caused a return to the Old Testament in denial of the New Covenant revealed through our Lord and Saviour. Over and over in the New Testament we are told that God **is no respecter of persons**, and that in His sight **there is no difference between the Judaean** [Jew] **and the Greek** (Romans 10:12) because all are sinners in need of salvation. Our Lord told a Judaean Pharisee named Nicodemus that **except a man be born again** by the Holy Spirit **he could not see the kingdom of God**. But today's prophecy teachers, in denial of New Testament revelation, are saying that millions of unsaved people have a special relationship with God, no matter how deep in sin their lives may be.

18

The New Testament Messiah also told that Hebrew Pharisee that an unbeliever **shall not see** [eternal] **life, but the wrath of God abides on him** (John 3:36). But in denial of this clear proclamation, certain prophecy teachers are now saying that thousands of professed atheists have a covenant relationship with God, even though they may deny that He exists.

The New Testament warns us about being led away from the **spirit of truth** by **the spirit of error** (I John 4:6); and those teachers who are leading immature Christians back under the Old Testament are causing immeasurable damage to the spiritual lives of their followers.

Here let me say that God's revelation in the Old Testament is of tremendous value for all Christians. During that period He demonstrated that all men are dead in sins, unable to keep His Law or merit His favor. Thus every man and every woman on this earth deserves God's righteous judgment and, according to Moses, is under His curse. Moses said, **Cursed be he that confirms not all the words of this law to do them** (Deuteronomy 27:26). But none have been able to keep that law in their own strength. There is only one way that this curse can be lifted, and that is by faith in the sacrificial **Lamb of God** who was **made a curse for us** (Galatians 3:13).

In Deuteronomy Chapters 27 and 28 Moses pronounced more than 50 different curses that would befall the Israelites if they failed to keep God's law. True, he also promised corresponding blessings, but they are always conditional. Failure to meet God's conditions under the Old Testament law would always negate the promised blessings. But, strangely, certain Christian Bible teachers of the past century have ignored this truth. They pronounce unlimited blessings to a certain group of unsaved people regardless of whether or not God's conditions have been met. Such teachings are a denial of the clear declarations of God's word in the Old Testament as well as the New.

The Old Testament repeats God's curses against sinful men from beginning to end. The first curses are in Chapter Three of

Genesis and the final one is the very last word of the Old Testament (Malachi 4:6). No one is spared, because all are sinners who stand condemned before a holy God. That's why we are told in Romans 3:22-23 that **there is no difference, for all have sinned and come short of the glory of God.** But certain teachers of Bible prophecy talk as though events and revelations of the New Testament had never happened. They are telling their followers that God does make a difference between unsaved people, based on their ethnic origin. Before you finish reading this book you will see the fallacy of this error, as well as some of the tragic results it has brought upon millions of people.

Most important of all, I trust you will come to understand the one prophetic event that really matters. In fact, I'll tell you now what it is. You will find it in the 24th Chapter of Matthew.

Our Lord had come to Jerusalem to offer up His life as a sacrifice for our sins, in fulfillment of the symbolism of animal sacrifices that were taking place in the temple. While there, some of His disciples wanted to show Him the magnificent buildings of the temple but, sadly, He had to tell them that those buildings were going to be destroyed. The angel Gabriel had foretold this event to the prophet Daniel five centuries earlier. Gabriel told Daniel that when **Messiah the Prince** came He would be killed **to make reconciliation for iniquity,** after which certain people would **destroy the city and the sanctuary** [temple] (Daniel 9:26). The **Lamb of God** knew that when His death for our sins took place **the veil of the temple** would be **rent in twain from the top to the bottom** (Matthew 27:51), and animal sacrifices would serve no further purpose. He knew also that He would arise from the dead to become our heavenly **High Priest**, and that all who believed in Him would also be **priests with direct access into the Holy of Holies**, which is **Heaven itself** (Hebrews 10:19-22). The earthly temple was but **a figure of the true** (Hebrews 9:24).

So the temple in Jerusalem would become meaningless when our Saviour and High Priest entered Heaven **with His own blood**. Therefore the earthly temple would have to be destroyed. That's one reason why Christ said, sadly, **There shall not be left here one stone upon another, that shall not be thrown down** (Matthew 24:2).

The disciples were frightened at His words, no doubt fearful of retaliation from the chief priests of the temple. But around that time He had been teaching them not only about His approaching death but also of His resurrection, ascension and second coming in power and great glory. So privately they asked Him two questions: 1) **When shall these things be?** and 2) **What shall be the sign of your coming and of the end of the age?** No doubt they thought He was going to destroy the temple at His second coming. But they were wrong. It would be done in their generation.

The Lord Jesus answered their second question first (verses 4-14), the one about **the sign of His** [second] **coming**. Then, beginning with verse 15, He answered their first question about **these things**, the destruction of the temple. To help them distinguish between **these things** (the destruction of Jerusalem) and His second coming, He explains further beginning with Verse 26 and then contrasts the two events back and forth to the end of the chapter. I will clarify these verses later.

So what is the sign of His coming? I have a deep feeling of sadness when I hear my Christian brothers and sisters saying that wars, famines, earthquakes, false messiahs, pestilences and persecution are signs of His coming. What He said was just the opposite. All such events have been going on for 2000 years. None are signs of His return. He listed them for the express purpose of saying that they were not signs of His coming again.

Regarding His return to this earth, our Lord gave only one sign: **This gospel of the kingdom shall be preached in all the world for a witness unto all nations; and then shall the end come** (verse 14). No other signs are given in the New Testament.

I have often expressed this truth when speaking to student audiences, praying that they might be motivated to become involved in foreign missions. But my emphasis has not always been appreciated by faculty members who have returned to the Old Testament in their thinking. After I had given an impassioned plea to the student body of a Bible college in Philadelphia about 50 years ago, some of the faculty backed me into a corner to straighten me out on my teaching.

"That verse [Matthew 24:14] is not for today," they said. "This is the church dispensation, not the age of the kingdom. The gospel of the kingdom will be preached by 144,000 Jews during the tribulation period after the church has been raptured. The gospel of the kingdom in the New Testament is for Jews only. In the church age we preach only the gospel of grace."

"Then please tell me," I asked, "who is the chief spokesman of the gospel of grace for the church age in the New Testament?"

"Oh, it's the Apostle Paul, of course," they replied.

"Then I'm afraid you haven't really studied what Paul was preaching," I said, as I proceeded to tell them that the very last verse of the Book of Acts leaves Paul in Rome, near the end of his ministry, **preaching the kingdom of God.** He told the elders of the church at Ephesus that for three years he had worked among them **preaching the kingdom of God** (Acts 20:25,31). Twenty-one times in The Acts and in his epistles, Paul speaks of believers being in relation to the **kingdom of God**, or the **kingdom of His dear Son**, or the **kingdom of Christ**.

"Yes," the returnees to the Old Testament will say, "but while Paul was speaking of the kingdom of God, in Matthew it's the kingdom of heaven." They try to make a distinction between the two.

Here again is a sad example of lack of knowledge. Identical passages in the synoptic Gospels have **the kingdom of God** in Mark and Luke, while Matthew has **kingdom of the heavens.** It should be obvious to anyone who has done research on ancient manuscripts that Matthew was originally written in the Hebrew language and would not use the "divine name." At that time the Hebrews avoided its use due to their legalistic perception of the Old Testament. That's why in our Greek translation of Matthew we usually find **kingdom of the heavens** instead of kingdom of God. I once heard Michael Rood say in his television program that he had found untranslated copies of the original Hebrew manuscripts of the Gospel of Matthew in a library in Saint Petersburg, Russia.

So when the disciples wanted to know what sign to look for regarding their Lord's return, He gave them only one sign: that in Matthew 24:14, repeated in Mark 13:10 as **THE GOSPEL MUST FIRST BE PUBLISHED AMONG ALL NATIONS.** Other events (tribulation, wars, persecutions, earthquakes, etc.) have no relevance regarding His second coming.

So to gain insight into when Christ will come again, we should watch the spread of the kingdom of God among unreached nations. In the Bible a "nation" is an ethnic group having a distinct culture and their own language. According to National Geographic magazine, over 6000 nations are generally recognized throughout the world. A witness for Christ may be found among probably 4000 of them. So there is still much work to be done to complete our Lord's eternal purpose regarding the many nations of people on this planet.

The coming of the Messiah marked a new beginning in God's dealings with human beings, as the Book of Hebrews states repeatedly: **He taketh away the first, that He may establish the second** (Hebrews 10:9). **The law and the prophets were until John** [the Baptizer]: **since that time the kingdom of God is preached** (Luke 16:16).

Essentially, the kingdom of God is this: **Our citizenship is in heaven** (Philippians 3:20); **We are strangers and pilgrims on the earth** (Hebrews 11:13, I Peter 2:11). So, in contrast with the Old Covenant kingdom of David, the New Covenant kingdom of the **Son of David** is non-political. Whereas the kingdom of David had an earthly government and territory, citizens of the New Covenant kingdom are dispersed among all nations, **as lambs in the midst of wolves** (Luke 10:3). Our King said, **My kingdom is not of this world: if my kingdom were of this world, then would my servants fight** (John 18:36). From the time of Moses onward under the Old Covenant there was continual fighting and killing. Then Christ came, **not to destroy men's lives, but to save them** (Luke 9:56).

Now then we are ambassadors for Christ (II Corinthians

5:20). During the 22 years I lived in Washington, I was frequently invited to receptions at foreign embassies. As I entered the impressive gates of one on Massachusetts Avenue, I left my own country and entered the United Kingdom. Once inside those gates I was on foreign soil. The ambassador was not there to fight with the USA, or to change it. His sole purpose was to represent the kingdom of Her Majesty, Queen Elizabeth. His citizenship was in Great Britain. He was a stranger and a pilgrim within that embassy compound, surrounded by people outside whose interests and loyalties were different from his. That's what it means to belong to the kingdom of God, except that we don't isolate ourselves from those around us. We **go into all the world and preach the gospel to every creature**. There was no parallel to this under the Old Covenant.

Also, in contrast with the Old Covenant, the kingdom of God does not recognize ethnic origin. **There is no difference** [between nationalities]**, for all have sinned** (Romans 3:22-23). **There is no difference between the Judaean and the Greek . . . the Scripture hath concluded all under sin** (Romans 10:12, Galatians 3:22). All men are sinners, and stand condemned before our Holy God. The giving of the Law under the Old Covenant was to establish that fact, and demonstrate the necessity for the **Lamb of God** to be sacrificed in order that those who believe in Him might be **reconciled to God**.

From the time the Messiah died for us and rose again, a person's ancestry meant absolutely nothing in the sight of God. Prophecy teachers who are trying to lead people back under the Old Covenant by making a distinction among people based on their ancestry do so in denial of God's revelation under the New Covenant. I repeat, our Lord told **a ruler of the Judaeans and a teacher in Israel, Nicodemus**, that regardless of his ancestry he was **condemned already** (John 3:18), and that the **wrath of God abides on him** (John 3:36) unless he believes in the Son of God and is **born again** (John 3:3). **All men are dead to God** (Romans 5:12) until they are reconciled to Him by faith in Christ and **made alive** (Ephesians 2:1-6) by His Holy Spirit. The whole point of the Old Testament was to demonstrate these facts. And those who are trying

24

to convince people otherwise today do so in denial of both the Old Testament and the New Testament.

The Eighth and Ninth Chapters of the Book of Hebrews explain how the New Covenant (foretold in Jeremiah 31:31), based on the new birth by the Holy Spirit, would render meaningless the Old Covenant based on natural birth by the flesh. **In that He sayeth, A new covenant, He hath made the first old. Now that which decayeth and waxeth old is ready to vanish away** (Hebrews 8:15). How sad that immature Bible teachers are trying to bring it back.

When the kingdom of God came with power on the Day of Pentecost, and the Holy Spirit baptized those disciples into one body, then and there God ended forever any and all distinctions among people based on their human ancestry, even though those disciples did not fully comprehend it at that time. It was revealed to Peter some time later when he went to the house of Cornelius and said, **Of a truth I perceive that God is no respecter of persons: but in every nation he that feareth Him, and worketh righteousness, is accepted of Him** (Acts 10:34-35).

The full revelation of this fact was given later through the Apostle Paul, who wrote, **In Christ Jesus neither circumcision availeth anything, nor uncircumcision, but a new creature** (Galatians 6:15). In the kingdom of God, in Christ Jesus, **there is neither Greek nor Judaean [Jew}, circumcision nor uncircumcision, male nor female, Barbarian, Scythian, bond nor free, but Christ is all and in all; for ye are all one in Christ Jesus** [the son of Abraham], **and if ye be Christ's, then are ye Abraham's seed and heirs according to the promise** (Colossians 3:11, Galatians 3:28-29). And, regardless of his ancestry, until a man is born again into the kingdom of God by the Holy Spirit he is simply a lost soul, dead in sins, having no promise from God except new life in Christ if he repents and believes the gospel. Other Old Testament promises were canceled forever at the cross of Christ (Colossians 2:14).

I will provide more in-depth details on this subject in later chapters.

Chapter 3

Loving Words for our Jewish Friends, and Roman Catholics

A re the gentle citizens of Norway and Sweden upset when historians recount the murderous exploits of Viking raiders a millennium ago? Are the genteel people of Japan offended when they read accounts of the millions of Chinese killed, injured or displaced by the Japanese conquest and occupation of eastern China seventy years ago? Do we insult docile residents of Mongolia if we portray the horrors inflicted on millions of Asians and Europeans by Genghis Khan and his murderous horde eight hundred years ago? Will the amiable citizens of France hate us if we mention the Reign of Terror in 1793; or discuss the victims whose heads were chopped off by the guillotine; or the murderous, inhuman treatment of prisoners on Devil's Island? Will the football fans of Italy, who cheered their team to victory in the World Cup contest of 2006, vehemently protest against any who speak of the bloody events of 2000 years ago when Roman spectators cheered the slaughter of gladiators and other victims in the Colosseum?

I think not.

So will our Jewish friends be offended if we repeat what the Bible says about the ancient Israelites? Or the misdeeds of some Jewish people in more recent times? I hope and pray that none will be that unrealistic. But I also realize that many are very sensitive regarding any negative comments concerning those we fondly call "the Jewish people."

With good reason. Collectively, some Jews have suffered the brunt of physical and verbal abuse in many countries for many years. They have been made victims of stereotypes that have resulted in the innocent majority being punished for the offenses of the few. Many have died for no offense at all. So we can easily understand why some within the Jewish community are constantly on the lookout for anyone who may say unfavorable things regarding any Jewish person, or the Jewish people in general, even those who lived long ago.

But how far back should we go in being careful not to repeat negative comments regarding this ethnic group which some may regard as being special above other people?

How about Moses? Do we dare quote him? Seven times in the Torah he called the Israelites **a stiff-necked people**. Twelve times he accused Israel collectively of spiritual **whoredom**. No doubt if some of the Jewish extremists we have today were living then they may have accused Moses of being "anti-Semitic."

And that same dreaded label would have been laid on the prophet Ezekiel, who called Israel a spiritual whore no less than thirty-eight times. The prophet Hosea did likewise eleven times. Other Old Testament prophets including Isaiah, Jeremiah and Nahum also spoke of collective Israel as being a spiritual whore which **played the harlot** against God.

And that's only the beginning. Most of the Old Testament prophets condemned the Israelites for being, what Isaiah called, a **sinful nation, a people laden with iniquity** (Isaiah 1:4). And then he thundered out to those wicked sinners, **Hear the word of the Lord, ye rulers of Sodom, give ear unto the law of our God, ye people of Gomorrah** (Isaiah 1:10). It will be remembered that God destroyed those two cities for their extreme wickedness, and Isaiah said the Israelites were equivalent to them.

The prophets also promised blessings from God, but they were dependent upon repentance and future obedience of the law. As Moses said to the Israelites, **If thou shalt hearken diligently unto the voice of the Lord thy God, to observe and do all His**

commandments which I command you this day . . . all these blessings shall come upon thee (Deuteronomy 28:1-2). **But if thou shalt not hearken unto the voice of the Lord thy God, to observe and do all His commandments . . . all these curses shall come upon thee** (Deuteronomy 28:15). **And it shall come to pass, that as the Lord rejoiced over you to multiply you and do you good; so the Lord will rejoice over you to destroy you, and bring you to nought** (Deuteronomy 28:63).

It is recorded in the chronicles of the kings of Israel that Pekah, the son of Remaliah, king of Israel, **smote the Judaeans [Jews] with very great slaughter,** in that he killed 120,000 Judaeans in one day (II Chronicles 28:6). If I were a Jewish person I certainly would not want to be identified with any Israeli such as Pekah, a monstrous tyrant who slaughtered 120,000 Jews in one day. He was really an anti-Semitic Hebrew.

It has been my joy and privilege to develop personal friendships with many, many Jewish people during the past 68 years, especially during the 22 years I lived in Washington. I have known them as employers, classmates, fellow athletes, educators, neighbors, physicians, attorneys, landlords, journalists, financiers, and merchants. But I have never had an unpleasant experience with any Jewish person I have known. I cannot imagine any one of them conniving the way the sons of Israel did 4000 years ago. By lying, deceit and trickery they murdered every man in the city of Shalem, then took all their wives for use as concubines, their children to be slaves, and stole all of their property (Genesis 34:15-29). I cannot believe that any of my Jewish friends would kill another man in order to take that man's wife, but that's what King David did, even though he had several wives already. Or attempting to kill his own father for personal gain, as Absalom, David's son did. Or having 700 wives and 300 concubines as King Solomon did. Or killing his own half-brother as Solomon did because that brother wanted a girl that Solomon had planned to add to his personal harem (I Kings 2:13-25).

The way Israelites lived 4000, 3000 or 2000 years ago has

nothing whatsoever to do with the Jewish people of today. To make such an association would be like identifying Queen Victoria or Queen Elizabeth with earlier kings and queens of England who were continually killing anyone who stood in their way.

Having made this point clear, I must also mention the fact that during times of war and military conquest, the genteel people of any nation can become murderous villains. The most refined *Dr. Jekyll* can morph into a *Mr. Hyde* rapist or terrorist at any moment. Nowhere has this been more evident than in Palestine since 1933, including both Jewish immigrants and native Palestinians. Hundreds of thousands of conscientious Jews inside and outside of Israel have vigorously protested against inhumane treatment of Palestinians by their fellow Jews. But this aberration does not in any way cast an unfavorable reflection upon Jewish people elsewhere in the world, or even upon a majority of those now living in Israel. And terrorist attacks against Israelis by Palestinian Muslims should not be construed as justification for condemning other Muslims, such as Muhammad Ali or Kareem Abdul-Jabbar.

We should note here that the ancient Israelites were not necessarily worse in the sight of God than other nations. The main point of the Old Testament period was to demonstrate that all men are sinners in need of salvation. The whole world of mankind was in rebellion against the Creator, and their only hope for reconciliation was for the Son of God to come and take their sins upon Himself, thus to pay the price for their guilt and shame. Only then could any man have peace with God. Prophecies in the Old Testament pointed forward to His coming, and the sinful Israelites were the one nation God was using to show why there was no other way. The problem was that **The heart is deceitful above all things, and desperately wicked** (Jeremiah 17:9). The Hebrews were wicked sinners the same as all other people on earth at that time. All were in need of a Saviour to reconcile them to God.

The prophets also explained that God would not be righteous unless He judged and punished those who sinned against Him, including the Israelites. And the main thrust of most prophecies in both the Old Testament and the New Testament has to do with God's judgments upon the Hebrews for their sin and rebellion. John the Baptizer, last of the prophets under the Old Covenant, said to the Pharisees and Sadducees, **O generation of vipers, who hath warned you to flee from the wrath to come** (Matthew 3:7). The subject matter of this book deals to a great extent with **the wrath of God** that was coming when He executed a terminal judgment upon the Hebrew nation. Over and over in the Four Gospels we are told that Jerusalem was going to be destroyed and that the Hebrew people would go through a time of tribulation worse than they had ever experienced before. But it didn't happen right away. It was delayed almost forty years, and finally came beginning in the year 66 A.D. This book explains why it was delayed, and tells some of the things that happened when, finally, God declared **THE TIME IS AT HAND** (Revelation 1:3, 22:10) for that judgment to fall.

My point in this chapter is to remind our Jewish friends that the fearful retribution of Almighty God upon the Hebrews of that generation is in no way related to or a reflection upon the Jewish people of today. I can see no connection whatsoever. So please do not say that either the Old Testament or the New Testament prophecies are "anti-Semitic." The characters are nearly all Semitic Hebrews. Chief among them is **Jesus the Christ, the son of David, the son of Abraham** (Matthew 1:1); and, most importantly, **the Son of God** (Mark 1:1).

New Testament prophecies also foretell events to come in the centuries that followed, which would necessarily include Roman Catholics. I have Catholic friends and even relatives who don't want to believe that 900 years ago their church sponsored murderous crusades during which hundreds of thousands of people were butchered in the name of God. Or that Popes instigated "the Inquisition" to torture and burn alive many thousands of nonconformists who could not, in good conscience, subscribe to the doctrines of the Vatican. I am convinced that many forthcoming (but now past) events in church history were foretold in the New Testament, and that we must consider them if we are to understand

31

biblical prophecy.

But prophecies concerning Catholicism during the "dark ages" of medieval church history should in no way be interpreted as an unfavorable reflection upon Roman Catholics living today. Things have changed dramatically since those evil days, and I do not find any New Testament prophecy which relates to Catholicism of the present time. So please don't brand me as being anti-Catholic. I'm simply trying to teach what I believe was included when a voice said to John, **Come up hither, and I will show you things which must be hereafter** (Revelation 4:1).

But before going further, let me share with you a bit about how, by God's grace, I have grown in knowledge over the past 69 years to arrive at my present level of understanding of His Word and the facts of history. God has arranged things so that every person who is saved from eternal death by faith in Christ must begin his or her spiritual life as a newborn babe. How much we grow from that point is determined by our consecration to God, our study of His Word, by the influence of our fellow believers and many other factors. There is no limit to how much we can grow, because the truth of God is inexhaustible.

I rejoice in the Lord that after 69 years as a believer I am still learning and still growing. As we mature we must lay aside some of the errors we picked up in our spiritual childhood and replace them with new knowledge gained from God's Word. I hope you will read the next chapter in its entirety to help you understand where I am coming from in the things I am teaching.

Chapter 4

My Pilgrimage in Pursuit of Prophecy Perception

My first exposure to Bible prophecy occurred more than seventy years ago (around 1934) when some nice ladies came unexpectedly to our family farm in Virginia and told my mother about a monstrous calamity called "Armageddon" which could break forth upon the earth at any moment. They warned her that she faced inevitable destruction unless she joined up with them. At the inquisitive age of twelve I listened in awe as these ladies kept saying, "It's right here in the Bible." My mother, a nominal Presbyterian, didn't buy it, although after they left she did comment that these visiting strangers "were very sincere." She said they were called *Jehovah's Witnesses*.

Prophecy was never mentioned in the boring sermons we endured whenever our father dragged some of his eight children off to the Presbyterian church in Charlottesville aboard our Model-T Ford truck (we didn't own a car). A decisive year in my life came when I was fourteen. Due to my father's illness I stayed out of school for a year to work on the farm: milking cows, feeding chickens, growing crops and cutting the firewood that was our only source for heat, cooking and cash income. I was virtually alone all day while my siblings were in school, and from time to time began to read a pocket-sized New Testament which my Aunt Mary, a school teacher, had given to me.

At first it fascinated me, then I became frightened by prophetic passages such as Matthew 24, Mark 13, Luke 21 and the Apocalypse (Revelation). At that time I was so shy that I could not bear to let anyone know what was happening in my life. I was praying continually in secret, seeking to find meaning and purpose to life on this earth, and beyond. Out on a pasture hill alone one starry night I received a clear revelation similar to what God gave to Abraham: **Get thee out of thy country . . . from thy father's house, unto a land that I will show thee** (Genesis 12:1). Included was an indication that I should go toward the south. No one knew that these things were happening in my life.

Soon after graduation from high school I arose before daybreak one morning and walked down to the gravel road that led to Charlottesville. The first car that came along offered me a ride into town, where I stood for a while on Route 29, going south. Soon a fellow came along who picked me up and gave me a ride into North Carolina, over 200 miles away. Two weeks and many rides later I arrived in Miami, about as far south as I could go.

There a series of events took place which can only be explained as supernatural. God had picked out numerous key persons whom He placed in my pathway, each one specially fitted to meet me where I was in spiritual growth and lead me on step by step toward maturity in faith and the knowledge of God's Word.

Up until this time I knew next to nothing about assurance of salvation by grace through faith. I had never met an evangelical Christian who could testify of having been born again. My chief direction came from Luke 10:1-9 where our Lord sent out seventy disciples to proclaim **the kingdom of God is come nigh unto you.** I was burning with zeal to urge people to save their souls by doing good works and joining a church. I found a job working in a parking lot during the day and went to a church meeting wherever I could find one almost every night. I didn't know the difference between a Protestant and a Catholic or a modernist and a fundamentalist. I visited every kind.

One night I went to hear a lecture (on socialistic politics) at

Trinity Methodist Church, Northeast First Avenue and Third Street in Miami. Just as the proceedings started, a young fellow came in and sat down beside me. When it was over he introduced himself as Bernard Bowker from Binghampton, New York. He was a recent graduate of Practical Bible Institute there, and had come to Miami looking for work. He had found a cheap place to stay directly across Sixth Street from the parking lot where I was working. And he was the first born again evangelical I had ever met in my life.

Bernie and I spent many hours together, and from him I learned the difference between those who, at that time, were called "fundamentalists" (true believers) as opposed to "modernists" who were not Bible believers but denied many basic truths of the Scriptures. Bernie told me that I should be going to a fundamental church, and he soon found one: Shenandoah Presbyterian on S.W. Eighth Street. When he first took me there he said, "Look at all the young people," a rare sight in churches during those days.

Daniel Iverson, the pastor, was a graduate of Moody Bible Institute in Chicago who preached the Bible as being the Word of God. And at that church I was introduced to a whole new world of faith and love among born again, Bible believing Christians who were not ashamed of the gospel of Christ. It became my spiritual home for almost two years.

At Shenandoah Church I was introduced to Bible prophecy for the first time, always from what was called a "dispensationalist" point of view. Pastor Iverson would bring in speakers from Moody and other Bible institutes, as well as from Dallas Theological Seminary and from missions that worked among Jewish people. A chief emphasis of many of them was to point out how Bible prophecies were being fulfilled "in our day" (1940). So I began to study the subject with great interest, eagerly believing all that these dispensationalist teachers were saying.

A new friend in Shenandoah Church gave me my first *Scofield Reference Bible*, and I began to eagerly follow the notes in it, especially those dealing with prophecy. Whenever I won another fellow to Christ, I would include teachings on "the seven dispensations" when I discipled him. I read every book on prophecy that I could temporarily borrow. And my new-found friends in Christ urged me to attend Dr. Thompson's Bible class, which I did every Monday night for almost a year.

Harry Thompson was a retired Presbyterian evangelist who had been a disciple of C. I. Scofield and other dispensationalists. He was teaching the book of Zechariah, and was telling us that almost all the prophecies there were yet to be fulfilled during the coming "tribulation period." He continually talked about "Israel" as though nothing had changed regarding the Hebrew nation of Old Testament times. I dutifully accepted all he was teaching us, strange though it seemed to me at the time.

I had found a new, better-paying job in the city of Miami Beach, where about 90% of the 50,000 winter season residents were Jewish people. Most of those for whom I worked were multi-millionaires. Humanly speaking, they were great people to work for -- friendly, honest and generous. But they showed no interest in the things of God. I never did see a synagogue in Miami Beach, although no doubt there must have been a couple of them there. Almost everyone was preoccupied with earthly things: money, business, pleasure, friends and family. Yet Dr. Thompson was teaching that these were God's chosen people, who would soon fulfill the prophecies of Zechariah. So I had to believe him even though, from a spiritual point of view, I could detect no essential difference between the Jews and the general population of unsaved people in the Miami area.

One Sunday in 1940, when Pastor Iverson was away, Dr. Thompson was asked to preach at Shenandoah Church. His subject was the soon-coming seven year period of "great tribulation." But, he said, we Christians would be taken away in the rapture of the church before it happened, and those left behind would suffer, especially the Jews. He called it **the time of Jacob's trouble,** based on Jeremiah 30:7. It caused me to worry about all those nice Jewish people I had met at their palatial homes on the island of Miami Beach.

Another man who had a great influence on my life during

my two years in Florida was Clifton L. Fowler, founder of Denver Bible Institute (now Colorado Christian University) and one of the co-founders of Independent Fundamental Churches of America (IFCA). Due to heart problems he had to give up living in high altitudes and at the age of 60 had relocated to Miami to live in retirement. One Wednesday night he was the guest speaker at Shenandoah, and when I approached him with questions he quickly perceived my hunger for the Word of God and added me to his company of personal disciples. He was much in demand as a Bible class teacher and I went to hear him often, as did Bernie Bowker. Frequently he gave us rides back to where we were staying, and taught us along the way. I still have several of his books which he gave me, one of which is BUILDING THE DISPENSATIONS, published in 1940, the year he gave it to me.

Unique in that book, he wanted me to see, was that he had eliminated the "Dispensation of Promise" taught by Scofield and others. They had generally taught that "God's Dispensations" covered seven periods of human history. They were:

1. Innocence – Adam and Eve in the Garden of Eden.
2. Conscience – from expulsion from the Garden to the Flood of Noah.
3. Government – after the Flood to the Tower of Babel.
4. Promise – From the call of Abraham until the time of Moses.
5. Law – From the giving of the Law until the resurrection of Christ.
6. Grace, or Church Age – from the Day of Pentecost until Christ's return.
7. Kingdom – the Millennium Age, with Christ reigning on earth.

Dr. Fowler taught that there was no Dispensation of Promise. Instead, he said, the Dispensation of Law began with the call of Abraham and ended with the destruction of Jerusalem 70 A.D. But the Church Age, which he called "The Body" [of Christ] began on the Day of Pentecost, so there was an overlap of 40 years between the fourth and fifth dispensations, according to Fowler. He called this a "transition period," a concept which was unique to Dr. Fowler until that time.

Also unique was his teaching that the seven year "tribulation period" following the Church Age was to be the Sixth Dispensation. Other teachers had included it within the Church Age as a period of God's judgment on an evil world.

Throughout my Christian life I have always felt a deep debt of gratitude toward Clifton Fowler for the many precious hours he spent tutoring me in the Word of God, even though, by God's grace, I would later grow in knowledge to understand that he missed the mark in many of his interpretations of prophecy.

Although my Christian friends in Miami all urged me to go to a Bible institute or Christian college, God led me to return to my home town and enroll at the University of Virginia in September, 1941. None of my professors were evangelical Christians, so I wasn't brainwashed with specific dogmas as might have been the case in a fundamentalist school. I took courses in Greek for three years and began reading my New Testament almost daily in its original language, as I have continued to do for more than 65 years.

Out of 50 fellows living in my dormitory, eleven were Jewish students from wealthy families in New York and other cities. All professed to be atheists except one, who was from an Orthodox family. Two of my Jewish classmates would later become famous movie producers in Hollywood. At every opportunity I talked with these Jewish fellows about Christ, but none showed any interest in the gospel. Yet, according to my teachers in Miami, I was supposed to believe that all of them were "covenant people of God."

During three summer months of 1942 I went to Philadelphia and did missionary work full time, my first experience in Christian service with an organization. I worked for THE MILLION TESTAMENTS CAMPAIGN, founded and directed by Dr. George T. B. Davis. Along with two friends who were students at a Bible institute, I went door to door distributing New Testaments to Jewish people, who tended to live next to one another in various sections of the city.

Dr. Davis was an "evangelical Zionist." His goal, as I understood it, was to place New Testaments into the hands of Jewish people so that after the rapture of the "church" (meaning all born again Christians), these Jews would be converted to Christ through reading those Testaments. Those who believed would then be part of 144,000 Jews who were destined to preach the gospel of Christ's kingdom during the coming "Tribulation Period." Or so said Dr. Davis.

As I was told, Dr. Davis was not Jewish himself, but his wife was. He had married her after she believed in Christ. Among the numerous books and articles which Dr. Davis published was one entitled SEEING PROPHECY FULFILLED IN PALESTINE. It had to do with how some Jewish people were leaving Europe to go live in Palestine. He had written it after he and Mrs. Davis had spent seven weeks there in 1937. He was impressed with changes being implemented by Jewish settlers who had recently arrived in Palestine as immigrants from other countries. *All this modern development of Palestine,* he wrote, *is the growing fulfillment of the predictions of the Old Testament prophets.* I was a baby Christian at that time, so it was only natural that I would accept everything Dr. Davis was teaching, and use it enthusiastically in trying to win Jewish people to Christ in Philadelphia. Later, as I grew in knowledge, I would learn that all of those prophecies had been fulfilled either in the days of Ezra and Nehemiah, or during the CENTURY OF RESTORATION that began with the Maccabee brothers in 165 B.C. I would also come to understand why Dr. Davis wrote that what he saw was the fulfillment of OLD TESTAMENT prophecies only. There is no mention, hint or suggestion anywhere in the NEW TESTAMENT regarding "Jews going back to Palestine."

Dr. Davis wrote that the dramatic increase in the number of Jewish people in Palestine after 1933 must have surely been by the hand of God. Little did he realize that it was a gift from the government of Germany which arranged for 60,000 Jews to emigrate to Palestine beginning in 1933. In addition, the German government also gave one hundred million dollars ($100,000,000) to the Zionist colony in Palestine: adjusted for inflation, that's about two billion. These actions were documented in great detail by the award-winning Jewish reporter, Edwin Black, in a 400 page book,

The Transfer Agreement, published by Carroll & Graf in 1984.

In 1942 I had no knowledge of what was actually happening in Palestine, and now I realize that Dr. Davis didn't either. He wrote, *The period from 1933 to 1935 was a time of unparalleled prosperity; new people flocked into Tel Aviv and new industries were started.* Page 97 of his book is taken up by a full page photograph of a shipload of prosperous immigrants arriving from Germany at the port of Jaffa. Some of the 60,000 Germans who emigrated to Palestine in 1930's were quite well-to-do, and all were allowed to take their assets with them. Dr. Davis never mentioned the benevolence of Adolph Hitler and the German government in this development.

In keeping with Dr. Davis' teaching, I tried to tell the Jewish people in Philadelphia that one proof of the truth of the Bible was "the Jews going back to Palestine." While it was true that many thousands of Jewish people had emigrated there from Europe since 1930, I did not realize at that time (1942) how many more had come to the "promised land" of America than had gone to Palestine. Some of them, such as Albert Einstein of Germany, Enrico Fermi of Italy and Edward Teller of Hungary, were brilliant physicists who played a major role in the production of the first atomic bomb. From among the tens of thousands of Jews who emigrated to America, hundreds rose to prominence as scientists, physicians, investment bankers, stock brokers, merchants, writers, actors, movie producers, musicians and many other vocations through which they profoundly influenced the culture of the country.

It is well known that the Roosevelt administration, in which many prominent posts were filled by Jewish persons, was very helpful in enabling European Jews to emigrate to America. When I tried to tell one recent immigrant (who could barely speak English) about the Messiah, she responded excitedly, "Yes, the Messiah has come! His name is Rosenveldt!"

Many thousands of Jewish people who came from Europe before the outbreak of World War II did so by coming as tourists to attend the New York World's Fair in the spring and summer of 1939, and then staying on in America rather than returning to

Europe. Those who did not already have relatives to take them in were, nevertheless, absorbed into Jewish communities in New York, Chicago, Los Angeles, Washington and other cities. I met hundreds of them sitting on front porches in Jewish neighborhoods of Philadelphia reading Yiddish newspapers or other materials in European languages which I could not understand.

For three months in the summer of 1942, sometimes for ten hours a day, five days a week, I was engrossed in conversation with Jewish people about the contents of the OLD TESTAMENT PROPHECY EDITION of the New Testaments which we were trying to give them. Each New Testament had quotations from the Old Testament at appropriate places to show how they were fulfilled in or by Jesus the Messiah. The problem was, hardly any of these friendly, highly intelligent people had any knowledge of the Old Testament. And to many of them, the New Testament was considered a book of blasphemy. Nevertheless, most of them were willing to talk. These were not millionaires like those I had known in Miami Beach. Most were middle-class professional types living in row houses, each with a porch in front. None of the homes had air conditioning in those days, so whoever happened to be at home would welcome the opportunity to come out and sit with me on the porch to "discuss religion." They seemed to like the interlude, since life could be boring on hot days in the city. Those were the days before television.

Since schools were out for the summer, I found hundreds of young people at home, and had great discussions with them. Those of college age were nearly all atheists, so rather than talk with them about our Lord Jesus being the Messiah, I spent most of my time trying to convince them why they should believe in God.

I stayed with a Christian family in the Olney neighborhood of northern Philadelphia, and a near neighbor and friend of theirs was Harry J. Burgen and his lovely wife, Rebecca. They were the first Jewish people I had ever known who were born again Christians. Their daughter, Helen, was about my age and we had some lively discussions together whenever they invited me to their home.

Harry had come from Lithuania in 1910, and while aboard ship en route someone had given him a New Testament in his native Yiddish language. Then after his arrival in New York he found a job in a pipe factory where another Jewish fellow invited him to attend a mission operated by Leopold Cohn, whose work eventually developed into *The American Board of Missions to the Jews*. My fascination with the Jewish people was greatly increased through my contacts with this mission. Every time I heard Leopold Cohn speak, he weaved in a prophetic emphasis regarding the ethnic group to which he belonged. At that time I knew nothing of the Khazar origins of Ashkenazi Jews, or the Yiddish language which they spoke.

Harry and Rebecca Burgen had both came to faith in Christ through the ministry of Leopold Cohn, and I was deeply touched by things they shared regarding the vicious persecution and savage hostility they suffered from their relatives after they confessed their faith in Christ as Lord and Saviour.

Those three months of missionary work among Jewish people of every sort increased my confusion as to how these unbelievers could be "God's chosen people," as my teachers had said. They seemed to me to be just plain lost sinners like all the other unsaved people I met who were of differing ethnic origins.

During that summer I attended Tenth Presbyterian Church where I began a long and enduring friendship with its pastor, Donald Grey Barnhouse, another evangelical Zionist. He taught public Bible classes in various cities on weekdays, and for several months in 1944 I arranged for him to speak in Charlottesville for large audiences every Thursday evening. Then when I returned from missionary service overseas and in 1953 launched International Students, Inc. (ISI) as a missionary ministry among foreign students, Dr. Barnhouse invited me to make Philadelphia a base of operations with his church as one of our main supporters. He served on the Board of Directors of ISI from its inception. I spent many valuable hours with him, asking him questions and gaining valuable new insights from his brilliant mind. He was a dispensationalist like Dr. Fowler, and taught prophecy along lines very similar to those in the Scofield Bible. I shall ever be indebted to Donald Barnhouse for all the great storehouse of Biblical knowledge which he shared with me.

Following my graduation from U.Va. in 1944, I became a "field evangelist" with two ministries simultaneously, Youth for Christ (YFC) and InterVarsity Christian Fellowship (IVCF), both based in Chicago. One of my co-evangelists in YFC was Billy Graham. At that time I gathered that he knew less than I did about Bible prophecy, although later (possibly with help from ghost writers) he would author books on the subject. Both of us traveled continually throughout the U.S. and Canada speaking in YFC rallies, church services, Christian colleges, theological seminaries, Bible institutes and even secular universities. During a three year period I had an unparalleled opportunity to meet outstanding evangelical pastors, professors, broadcasters, Bible teachers and ministry leaders. I became personally acquainted with men whom I had idolized, such as Lewis Sperry Chafer of Dallas Seminary, whose books had a deep influence in my life. He conducted a Bible conference at a church in Iowa for one full week while I was in the same town working with IVCF, so I got to know him then, as well as during several visits to the Seminary in Dallas. Later, in 1953, after I returned from missionary service overseas to launch the ministry of International Students, Inc., I immediately purchased the eight volume set of SYSTEMATIC THEOLOGY which Dr. Chafer had published in 1948. Then I hungrily devoured the fifteen chapters (184 pages) on ESCHATOLOGY in Volume IV. In succeeding years I would return to it again and again to compare what he had written with my ever increasing insights on the subject.

My soul had been nurtured during student days by the radio ministry of Charles E. Fuller whom I got to know in Los Angeles, and even had an opportunity in 1946 to sit with him and his staff during a live broadcast of *The Old Fashioned Revival Hour*. His teachings on Bible prophecy were similar to other dispensationalists.

During occasional stops in Chicago I rented a dormitory room at Moody Bible Institute where I had a chance to audit classes and meet faculty members such as Wilbur M. Smith. His just published (in 1945) book, *Therefore Stand,* encouraged me to forcefully defend the evangelical faith while speaking to university audiences throughout the country with IVCF. But, strangely, my most vivid memory of Dr. Smith is of a time when he spent almost half of a forty minute message trying to convince us that the name of the country of Russia came from the Hebrew word *ROSH* in Ezekiel 38:2, although it is typically translated as "chief." His point was that the prophet had foretold how the Russians were soon going to invade Palestine on horseback. Also in Chicago I occasionally attended Moody Memorial Church where I sought opportunities to pester the pastor, Harry Ironside, with questions about his teachings on prophecy. He was, like most others I met, an evangelical Zionist.

I also audited classes on prophecy in many other Bible institutes, Christian colleges and seminaries throughout the U.S. and Canada where I was invited as a chapel speaker. All the while I was learning and growing in knowledge, seeking to sort out the many inconsistencies of popular pronouncements on prophetic themes by the learned men whom I was coming to know.

While traveling continually I desperately needed a car, but in the aftermath of World War II they were almost impossible to obtain in 1945; but Billy Graham had wisely gotten on the waiting list early for a new Oldsmobile, so for $1300 he sold me his 1942 two-door Pontiac. It had a wide ledge between the back seat and rear window, and that became my library. Eventually I had about 200 books stacked there, and I studied them at every opportunity.

My collection had actually begun in 1942 while I was a student at U.Va. Elmo Stevens, the proprietor of a menswear store adjacent to the University grounds, was an evangelical who took an interest in my life and ministry. He gave me books by Dr. Chafer, Arno Gaebelein and several other dispensationalist teachers of prophecy. I still have *The Harmony of the Prophetic Word* which Arno wrote in 1907 and which Elmo had originally given to his own father in 1926. Gaebelein was one of the co-editors of the Scofield Reference Bible, and he spoke of "Israel" as though it was a monolithic people group like that which had existed in the days of King Solomon three thousand years ago.

Let us understand, he wrote, *that Israel is Israel, namely, the descendants of Abraham, the earthly people of God. There is a restoration of Israel coming which places that people at the head of the nations.*

Israel is a separated people. They are still a people dwelling alone and are not reckoned among the nations. Their separation and preservation is a divine miracle.

I dutifully followed this line of teaching because I knew next to nothing about the origin of "the Jewish people," particularly the Ashkenazim, or Yiddish-speaking segment who made up about eighty percent of the six million Jewish people living in America at that time. I had no idea that they were of Japhethite ancestry, rather than being related to the original Hebrews. Apparently Dr. Gaebelein didn't either, even though he made an effort to learn Yiddish in order to better relate to those he called *the seed of Abraham, God's earthly people.* Many scholars believe that Yiddish was originally the language of the empire of Khazaria in southern Russia where the entire population converted to Judaism in the Eighth Century. It became the second "Jewish state," the first having been the one in Palestine before 70 A.D.

Later I was given a copy of another book written by Dr. Gaebelein in 1933 and was thoroughly confused by its contents. He called it *The Conflict of the Ages,* and his concept of "Israel" had changed radically by that time. The turnabout in his thinking was brought on in a large measure by the participation of atheistic Jews in the Bolshevik (Communist) revolution which caused havoc in Russia beginning in 1917. Gaebelein was deeply concerned that millions of professing Christians had been killed or sent to slave labor camps by the Bolsheviks. These "Christians" were mainly Russian Orthodox but also included thousands of Mennonites, Baptists and other evangelicals. Chief among the perpetrators of this genocide, Gaebelein wrote, were Jewish men such as Leib Bronstein who had taken hundreds of young Jewish atheists from the New York area to lead the revolution in Russia. They were instructed to adopt Russian names after they arrived there, following Bronstein's example, who called himself Leon Trotzsky. In this later book Gaebelein filled many pages with details regarding Jewish atrocities in Russia. Here are a few excerpts from what he wrote:

Karl Marx had appeared as one of the most prominent Jewish leaders of the revolutionary activity. He was the son of a Jewish lawyer named Mordecai . . . [This] Jewish atheist issued the "Communist Manifesto" . . . the basis of the attempted world revolution of our times. He [also] wrote "Das Kapital" which Communists call their "Bible."

A Jew by the name of Apfelbaum, who changed his name to Zinovieff wrote: "The interests of the Revolution require the physical annihilation of the bourgeois class. Without mercy we will kill our enemies in scores of hundreds."

On September 3, 1918, the American Consul in Moscow sent [this] report to Washington, "Thousands of persons have been shot without a trial, many of them innocent of the political views which were supposed to be the motive for their execution." The Jew Trotzsky was the main instigator of this program of hell.

"The Communist," a newspaper published in Kharkoff, on April 12, 1919 [stated]: "The great Russian Revolution was accomplished by the hands of the Jews . . . the Jews are leading the masses to victory . . . the symbol of Jewry has become the symbol of the Russian proletariat, which can be seen in the adoption of the Red five pointed star, which in former times was the symbol of Zionism and Jewry."

Another Communist organ, the Red Gazette, says: "The fact is incontestable, the Soviet bureaucracy is almost entirely in the hands of Jews and Jewesses, while the number of [native] Russians who participate in the government of the Soviets is ridiculously small."

Dr. George A. Simons, superintendent of Methodist Missions in Russia, in a report to a Sub-Committee of the Committee of the Judiciary of the U.S. Senate, said: "Hundreds of agitators from the lower east side of New York followed in the trail of Trotzsky-Bronstein. As the American pastor in Petrograd I was impressed with the Yiddish element [of the Revolution] *right from the beginning. It soon became evident that more than half of the agitators in the Bolshevik movement were Jews. I am against anti-Semitism, but I have a firm conviction that the Bolshevik Revolution is Yiddish, and that one of its bases is in the east side of New York . . . In December of 1918, in the section of Petrograd under the presidency of a Jewish man named Apfelbaum (Zinovieff), out of 388 members of the Soviet Regime there, all but 17 were Jews. I remarked to my sister, "This all looks so Yiddish." All over Petrograd we had a predominance of Yiddish proclamations, big posters and everything in Yiddish.*

Gaebelein then gives a long list of the names of the Jewish leaders of the Bolshevik Revolution in Russia, and quotes an article which appeared in the *London Times* March 29, 1919: *Of the commissaries who provide the central machinery of the Bolshevist movement, not less than 75% are Jews.* Then he quotes a September 14, 1918 article from a French journal in which the author stated, *Almost all of the functionaries of the Bolshevist Government are Jews. In Moscow, in provincial districts, in district offices, in the Soviets, I have met nothing but Jews, and again Jews. Bolshevism is a Jewish movement.*

In the decade that followed the Communist Revolution in Russia there was wholesale slaughter of professing Christians, destruction of church properties, vile and blasphemous propaganda against Christ, and the dislocation of millions of people who were uprooted, deprived of possessions and forced into concentration camps as slave laborers. Gaebelein was appalled at the terrible suffering imposed by Jews upon Christians, especially the Mennonites and Baptists. And it did not go unnoticed that the first head of the Soviet Secret Police (originally the G.P.U., later the KGB) was a Yiddish man named Jogada; or that another named Simon Firin was in charge of 22 concentration camps holding hundreds of thousands of prisoners; and that Naftaly Frenkel, Chief of all Gulag prisons, was also Jewish. His deputy, also Yiddish, was Matvei Berman.

Arno Gaebelein struggled with the conflict of how such murderous, inhuman savages could be included among those whom he had previously taught were "God's chosen people." And so did I after reading his 1933 book, THE CONFLICT OF THE AGES. I never could figure out what Arno's solution was to this enigma, because he was determined not to turn loose of his previous doctrine that the Jews were "the earthly people of God." His conclusion seemed to be that only the Orthodox Jews, or at least those who believed in God, should be considered as part of "the chosen." I presume that Gaebelein was aware that when Nicolai Lenin displaced Leon Trotsky as the top leader of the Communist revolution, he continued to deploy the large contingent of atheists from New York in his persecution of Christians. Later, however, Joseph Stalin succeeded Lenin and gradually purged many of the Jews from their previous positions of power.

My personal experience with Jewish people, even those who were atheists, had been just the opposite of the ones who followed Bronstein to Russia from New York. I couldn't imagine how any Jewish person could turn into such murderous monsters as those who led the original Bolshevik Revolution after 1917.

In the summer of 1948 I found an answer to this dilemma. I was in Europe speaking at an all male camp/conference of about one hundred German students, sponsored by the International Fellowship of Evangelical Students. Nearly all of these fellows had been in Nazi military service just three years earlier. During the war, we in America were continually bombarded with reports of how Nazi military personnel were fiendish monsters. But the war was over, and these guys were as friendly and amiable as any I had ever met. I had a great time of friendship with them, and fellowship in Christ with those who were believers. Needless to say, they had come to the conference with some trepidation about Americans. How could we have been so cruel as to bomb non-military targets in cities like Dresden, where hundreds of thousands of innocent civilians were killed, mainly women and children and the elderly?

A year later in Japan I had a similar experience. I found the

Japanese to be just as friendly and peace-loving as the Germans, including many university students to whom I ministered in Christian fellowship groups. Sometimes I asked about their war experiences, but they didn't like to talk about them. But those who hadn't been overseas in military service, especially the women, positively refused to believe that any Japanese person could be guilty of such atrocities in China, Korea or the Philippines as had been reported in the foreign press. On the other hand, they thought all Americans were monsters because of the terrible air raids on residential areas that had killed hundreds of thousands of women and children, as well as the sick and elderly. Not to mention the atomic bombs which had obliterated two Japanese cities. They were sure that when occupation forces arrived the Americans would kill off half the population that still remained alive. Needless to say, they were absolutely astounded when 100,000 U.S. troops came ashore and many of them started giving out toys and candy to homeless children, as well as food and clothing to destitute adults.

My experiences with German and Japanese students who had been in military service helped me to understand how Jewish people who were, humanly speaking, as nice as any persons I had ever known, could also become fiendish monsters in the heat of conflict and lust for power that develops during times of military conquest. After I had visited Palestine in 1951 I came to realize that Jewish people in general are no different from human beings of other nationalities, as David and other Old Testament prophets wrote so long ago. The Hebrew apostle named Paul quoted several Old Testament passages regarding his own people: **Their throat is an open sepulcher; with their tongues they have used deceit; the poison of asps is under their lips; whose mouth is full of cursing and bitterness; their feet are swift to shed blood: destruction and misery are in their ways; and the way of peace they have not known** (Romans 3:13-17).

Just outside the wall of the old city of Jerusalem I took a photo at *Golgotha* which in 1951 still looked like a human skull. Then on the left side of it I visited *The Garden Tomb* where,

I believe, our Saviour's body was laid after His crucifixion. The proprietor was a devout evangelical who helped me take photos of myself lying in the empty sepulcher out of which Christ arose on the third day. It was a great joy to have fellowship with this precious brother who had devoted his life to caring for that historic site. But, sadly, later on two militant Zionists came to the Tomb and murdered that dear man of God in cold blood. Why? Presumably because he bore witness to Christ's resurrection. He had violated no other law of the state of Israel.

Still later I would meet Bishwa Awad, president of Bethlehem Bible College, whose childhood home was in Jerusalem. When he was ten years old some militant Zionists came to their home and demanded that Bishwa's father come outside. Then, as that little boy watched in horror, those wicked men pumped his father's body full of bullets and left his lifeless corpse lying there on the ground. Bishwa's mother had to flee for her life, taking her children to the neighboring country of Jordan. To this day, neither she nor her children have been allowed to return to their ancestral home in Jerusalem, which was stolen by Zionist immigrants. Why was her husband murdered, and his family made refugees? Presumably because they were not Jewish! They had committed no offence that was legally punishable.

In their zeal to take over and occupy the land of Palestine, Jewish immigrants since 1933 have killed many thousands of the indigenous people whose families have lived there for centuries. I am not speaking here of those killed in wars since the State of Israel was proclaimed in May 1948. And I am not unaware that many Jewish people have died at the hands of the Palestinians, who have fought back against what they perceive to be an invasion of their homeland. My point is that military conquest produces ruthless actions by both sides. Four hundred years ago what is now my hometown of Charlottesville was peacefully owned by the Monacan nation, but they had all been killed or driven out by the time Thomas Jefferson established his fabulous plantation at Monticello.

In addition to the tens of thousands of native Palestinians

killed, wounded or injured, probably two million or more have fled or been driven out of their homes and suffered the loss of all their property. Hundreds of thousands have been forced to live in the squalor of refugee camps. Unless some provision is made for them, I can see no hope for peace there in the foreseeable future.

Since the end of World War II, Jewish people who suffered losses of family members or property at the hands of the Nazis have received billions of dollars in reparations, over thirty billion from Germany alone. But dislocated Palestinian natives have received next to nothing from the Zionists who displaced them. Is it any wonder they fight back, even if they must sacrifice their own lives in order to exact revenge?

What God revealed about human beings in the Old Testament is just as true today as it was then. The constraints of our culture keep us civil toward one another, but under the duress of political power and military conquest, any person can turn into a monster, whether American, Bolshevist, Maoist, Nazi, Zionist or Al-Qaida.

The head man of Inter-Varsity in 1945 was C. Stacey Woods, who was in fellowship with assemblies of Christians called "Plymouth Brethren." As I traveled from one university to another, Stacey often arranged for me to stay in the homes of Brethren families. From them I learned the origins of dispensationalism, beginning with John Nelson Darby in England, who was one of the Plymouth Brethren. I can't remember who it was that gave me a copy of Darby's 19th Century *Lectures on the Second Coming*, but I still have it. Also several books by William E. Blackstone (known as WEB), including *Jesus is Coming* (published in 1878), and others by C. H. Mackintosh (CHM) including *Papers on the Lord's Coming*.

One thing that fascinated me about Blackstone was his determination to personally bring about the fulfillment of his prophetic beliefs. Like most other naïve, uninformed, idealistic dispensationalists of his time, he regarded "Israel" as being a monolithic people group identical to the unified nation that existed in the days of King Solomon. *Their wonderful preservation,* he wrote, *as a distinct people through all the persecutions and wanderings of the past eighteen centuries is a standing miracle. Other nations come and go, but Israel remains.* Then quoting Old Testament passages he argued that "Israel" will "return to Palestine" before the Messiah comes again. He ignored the fact that these prophecies had already been fulfilled twice, first in the days of Ezra, Nehemiah and Zechariah, and again during the CENTURY OF RESTORATION that began in 165 B.C. when the Maccabee brothers drove the Greeks out of Jerusalem. Anyway, since Blackstone believed that "Israel" should occupy Palestine again, he set about to make it happen. And thus he became the first of the Zionists, even before the appearance of Jewish Zionists such as Theodor Herzl who was born in Budapest and later lived in Vienna and Paris. In 1896 Herzl wrote *The Jewish State* in which he proposed that Jews should have their own country somewhere, perhaps in Argentina, or even in Palestine. He then organized a *Zionist Congress* which was held in Basle in 1897 and attended by 200 European Jews. But W. E. Blackstone was way ahead of him. Having visited Palestine and seen Jewish settlements there, WEB conducted a Zionist conference in Chicago in 1890 at which he urged the formation of a Jewish state in Palestine. For the next several years, WEB campaigned vigorously on behalf of his concept of political Zionism, circulating petitions signed by prominent people in business and government and submitted to three U.S. presidents in hopes of gaining their endorsement. When Jewish Zionists held a conference in Philadelphia in 1918 they recognized Blackstone as a *Father of Zionism*. And I am told that today a small forest in Israel bears his name to honor his contribution toward the cause of political Zionism.

The first time I was invited to preach at The People's Church in Toronto, the pastor, Oswald J. Smith, gave me a complete collection of his books, including *Prophecy — What Lies Ahead* which he first published in 1943. Many others whom I met in my ministry travels also gave me copies of their prophetic books, including Salem Kirban, Harry Rimmer and Donald Barnhouse.

At a church conference in later years I shared the pulpit with John Walvoord while he was president of Dallas Seminary. It was almost amusing to see how he had adapted the views of his predecessor, Lewis Sperry Chafer, to incorporate current events. He still believed that eventually Russia was going to invade Israel. He also held on to the idea of a "revived Roman empire," and saw its possible fulfillment in the European Common Market. But unlike Chafer, Scofield, Darby and others who came before him, Walvoord added Islamic countries to the mix. In fact, his Antichrist was predicted to begin his reign as the strong man of a Mediterranean Confederacy. Arab oil wealth now became a major theme of prophetic teaching, and in one of his books Walvoord associated *Oil and the Middle East* with *Armageddon*.

I was fascinated with the really weird dispensational charts which were created by various authors, such as those of Clarence Larkin in his 1918 book, *The Second Coming of Christ*. I used several of them in Bible classes which I taught. Also those of David L. Cooper, published in 1942.

Just about all of the evangelical teachers and writers whose ideas I followed were in general agreement about prophetic revelations in the Word of God. They said that the Old Testament prophets spoke mainly about things that were yet future, rather than what was going on in their day. The main focus of my mentors was on "Israel," as though it was still one united nation equivalent to what it was three thousand years ago. None seemed to realize that a unified "Israel" had not existed since Jeroboam split the country into two factions after King Solomon died. The Messiah, my teachers said, had offered to restore the kingdom of Israel as it was in Solomon's time, but since the Hebrew leaders rejected Him, the kingdom was postponed until the Messiah's second coming. Meanwhile, the church age was inserted as a sort of parenthesis in God's prophetic plan, and no prophecy revelations concerned it. Rather, there would soon come the rapture of the church and then God's prophetic clock would start ticking again with the conversion of Israel, the coming of the Antichrist, and **the great tribulation**. Seven years later Christ would come again to defeat the Antichrist at the battle of Armageddon and set up a Jewish kingdom based in

Jerusalem for **a thousand years** (the millennium).

I often included this standard dispensational formula in my preaching and teaching. As a youthful, immature evangelist who liked to get a response from my audience, I would make a joke about the "secret rapture" when true believers would be caught up to be with the Lord in the skies and leave everyone else behind. "Think of those who will be flying planes or driving cars, trucks, trains and buses," I said. "When all of those vehicles crash it will really start the tribulation off with a bang."

A turning point came in my perception of prophetic truth when I went overseas as a missionary. I conducted evangelistic meetings in China during 1948-49, and in Korea just before the outbreak of the terrible war that devastated most of the population there beginning in 1950.

Foolishly, I tried to teach believers in China about The Seven Dispensations. "We are in the Fifth Dispensation now," I said, "and it will be followed by the Sixth, The Great Tribulation, which will be a time of terrible suffering. But don't worry, all of us who are believers in Christ will be raptured out of the world before the Tribulation begins."

Imagine how ridiculous all of this must have sounded to an audience of holocaust survivors in China. For many years they had suffered pillage, plunder, violence, torture, terror, bombings, rape, robbery, murder, genocide and other horrors at the hands of Buddhists, Boxers, bandits and Japanese invaders. There was never even one person in my audience who had not suffered personally or had lost family members to the Japanese army during its invasion and occupation.

And even as I was speaking the forces of atheistic Communism were storming across the Yangtze en route to overrunning all of China and imposing another reign of terror which would continue for more than half a century.

Still, like most Bible believing Christians, I was slow to change any of the ideas, dogmas and doctrines which I had learned from eminent Bible teachers I had known and loved during my first ten years as a born again Christian. So, when the Communists put all foreign missionaries out of China, I went on to Korea where in 1950 Bob Pierce (founder of World Vision and Samaritan's Purse) and I were co-evangelists in huge evangelistic meetings with audiences up to 50,000 in major cities. I preached Christ to entire student bodies of public schools, colleges and universities all over the country. And in smaller groups I would include some teaching on Bible prophecy, with my usual formula. Many times I would be asked questions, especially by university students.

One of them, a refugee from Communist persecution in North Korea, was puzzled by my reference to "seven years of tribulation." He commented that when the gospel first spread into the then closed land of Korea from China, those who believed suffered great tribulation from the Buddhists, which lasted about seven years. Then came the terrible time of suffering at the hands of the Japanese during World War II. That had lasted about seven years also. Now the Communists had occupied North Korea and brought horrific suffering to tens of thousands of consecrated Christians who had been conducted daybreak prayer meetings in hundreds of churches throughout the country.

"Are you saying," asked this refugee from tribulation, "that this terrible time my people are going through will be over after seven years?"

Tragically, it was to continue without interruption for more than 60 years from the time Communist dictatorship was imposed at the end of World War II.

Then and there I came to my senses. I had been blindly following, and teaching, an unbiblical concept developed by John Darby and others during the peaceful reign of Queen Victoria, who professed to be an evangelical believer. That was "the age of certainty" when Britain ruled the seas and there was no persecution of Christians in England. So how could Darby and his followers relate to New Testament teachings about the sufferings which believers must endure? They projected it all into the future. And millions of Christians in America, influenced by this erroneous teaching, have been glibly saying, "The church won't go through the tribulation." Such teaching is pure nonsense. Millions of Christians have gone through great tribulation for almost two thousand years, and still do in Communist, Hindu, Buddhist and Islamic countries.

When my eyes were opened in 1950 I came to realize that teaching about the so-called "Tribulation Period" was not in the New Testament. In fact, many times on nationwide radio broadcasts I offered a thousand dollars to anyone who could show it to me. I had no takers, because it is not there.

Once I saw how I had been misled on the subject of the "Tribulation Period," my prophecy house of cards began to crumble. Much of what I had followed and taught as prophetic truth turned out to be fictitious nonsense, in many ways similar to what the Jehovah's Witnesses were trying to teach my mother more than 70 years ago.

Fictitious prophecy concepts are now being followed by millions of evangelical Christians. For some they are rigid dogmas, and disagreements about them have caused splits in churches, firing of preachers and bitter quarrels among the people of God. Such actions are of the flesh, not blessed by the Spirit of God. I have great love and deep respect for my peers in the evangelical community who still hold to teachings which I now believe to be erroneous. I continue in fellowship with all who will receive me. My daily prayer is that things I have learned and now teach will not cause bitterness, hostility or divisions among God's people. His Word says that **we, being many, are one body in Christ, and every one members one of another** (Romans 12:5). **Therefore, be ye kind one to another, tenderhearted, forgiving one another, even as God for Christ's sake hath forgiven you** (Ephesians 4:32).

So as I proceed to dismantle the collection of errors which so many evangelicals blindly follow, I do so in love, with the prayer that it may contribute to the spiritual growth of those who read. Then, after dealing with some major mistakes which are popularly taught, I will explain what God's Word actually says on the subject of prophecy.

Chapter 5

The Great Tribulation Fantasy

A new doctrine emerged among evangelical Christians toward the end of the Nineteenth Century and throughout the Twentieth Century. It was the belief that at the end of what's called "The Church Age," or "The Age of Grace," there would come a seven-year period of unparalleled suffering on the earth, during which a mythical figure called "The Antichrist" would seize power over the nations of Europe and rule there as well as in other parts of the world. Several volumes of the LEFT BEHIND series of books (mentioned earlier) are devoted to this imaginary period. I have already mentioned also how my mentor, Clifton L. Fowler, taught that "The Tribulation" would be one of the Seven Dispensations, even though it was due to last only seven years. Also, I have mentioned how I myself taught this erroneous doctrine until my knowledge of God's Word increased to the point where I realized that I had been teaching something that had no basis in Scripture.

Credited with the formulation of the doctrine was John Nelson Darby who, as previously mentioned, lived in England during the Nineteenth Century. As I have said, I honestly believe that the peace, protection and security which evangelicals enjoyed during the reign of Queen Victoria was a contributing factor. And, whereas the book of Revelation was written, in large measure, to inspire believers going through tribulation to **be faithful unto**

death, Darby and his followers had no opportunity to experience trials of faith. So they projected it all into the future.

Thousands of Christians in the United States, where there had been no major period of internal tribulation since the Civil War, seized upon the doctrine following the publication and wide distribution of the Scofield Reference Bible in 1909. It was picked up by the many Bible institutes which proliferated during the century and also by some seminaries such as Dallas Theological. Soon it became a dogma over which fundamentalist Christians would fight like opposing packs of hyenas. Affirmation of the fine points became essential to graduation in some schools. Deviation from particular aspects of the dogma caused many pastors to be expelled from their churches. Some took along half their congregations to start competing assemblies which gave assent to the point in question.

All agreed that the so-called Tribulation Period had to do with "the end times" of the Church Age, but there has been wide disagreement regarding the details, especially as to when the rapture of the [true] church will take place.

Some, like Tim LaHaye, say it will come before the Tribulation Period begins. This is called "pre-tribulation rapturism," meaning that Christians will be spared from the horrors of the period, and only those "left behind" will suffer.

Others teach that the rapture won't take place until three-and-a-half years of the Tribulation Period have transpired. This is called "mid-tribulation rapturism."

A third group thinks that today's anemic Christians need a bit of suffering to refine their faith, so they will have to "go through the tribulation." This is called "post-tribulation rapturism."

So you must choose to be either pre-trib, mid-trib, or post-trib, unless you realize that according to scripture there is NO TRIB.

As I have already mentioned, I followed this silly teaching until I went to China in 1948 and met precious saints who had endured horrible tribulation and suffering all their lives. Then in Korea, in 1950, I lived among believers who had never known any kind of existence other than "great tribulation."

While there my mind went back to a wealthy family I had known in Iowa. They had me as a guest in their palatial home overlooking the Mississippi river. Humanly speaking, they had everything money could buy, but the wife was troubled. Her pastor had begun to teach that "the church will go through the tribulation," and she was fearful as to what might happen to her. Three months in their fabulous winter home on an island off the coast of Florida didn't help. I saw her again after they returned to Iowa and she was still worried.

During my four years of living in Asia I became aware of multiplied thousands of poverty-stricken Christians who had been put out of their homes and deprived of their property. They had been beaten, imprisoned and tortured for Christ's sake. Many family members had been killed. And it made me realize that the tribulation nonsense being taught in American churches was contrary to biblical truth regarding persecution of believers.

After my return to the USA I was invited to speak in many churches and Christian schools. One was the Washington (D.C.) Bible College. There I tried to challenge the students to sacrifice for Christ by telling them about how God's people in Asia were going through terrible times of suffering for the sake of the gospel. Later I learned that the president of the college had said I would never speak there again. Why? Because he thought I had been trying to sneak in "post-tribulation rapturism," while the official position at WBC was "pre-trib." Actually, the "great tribulation" dogma never entered my mind while I was preaching to those students. But it has become an obsessive preoccupation for millions of evangelical Christians, especially in the USA.

So where does it come from, other than the fact that it is held mainly by Christians who have never suffered persecution for the sake of the gospel?

Essentially, it originated with a failure to understand the Twenty-fourth Chapter of the Gospel of Matthew, and neglecting to fill in the words of our Saviour there with other New Testament passages which deal with the same subject matter.

As I have already mentioned, in that chapter our Lord was answering two questions raised by His disciples: 1) **When shall these things be?** (the destruction of the temple), and 2) **What shall be the sign of your coming and the end of the age?** Up until that point they had never imagined that the two events would be 2000 years apart.

Three times, in answering their two questions, our Lord used the word which has been translated into English as "tribulation." In verse 21 it refers to **these things,** the destruction of the temple, which they had asked about. In verse 9 He used it to describe what His disciples would be going through for the next two thousand years. Then in verse 29 He referred to what He will bring upon the earth at His second coming. Failure to understand and differentiate between these three uses is what, in large measure, has resulted in the fabrication of the "Tribulation Period" dogma which is now so prevalent among evangelical Christians.

The original Greek word that is usually translated "tribulation" or "affliction" in the New Testament is *thlipsis,* meaning "grapes in the winepress." It is used primarily to denote the experience of suffering which believers in Christ must endure in this present evil world.

In Matthew 24:4-14 our Lord informed His disciples of all the difficulties believers would be going through during the centuries that followed, before His coming again and the end of the age.

Then in verses 15-24 He mentioned some things that would take place leading up to the destruction of the temple 40 years later, while in verses 25-51 He provided numerous details to help them separate that event from His second coming.

To get the full picture of what is revealed in Matthew 24, we should compare portions of Mark 13, Luke 21, I Thessalonians 4, II Thessalonians 1 and Revelation 19. By interspersing them with passages in Matthew 24, it will become clear that no future seven year "tribulation period" is taught in the New Testament. Rather, the **great tribulation** mentioned in verse 21 pertains to what was coming 36 years later from 66-70 A.D. It is in no way related to events that will take place centuries later when Christ returns in power and great glory.

BIBLE VERSES PREDICTING THE DESTRUCTION
OF JERUSALEM AND GOD'S TERMINAL
JUDGMENT UPON THE UNFAITHFUL HEBREWS

O Jerusalem, Jerusalem, thou that killest the prophets and stonest them which are sent unto thee, how often would I have gathered thy children together as a hen gathereth her chickens under her wings, and ye would not! Behold your house is left unto you desolate. You snakes, you generation of vipers . . . (Matthew 23:33, 37-38).

The kingdom of God shall be taken from you and given to people bringing forth the fruits thereof (Matthew 21:43).

He will miserably destroy those wicked men, and let out His vineyard to others (Matthew 21:41).

He sent forth His armies and destroyed those murderers, and burned up their city (Matthew 22:7).

Verily I say unto you, there shall not be left here one stone upon another, that shall not be thrown down (Matthew 24:2).

And when you shall see Jerusalem compassed with armies, know that the desolation thereof is nigh. Then let them which are in Judaea flee into the mountains; and let them which are in the midst of it [Jerusalem] depart out; and let not them that are [out] in the country enter thereinto. For these be the days of vengeance . . . there shall be great distress [tribulation] in the land and wrath upon this people (Luke 21:20-23).

Woe unto them that are with child, and to mothers that are nursing babies in those days . . . for then shall be great tribulation, such as was not since the beginning of the age until now, no, nor ever shall be (Matthew 24:19,21).

Daughters of Jerusalem, weep not for me, but weep for yourselves, and for your children. For, behold, the days are coming when they shall say, Blessed are the barren, and the wombs that never bare, and the breasts which never nursed a

child. Then shall they begin to say to the mountains, Fall on us, and to the hills, Cover us. For if they do these things [crucify] **to a green tree** [the Son of God], **what shall be done to the dry** [that generation of vipers who condemned Him to death] (Luke 23:28-31).

And the kings of the land [of Israel], **and the great men, and the rich men, and the chief captains, and the mighty men, and every bondman, and every free man, hid themselves in the rocks and the mountains; and said to the mountains and rocks, Hide us from the face of Him that sitteth on the throne, even from the wrath of the Lamb: for the great day of His wrath is come, and who shall be able to stand?** (Revelation 6:15-17).

But those mine enemies, which would not that I should reign over them, bring hither and slay them before me (Luke 19:27).

All of these verses have to do with a three-and-a-half year period of great tribulation for the Israelites from 66 to 70 A.D. when civil war broke out in Palestine and mass killings brought untold agony upon the population. It began in Galilee and spread throughout the land.

Since Palestine was a Roman territory, troops were dispatched under the command of General Vespasian to quell the uprising. As his forces advanced, many of the Hebrews left off fighting each other and turned to fighting the Roman legions instead. Nevertheless, Vespasian advanced until he came within sight of Jerusalem. Then word came that Emperor Nero was dead, so Vespasian withdrew until he had more news from Rome. During his absence, believers in Christ fled Jerusalem to seek refuge in the mountains, remembering how Christ had said, **When ye see Jerusalem compassed with armies, know that the desolation thereof is nigh. Then flee to the mountains** (Luke 21:20-21).

When Vespasian was proclaimed Emperor, he went to Rome and dispatched his son Titus to clean up the mess in Palestine. Those were the days of the *Pax Romana*, the "peace of Rome." Relative peace and stability had prevailed throughout the empire since the days of Julius Caesar, a century earlier. But now all hell had broken loose in Palestine, and the Romans were determined to put an end to it. Detailed records of what happened were written and preserved by Flavius Josephus, a brilliant Hebrew scholar of Galilee whom Titus recruited to be his interpreter. Every student of Bible prophecy should have a copy of WARS OF THE JUDAEANS which Josephus wrote. My first copy was translated by William Whiston of Cambridge University in 1737 and published by The John C. Winston Company of Philadelphia. A more recent translation by Paul L. Maier was published in 1988 by Kregel Publications of Grand Rapids, Michigan.

As the Roman forces advanced southward from Galilee, hundreds of thousands of Judaeans rushed to Jerusalem and took refuge inside its massive walls. The number of people who were crowded within the city walls for three years was estimated by Josephus to have been well over three million. There was no sanitation, no extra beds or blankets, no medical care, inadequate shelter from cold, sun or rain. The refugees had hardly any food to eat and only occasional rainwater to drink. The resulting mass starvation caused those pitiful, desperate people to resort to cannibalism. Women were reported to have eaten their own children. Like **grapes in a winepress**, that suffering mass of humanity endured a time of tribulation the likes of which has never been equaled by so great a number within the confines of such a relatively small area (Matthew 24:21).

Had the Judaeans been willing to give up and surrender the city, no doubt the Romans would have been merciful and spared the lives of all except the ringleaders of the rebellion. But just as our Lord had foretold, they were deceived by false reports. Men who claimed to be prophets cited Old Testament promises such as, **Alas! For that day is great, so that none is like it: it is even the time of Jacob's trouble; but he shall be saved out of it** (Jeremiah 30:7). "God will save us from the Romans," the false prophets proclaimed. And like sheep bound for slaughter, the people believed them.

One of the most widespread of the false hopes was the cry

that the time had come when God was going to send the promised Messiah to deliver Jerusalem. Mass hysteria erupted when reports were circulated that the Messiah had appeared in the temple. Other mobs were set to rush out of the city when it was reported that the Messiah had appeared in the desert and was on his way to Jerusalem. Even some of our Lord's disciples were deceived, thinking that the time for His second coming had arrived. Others, who had heard Him speak, were not misled: **Then if any man shall say unto you, Lo here is Christ, or there, believe it not . . . if they shall say unto you, Behold He is in the desert; go not forth: Behold He is in the secret chambers; believe it not** (Matthew 24:23, 26).

This leads us to the third period of tribulation which our Lord mentioned while telling his disciples about events associated with the soon-coming destruction of Jerusalem. He wanted to make it very clear to them that the armies which He would send to bring His conclusive judgment upon the unfaithful Israelites would be within that generation, and were in no way to be associated with His second coming in power and great glory. He told them to pay no attention to reports of false messiahs. Even if they were said to do signs and wonders, they could never be compared with the splendor of His return to this earth.

For as the lightening cometh out of the east, and shineth even unto the west; so shall the coming of the Son of Man be (Matthew 24:27).

The Lord Jesus shall be revealed from heaven with His mighty angels, in flaming fire taking vengeance on them that know not God . . . when He shall come to be glorified in His saints (II Thessalonians 1:7-10).

And I saw heaven opened, and behold a white horse; and He that sat upon it was called Faithful and True, and in righteousness He doth judge and make war . . . and out of His mouth goeth a sharp sword, that with it He should smite the nations; and He shall rule them with a rod of iron: and He treadeth the winepress [causes tribulation] **of the fierceness and wrath of Almighty God. And He has on His vesture and on**

His thigh a name written, **KING OF KINGS AND LORD OF LORDS. And I saw an angel standing in the sun; and he cried with a loud voice, saying to all the fowls that fly in the midst of heaven, Come and gather yourselves together unto the supper of the great God; that ye may eat the flesh of captains, and the flesh of mighty men, and the flesh of horses, and of them that sit on them, and the flesh of all men, both free and bond, both small and great** (Revelation 19:11-18).

For wheresoever the carcass is, there will the eagles [vultures] be gathered together (Matthew 24:28).

Immediately after the tribulation of those days shall the sun be darkened, and the moon shall not give its light, and the stars shall fall from heaven, and the powers of the heavens shall be shaken: and then shall appear the sign [wonder] of the Son of Man in heaven: and then shall all the tribes of the earth mourn, and they shall see the Son of Man coming in the clouds of heaven with power and great glory (Matthew 24:29-30).

From these verses it is clearly obvious that when our Lord used the word "tribulation" the third time in Matthew 24 He was referring to events that will transpire at His second coming. And, in summary, let me repeat that not one of the three uses in Matthew 24 can logically be applied to the hypothetical seven-year "tribulation period" invented in England more than a century ago by John Darby and now taught as dogma by thousands of evangelical Christians. In fact, not one time in the entire New Testament is the Greek word *thlipsis* so used.

HOW THE GREEK WORD "THLIPSIS," USUALLY
TRANSLATED "TRIBULATION" IS USED IN THE NEW
TESTAMENT
The word appears in 44 verses of the New Testament, and the ways it is used refer to the following subjects:

2 — God's judgment on lost souls and false prophets
2 — Suffering of Hebrews in Old Testament times
2 — Suffering of wives, widows and orphans

2 — War in Palestine and the destruction of Jerusalem, 67-70 A.D.

3 — What Christ will bring at His second coming

33 — Suffering which Christians have endured through 20 centuries

Not one usage can logically be applied to the hypothetical seven-year period that many teachers say will occur at the end of the church age. Here is a listing, in chronological order, of how the word is used.

Matthew 13:21 — What Christians suffer

24:9 — What Christians will suffer through the centuries

24:21 — Destruction of Jerusalem, 66-70 A.D.

24:29 — What Christ will bring at His second coming

Mark 4:17 — What Christians suffer

13:19 — Destruction of Jerusalem

13:24 — What Christ will bring at His second coming

John 16:21 — Suffering of a woman during childbirth

16:33 — What Christians will suffer in the world

Acts 7:10 — Joseph in Egypt

11:19 — Persecution of Christians

14:22 — Suffering of Christians

20:23 — What Paul suffered

Romans 2:9 — Lost souls in hell

5:3 — What Christians suffer

8:35 — What Christians suffer

12:12 — What Christians suffer

I Corinthians 7:28 — What wives (and mothers) suffer

II Corinthians 1:4 — What Christians suffer

1:4 — What Christians suffer

1:8 — What Paul suffered

2:4 — What Paul suffered

4:17 — What Christians suffer

6:4 — What Paul's team suffered

7:4 — What Paul suffered

8:2 — What Macedonian Christians suffered

8:13 — Pain of sacrificial Christian giving

Ephesians 3:13 — What Paul suffered

Philippians 1:17 — What Paul suffered

4:14 — What Paul suffered

Colossians 1:24 — What Paul suffered

I Thessalonians 1:6 — What Thessalonian Christians suffered

3:3 — What Thessalonian Christians suffered

3:7 — What Paul's team suffered

II Thessalonians 1:4 — What Thessalonian Christians suffered

1:6 — What Christ will bring at His Second Coming

Hebrews 10:33 — What early Judaean Christians suffered

James 1:27 — What widows and orphans suffer

Revelation 1:9 — What the Apostle John suffered

2:9 — What Christians at Ephesus suffered

2:10 — What Christians at Smyrna suffered

2:22 — What Jezebel (false prophetess) and her disciples suffered

7:14 — What Christians have suffered through the centuries (including today)

A review of these uses of the Greek word *thlipsis* in the New Testament shows quite clearly that there is no biblical basis for the imaginary future "tribulation period" which has been taught by so many evangelical Christians during the past century.

Now let's move on to another fictitious subject that has been taught in relation to the hypothetical "tribulation period," and which has been made a dogma by many Bible believing Christians.

Chapter 6

The "Antichrist" Mythology

Speculation about a personage labeled "The Antichrist" has been rife among Christians, especially theologians and charismatic leaders, for many centuries.

When Roman pagans persecuted the Christian minority during the Second and Third Centuries, church leaders began to apply the term "Antichrist" to some of the chief persecutors, particularly to certain despotic emperors.

Then when Islam began to spread as a great religious revival throughout western Asia and northern Africa, Roman Catholic and Eastern Orthodox priests almost universally applied the Antichrist label to Muhammad.

In her book, *Muhammad: A Biography,* Karen Armstrong points out how in the Seventh Century Islam began to spread as consuming fire throughout Christendom, absorbing the churches and converting them to mosques. Then, she says, Muhammad was almost universally identified as being the Antichrist, and his coming a portent that the last days were at hand. Armstrong says that to most Christians, Muhammad appeared to be the perfect fulfillment of prophecies concerning the Antichrist.

The shameful Roman Catholic crusades that began in 1096 and continued for more than a century were motivated in large measure by a goal to free the "Holy Land" from occupation and control by followers of Muhammad, whom they called the Antichrist.

In writing of the medieval crusades, Dr. George Smith said that their goal was *to recover from the Antichrist the holy places of the Lord's birth, life and death* (Chapter IX, *Short History of Christian Missions,* Edinburgh, 1897).

As the Medieval churches of Europe became increasingly corrupt, Martin Luther and other conscientious theologians began to call for reformation. A decisive moment came on October 31, 1517 when Luther posted his famous *Ninety-five Theses* on the church door in Wittenberg. He barely escaped being put to death for his actions, and there ensued a bitter warfare between the Reformers and the Papacy. Luther and others said the Pope was the Antichrist, and the Pope reciprocated by saying that Luther was. The end result of the long conflict that followed was to forget about Islam and Muhammad, who previously had been identified as the Antichrist for 900 years by European church leaders.

In the famous *Westminster Confession*, officially adopted by Presbyterians of Scotland in 1647, we find this statement (in Article XXV,6): *There can be no other head of the church but the Lord Jesus Christ: nor can the Pope of Rome in any sense be the head thereof; but is that antichrist, that man of sin, and son of perdition, that exalteth himself in the church against Christ, and all that is called God.*

They based their doctrine on an assumption that the **man of sin**, whose coming was foretold by the Apostle Paul in II Thessalonians 2:3-4, was the same person as the Antichrist. A further explanation of this usage is discussed in detail in Chapter 13.

A similar presumption was made by the translators of the Authorized English Version of the Bible in 1611. In their *Epistle Dedicatory* to King James they wrote that their work *hath given such a blow to that man of sin* [the Pope], *as will not be healed.*

I believe prophecy teachers have made a big mistake for 500 years when they have ascribed the term "antichrist" to the "man of sin" character foretold in II Thessalonians 2:3-10. Why should we do so when the Apostle Paul never used the term "antichrist" nor did any other apostle except John in two of his epistles?

Some applications of the Antichrist label have been really ridiculous. During the Revolutionary War period a popular teaching was that King George III of England was the Antichrist and the colony of Virginia was the woman mentioned in Revelation 12 who fled from him into the wilderness. The twelve stars on her head were said to represent the rest of the original 13 colonies. A century later some Southern preachers were saying the Antichrist villain was Abraham Lincoln and the woman in the wilderness typified the Confederate states which seceded from the Union. John Wilkes Booth foolishly believed that he would be hailed as a hero when he assassinated the Antichrist President.

Meanwhile, as might be expected, prominent clergymen far and wide had accorded the Antichrist label to Napoleon Bonaparte when he crowned himself emperor of Europe. He probably deserved the title more than most others [besides Muhammad] who had received it before him or in the two centuries that followed.

The latter half of the 19th Century marked the development of Antichrist mythology by evangelical Christians. It has now grown into a worldwide political movement affecting millions of people and seriously impacting the cause of Christ in many countries. When John Darby started teaching dispensationalism among local assemblies of the "Plymouth Brethren" in England, he quickly gained a following outside of those Assemblies, including many prominent evangelicals in America. Followers of his teachings produced the *Scofield Reference Bible* which would become what was probably the most influential prophetic instrument of all time.

Another influential follower of Darby's teaching was Sir Robert Anderson of Scotland Yard who wrote *The Coming Prince* around the turn of the century. My copy, obtained more than 50 years ago, is the Tenth Edition, published in 1915. I presume that the first edition must have come out before 1900.

The anti-hero of Anderson's book is the coming Antichrist [Prince] which he thinks is portrayed prophetically in both Daniel and Revelation. Anderson took his title from Daniel 9:26-27, the fulfillment of which he projected into some future time after 1915.

Since then the teaching has taken off into a worldwide phenomenon, finding its climax in a fictitious antichrist character called *Nicolae Carpathia* created by Tim LaHaye and Jerry Jenkins in the *Left Behind* books.

Some other potential Antichrists which I have seen identified in print include Benito Mussolini, Adolph Hitler, Joseph Stalin, Leonid Breshnev, John F. Kennedy, Henry Kissinger and Sadam Hussein. Many itinerant preachers used Antichrist predictions to draw crowds 70 years ago, and a popular joke at that time concerned one of them who had to cancel his engagements because, as he said, "My Antichrist just died."

About 40 years ago I was invited by a fellow Virginian, Rev. Jerry Falwell, to visit nearby Lynchburg and preach in a rapidly growing church which he had started there. Thus began a long and enduring friendship, which included my participation in some of his telecasts and sending Christian foreign students to Liberty University, of which he was Founder and President. Jerry had a host of other guest speakers at Thomas Road Baptist Church, many of whom were evangelical Zionists. In 1972 he distributed copies of *The Late Great Planet Earth* by Hal Lindsey as a promotional give-away for his broadcast, *The Old Time Gospel Hour.*

I watched with great interest as Jerry became more and more absorbed into political Zionism, making frequent trips to Israel and taking sides with the Zionists in opposition to the Palestinians. He was admired and honored in Israel until he made a proclamation about "The Antichrist." He said he believed that the man who was destined to become the Antichrist was alive somewhere in the world, and that he was a Jew. You can imagine how that was received by newspapers and TV stations in Tel Aviv. Poor Jerry, one of the best political friends the Israelis ever had, suddenly found himself labeled "anti-Semitic." He was thenceforth rejected by many (but not all) of the people he favored because he was repeating popular misconceptions about Bible prophecy.

Most of the Antichrist myths that have been circulated during the past century have portrayed him as a superman (Clifton Fowler used that term before it appeared in a comic strip) who will rule the world during the fictitious "Tribulation Period." But nothing even remotely related to such a concept is associated with the use of the word "antichrist" in the New Testament.

It appears only in the Epistles of John: four times in his First Epistle and once in his Second Epistle. And none of these give any hint of, or reference to, a political ruler. Only three uses refer to an individual; the others refer to **many antichrists** and **the spirit of antichrist**. In a literal translation of the original Greek, the first usage says, **You heard that the antichrist is coming** (I John 2:18). So there was teaching at that time that someone was coming who would fit the description of an **antichrist**. Then in Verse 22, John says, **The one denying that Jesus is the Christ, this is the antichrist, the one denying the Father and the Son.** Then in II John 7 we read, **The one denying that Jesus Christ has come in the flesh, this is the deceiver and the antichrist.**

And that's it. There is no other reference to an antichrist anywhere in the New Testament. Yet hundreds of books have been written about a mythical world ruler who is supposed to bear that title. Not only books, but movies and TV dramas on major networks. I saw a full hour program about the supposedly coming Antichrist on the History Channel, and another on CNN. Other networks have also aired programs on the subject, and Christian TV stations have been full of it. Some critics have compared it to the *Harry Potter* series of books and films.

The one thing we can learn from John's epistles is that some influential person would come on the scene who would deny that our Lord Jesus Christ was the Son of God. So, obviously, he would be a religious leader. John says also that there would be many antichrists, and while on earth our Lord said, **There shall arise false Christs, and false prophets, and shall show great signs and wonders; insomuch that, it if were possible, they shall deceive the very elect** (Matthew 24:24). But John seems to be telling us that one antichrist would exceed the others in the breadth of his influence.

And for 900 years nearly all the Christians in the world knew who that man was. His name was Muhammad.

Here we must be careful to define the term **antichrist**. We can best understand it if we compare it to "anticlimax," something which follows a major event and replaces it, or detracts from it. Christ came and started His church, but 300 years later that church began to fall away, as the Apostle Paul had foretold in II Thessalonians 2:3-12. Following the professed conversion of the Emperor Constantine in the year 312, the churches began to merge with the pagan religion of the Roman Empire. Three hundred years later the churches were almost totally paganized, so God allowed Islam to come as His judgment on the idolatrous churches. In all of Western Asia, North Africa and much of Europe, Muhammad "took the place of Christ" as a religious leader who was followed by a majority of the population. An anti-climax replaced the climax of all history.

That's why he was called "the Antichrist" for 900 years by church leaders, until Martin Luther and other reformers began to call the Pope the Antichrist, and the Pope said the same of the reformers, and they forgot about Islam.

But Muhammad's cumulative influence was then, and continues to be today, a thousand times greater than all other so-called "antichrists" put together. He was the one who "took the place of Christ" for millions of people. Beginning in the Seventh Century the Qur'an replaced the Bible, the mosque replaced the church building and synagogue, and imams or mullahs replaced priests and rabbis for more than half of Christendom and nearly all of Judaism in Palestine at that time.

Here we must be very careful to note that Muhammad was not "against Christ," but rather took His place as his followers proclaimed him to be God's primary messenger for millions of people. Muhammad never said what his followers would consider one disrespectful word against the man he called, in Arabic, *Isa Masih,* Jesus the Messiah. An entire *Surah* of the Qur'an is devoted to Mary and the man called *Jesus the son of Mary*. Muhammad taught the virgin birth, sinless life, miracles, ascension and second coming of *Isa Masih*. But, as John had foretold concerning the coming antichrist, Muhammad said that God did not have a Son. Rather, says the Qur'an, our Lord was only a prophet, like Muhammad, even though it says He was conceived by a spirit in the womb of the Virgin Mary.

Essentially, Islam was a return to the Old Testament. In travels to Syria and Palestine, Muhammad had met many Judaeans and absorbed numerous Old Testament stories and quotations. About ten percent of his sayings, later written down as the Qur'an, are either references to or quotations from Moses. Many of Muhammad's earlier followers in the Mecca-Medina area were Judaeans [Jews], but when they turned against him he attacked them, as Moses did the Amorites (Numbers 21:21-31).

In following the Old Testament, Muhammad instituted universal circumcision, kosher foods, animal sacrifices, Sabbath keeping [on Fridays], salvation by deeds of the Law, and belief in the one God of the Old Testament Who, as the rabbis had said, he believed had no Son. Yet, unlike some Judaeans [Jews], who in the Talmud and elsewhere have blasphemed and vilified the Son of God, Muhammad showed great respect for the one he called *Isa Masih*.

Even today, whenever any educated Muslims mention the name of Jesus, they will add, "May peace be upon him." This expression of honor and respect is reserved primarily for Old Testament prophets such as Abraham and Moses and, of course, for the one they regard as God's final prophet, Muhammad himself. In contrast with other Arabs around Mecca, Muhammad was vociferously opposed to all forms of idolatry. He demanded exclusive belief in and worship of the unseen and invisible Creator God of the Old Testament. No icons or images were allowed. If anyone would make a statue or painting of Muhammad he would likely be killed, even today. Muslims regard Christians as being idolaters because they have made paintings and false images of Christ, and even of God in Heaven.

After the year 622 Islam began to spread out from Mecca as a great religious revival, sweeping millions into its orbit of

75

"submission to God" (the meaning of the term "Islam"). Multitudes at every level of human society began to kneel in prayer and worship God five times daily. Kings and beggars knelt together with no distinctions of rank or class. Islam was a great social equalizer. For use in their prayers, they had 99 attributes for God.

Here we must pause to define the term "God." I have heard some Christians ignorantly say, "We worship God; Muslims worship Allah." But our word "God" is akin to the German *Gott* which was originally ascribed to pagan deities. English speakers use it now to designate the supreme being, almighty creator of the heavens and the earth. Almost every language has a term for the Creator. In Spanish it is *Dios* while French is *Dieu*. New Testament Greek speaks of *Theos*, while in Old Testament Hebrew it is *Eloah* (plural: *Elohim*). In the Arabic language the term is actually a contraction of two words combined: *al* (the) and *Ilah* (God). The origin of *Ilah* is Old Testament Hebrew. When the original *Eloah* went into Aramaic it became *Elah*, which our Lord cried out when He hung on the cross (Mark 15:34). When this term then passed into Arabic, the language of Muhammad's time, it became *Ilah*. When he spoke of *Al-Ilah* (the God) he was using the term he had learned from Hebrews of his day and was referring to *Eloah*, the Almighty Creator spoken of in the Old Testament. Throughout the centuries, millions of Arabic-speaking Christians have used *Allah* as their term for God in their Bibles, literature and worship services.

The spreading Islamic revival reached Jerusalem around 630. I remember reading in Robert Ripley's *Believe it or Not* about 60 years ago how the city was delivered to Omar Al-Khattab in 637 without a struggle. That's because so many of the church clergy and Hebrew rabbis in Palestine had come to believe that Muhammad was "that prophet" foretold by Moses in Deuteronomy 18:18-19. They were astounded to see thousands of new converts to Islam from their own churches and synagogues kneeling in prayer to worship God five times daily. Eventually, virtually all the churches and synagogues in Palestine became mosques. Omar is credited with clearing the site of Herod's (and Solomon's) temple in Jerusalem, and making plans for the construction of a shrine over a huge rock located there. Some call it the "Mosque of Omar," but it is not exactly a mosque. Rather, a large mosque is located on the temple site nearby, where hundreds of Muslims gather for ritual prayers. The beautiful "Dome of the Rock" shrine stands today as the most outstanding building in Jerusalem, with its golden dome clearly defining the temple area. I went inside it for a visit in May, 1951 and was told by Muslims there how they believed the rock it commemorates was the site to which angels bore Muhammad when some portions of the Qur'an were revealed to him.

In the year 1099, so-called "Christian" crusader armies came from Europe and chopped off the heads of an estimated 100,000 residents of Jerusalem in one day. Raymond of Toulouse and other European knights boasted that the victims' blood flowed up to the horses' bridles in the streets of Jerusalem. Little did they realize that most of the Muslims whom they murdered during this holocaust were descendants of the original Hebrews, who in turn were descendants of Abraham, Isaac and Jacob.

Jerusalem was reconquered by Islamic armies under Saladin in 1187, and, except for two brief intervals when European crusaders returned in the 13th Century, remained a predominantly Islamic city until the Zionist occupation began in 1967. Muslims still regard it as their third most holy city (after Mecca and Medina) and until recently hundreds of thousands of Islamic pilgrims visited there annually.

When Islam originally spread as a mighty religious movement among the churches, Muslim missionaries would quote John 16:12-13 in attempting to prove that Muhammad had come to replace Jesus as God's final messenger: **I have yet many things to say unto you, but ye cannot bear them now. Howbeit when he, the spirit of truth, is come, he will guide you into all truth.** That spirit of truth, the Muslims said, was in Muhammad and inspired him to recite the words which were later written down and published as the Qur'an. Millions of men have memorized the Qur'an throughout the past fourteen centuries. Even today, in my personal conversations with

Muslims, I have had several of them quote John 16:13 to me, trying to prove that "the prophet Jesus" foretold the coming of the one who would take His place.

Beginning in the Seventh Century the Qur'an replaced the Bible for three quarters of the professing Christians in the world, and for two million or more Hebrews in Palestine and elsewhere. Churches and synagogues were converted into mosques while priests and rabbis became teachers of Islam. Greece was under Islamic dominance for 400 years, and Spain for 700. Of the so-called "Christian world," only Italy, France and Northern Europe remained free from Islam at that time.

The countries of Europe, largely controlled politically by the Popes of Rome, fought back against Islam with military force, and gradually expelled it from their lands. The last remaining Muslims were driven out of Spain by King Ferdinand and Queen Isabella in 1492, the year they sent Columbus across the Atlantic.

Although excluded from most of Europe, the religion of Muhammad then spread eastward, winning over entire populations of countries now called Iraq, Iran, Turkmenistan, Uzbekistan, Afghanistan, Pakistan, Bangladesh, Northern India, Malaysia, Indonesia and others.

One major country they failed to convert was the empire of Khazaria, which lay between the Black Sea and the Caspian Sea in regions now called southern Russia and southeastern Ukraine. The Khazars had no religion, and earnest attempts were made to win them over by Roman Catholics on the west and Muslims along their eastern borders. King Bulan knew that if his people embraced the religion of either of their neighbors, they would have war with the other. So around the middle of the Eighth Century (730-760) a choice was made to convert the population to Judaism. That move provided neutrality toward the two powerful religions on their borders. Many scholars believe that the Ashkenazi Jewish people of Russia, Ukraine, Poland and the rest of Europe originated in Khazaria. The six million or so Jews in the USA are nearly all Ashkenazim.

Some have said that Islam was spread by the power of the

sword, but that allegation is not generally true. It has always been primarily a religious movement, persuading people to believe in and worship the God of the Old Testament.

It is true that Muhammad personally combined warfare with persuasion in his struggle against the idol worshipers of Mecca, but they attacked him and his followers first. Islam was a return to the Old Testament teaching of revenge: **an eye for an eye and a tooth for a tooth**. Muhammad followed the examples of Moses, Joshua, David and other Old Testament warriors who fought continual battles against the indigenous peoples of Palestine. And whenever Muslims have gained a majority, they have almost always sought to combine their religion with political control over the population. And once they gained control, they imposed a special tax on non-Muslims. This, in turn, caused many more to convert to Islam in order to avoid the tax.

Nevertheless, throughout the centuries Muslims have generally been tolerant of religious minorities living in regions under Islamic control. My many Muslim friends have reminded me frequently of the horrors their ancestors suffered during the terrible days of the Roman Catholic Inquisition and Crusades a millennium ago. "We are more tolerant than Christians are," they say with pride. Of course there have been many exceptions. There has always been persecution of minorities by religious majorities, whether they be Muslims, Hindus, Buddhists, Jews, Roman Catholics, Greek Orthodox, or, sad to say, even Protestants.

Islam stands today as the most powerful religious and political force on earth in opposition to the gospel of Christ. It is growing and spreading at a rapid rate throughout the world, especially in Europe and Africa. And I maintain that Muhammad was the Antichrist foretold in the Epistles of John. We need look for no other. As I said earlier, his cumulative influence throughout fourteen centuries has been a thousand times greater than all other antichrists put together. And those who speak of a political antichrist superman who, they think, is yet to come are talking fictitious nonsense.

Chapter 7

But what about
Daniel's Seventieth Week?

For more than a century almost all evangelical students of Bible prophecy have been familiar with the marvelous prophecy of **SEVENTY WEEKS** found in Daniel 9:24-27. My introduction to it was when I was given my first Scofield Reference Bible in 1940. Then I began to hear about it from prophecy speakers and teachers, climaxed by reading *The Coming Prince* by Sir Robert Anderson. All agreed that the **seventy weeks** referred to SEVENTY SEVENS OF YEARS, which would mean that from the time of Ezra to the time of Christ would be 490 years. In order for us to understand this subject matter, we need to have the full text before us, so here is what the angel Gabriel said, beginning with Daniel 9:24.

Seventy weeks are determined upon thy people and upon thy holy city, to finish the transgression, and to make an end of sins, and to make reconciliation for iniquity, and to bring in everlasting righteousness, and to seal up the vision and prophecy, and to anoint the most Holy. Know therefore and understand, *that* **from the going forth of the commandment to restore and to build Jerusalem unto the Messiah the Prince** *shall be* **seven weeks, and threescore and two weeks: the street shall be built again, and the wall, even in troublous times. And after threescore and two weeks shall Messiah be cut off, but not for himself: and the people of the prince that shall come shall destroy the city**

and the sanctuary; and the end thereof *shall be* with a flood, and unto the end of the war desolations are determined. And he shall confirm the covenant with many for one week: and in the midst of the week he shall cause the sacrifice and the oblation to cease, and for the overspreading of abominations he shall make *it* desolate, even until the consummation, and that determined shall be poured upon the desolate.

Once we accept the fact that the seventy weeks represent 490 years, everything falls into place. Many excellent scholars have documented the accuracy of the prediction that from the time Cyrus, king of Persia, gave the order to restore and build Jerusalem (Ezra 1:2-4) until the beginning of the public ministry of Jesus the Christ was 483 years. But there has been great disagreement regarding the final seven years of the 490 total. Entire eschatological systems have been built on the basis of speculation regarding that seven year "week." But rather than review the various theories on this subject, let's just look at what Gabriel said and see how some of the prophecies relate to historical events since that time.

1. **Upon thy people** [the Judaeans] **and upon thy holy city** [Jerusalem]. Does this not mean that God will be finished with both within 490 years?

2. **To finish the transgression and to make an end of sins.** The main purpose of the Old Testament period was to show that all men are sinners in need of salvation. **There is none righteous, no, not one** (Psalm 14:1-3, Romans 3:10). To accomplish this purpose, God dealt primarily, and temporarily, with one nationality group, the Hebrews. To demonstrate that they were sinners, He gave the law through Moses, and when they universally failed to keep His law, God sent prophets such as Isaiah, who called them a **sinful nation, a people laden with iniquity, a seed** [generation] **of evildoers** (Isaiah 1:4). God was patient with them, but He had no intention of letting it go on forever. So Gabriel told Daniel that in 490 years this phase of God's dealing with one specific ethnic group of sinners would be finished, and that He would make an end to all of this sinning

as far as His people were concerned.

3. **To make reconciliation for iniquity.** From the beginning of creation, God had a plan to reconcile sinful mankind unto Himself. The **tabernacle** in the wilderness, the **sacrificial lamb**, and the **day of atonement** when the high priest would go into the **holy of holies** (all duplicated in Solomon's temple) served only one purpose: to foreshadow the day when God's only begotten Son would shed His own blood and then take it **into Heaven itself, there to appear in the presence of God for us** (Hebrews 9:24). This would be accomplished within the seventy weeks (490 years).

4. **To bring in everlasting righteousness.** Under the Old Covenant, no man could be accounted righteous before God, because none kept the law. But after Christ died and rose again, **the righteousness of God without the law was manifested . . . even the righteousness of God which is by faith of Jesus Christ unto all and upon all them that believe . . . whom God has set forth to be a propitiation through faith in His blood, to declare His righteousness for the remission of sins** (Romans 3:21-25). How marvelous that Gabriel would reveal to Daniel this glorious truth 490 years before it came to pass, and that it was fulfilled right on schedule.

5. **To seal up the vision and prophecy.** I believe that we are being told here that almost all of the visions and prophecies written by God's prophets in the Old Testament period would be fulfilled and completed before or when the Messiah came in 490 years. I think that many of my brothers and sisters in Christ make a big mistake when they try to find some fulfillment for Old Testament prophecies beyond the forty year New Testament period from 30 to 70 A.D.

6. **And to anoint the Most Holy.** This has to be a reference to the triumphal entry of the Risen Saviour **into Heaven itself** where He was anointed as **High Priest forever after the order of Melchisedec** (Hebrews 5:6), and proclaimed **KING OF ALL KINGS AND LORD OF ALL LORDS.**

7. **From the . . . commandment to restore and build Jerusalem unto Messiah the Prince shall be seven weeks, and threescore and two weeks.** We are being told here that it would be 69 weeks (483 years) from the time of Ezra until the Messiah appeared. Many excellent scholars have demonstrated that from the time King Cyrus gave the order until our Lord began His public ministry was 483 years. But there has been much speculation, disagreement, argument and fantasizing about the seventieth week. Some say that our Lord's ministry was completed by the end of the 69th week, and that the 70th has not yet happened. Others say that **until Messiah the Prince shall be** sixty-two weeks plus seven weeks; so, since His public appearing came AFTER sixty-nine weeks, the seventieth week would certainly include the three-and-a-half years of His ministry. So all that's unaccounted for is the second half of the seventieth week.

8. **After threescore and two weeks** [plus the first seven weeks when **the street and the wall of Jerusalem would be rebuilt** by Zerubbabel, Ezra and Nehemiah] **shall Messiah be cut off, but not for Himself.** This is a marvelous prophecy of the substitutionary, sacrificial death of the coming Messiah, even indicating the fact that He would be murdered. Truly, **He was the Lamb slain from the foundation of the world** (Revelation 13:8), **the Son of God, who loved me and gave Himself for me** (Galatians 2:20).

9. **And the people of the Prince that shall come shall destroy the city and the sanctuary; and the end thereof shall be with a flood, and unto the end of the war desolations are determined. And He shall confirm the covenant with many for one week: and in the midst of the week He shall cause the sacrifice and the oblation to cease, and for the overspreading of abominations He shall make it desolate, even unto the consummation, and that determined shall be poured upon the desolate.** Since the days of John Darby, failure to understand this passage has probably caused as much confusion as any other of the Old Testament prophecies which have been misinterpreted

by Bible teachers. The first big mistake was trying to say that **the Prince** mentioned here is not the same person as **Messiah the Prince** mentioned previously. I am really surprised that a brilliant Scotland Yard detective like Sir Robert Anderson should make such a colossal error, but the title of his famous book, THE COMING PRINCE, is based on the presupposition that **the prince that shall come** is not **Messiah the Prince.** Rather, says Anderson, he is the hypothetical "antichrist" who still hasn't come almost 2000 years later. To me, such interpretations seem extremely far-fetched. It was Messiah who wept over Jerusalem and said, **Behold, your house is left unto you desolate** (Matthew 23:38). It was Messiah who said, in a parable regarding the unfaithful Israelites, **the king . . . was wroth, and he sent forth his armies, and destroyed those murderers and burned up their city** (Matthew 22:7). The **king** in His parable can refer to none other than **Messiah the Prince,** as does the **nobleman** in another parable who **went into a far country to receive for himself a kingdom**, and whose citizens hated him, saying, **We will not have this man to reign over us** (Luke 19:14). None but Messiah the Prince could say, **Those mine enemies, who would not that I should reign over them, bring hither and slay them before me** (Luke 19:27). It was the Messiah who said, **There shall not be left here one stone upon another that shall not be thrown down** (Matthew 24:2).

It was Messiah who **confirmed the covenant** with the Israelites as He began His public ministry. When He healed a leper, He sent him to the priest for ceremonial cleansing according to the Law. It was Messiah who said, **Think not that I am come to destroy the law, or the prophets: I am not come to destroy, but to fulfill** (Matthew 5:17). His ministry was carried out under the terms of the Old Testament Covenant. He **confirmed** it for one week of years.

It was the death of the Messiah that **caused the sacrifice and oblation to cease.** When His blood was shed as **the propitiation for our sins, and for the sins of the whole world** (I John 2:2), the **veil of the temple** [in Jerusalem] **was rent in twain from top to**

85

bottom (Matthew 27:51), a supernatural act of God signifying that there would be no further purpose for sacrifices or oblations within that earthly temple.

A most significant fact is that it was **IN THE MIDST OF THE WEEK** that the sacrifice and oblation were caused to cease. This can mean nothing else but that our Lord was crucified **IN THE MIDST OF THE SEVENTIETH WEEK.** His public ministry, then, would have begun "after sixty-nine weeks," or at the beginning of the seventieth week. Some say His ministry was for only three years, but I believe there is ample evidence that it was for three-and-a-half years. So since it was ended **in the midst of the week**, there remains only the last half of that week to be accounted for.

WHICH BRINGS US TO THE TITLE OF THIS BOOK. **THE TIME IS AT HAND** VERSES IN REVELATION TELL US THAT THE TIME HAD ARRIVED FOR EVENTS TO TAKE PLACE WHICH HAD BEEN SCHEDULED FOR THE SECOND HALF OF DANIEL'S SEVENTIETH WEEK.

These events included the destruction of the temple, and of the city of Jerusalem, with a flood of blood and a war that would leave the Israelites **desolate** because of **the overspreading of** [their] **abominations**. The Apocalypse of John describes the fulfillment of this prophecy in Daniel, the second half of the **seventieth week** (of years).

Here we should note Matthew's comment, **Whoso readeth, let him understand** (Matthew 24:15). That's because there are several uses of "abomination" and "desolation" in Daniel. The first, which I believe is intended here, has to do with God's judgment upon the Israelites for **the overspreading of** [their] **abominations** and was fulfilled in 70 A.D. **The abomination that makes desolate,** as mentioned in Daniel 11:31 & 12:11, has to do with the desecration of the temple in Jerusalem by numerous invaders as well as the Romans. One of the most notorious was Antiochus Epiphanes of the Greek Seleucid empire in 170 B.C. We should keep in mind that our Lord would have made this reference regarding Daniel's prophecy while speaking in the Aramaic language, then Matthew wrote it down in Hebrew, after which it was translated into Greek, and now we have it in English. So Matthew cautions us to make sure we understand which **ABOMINATION** reference in Daniel was intended. I believe it definitely has to do with the Roman armies which came to "the holy place" to bring a conclusive judgment upon the Hebrews for **the overspreading of** [their] **abominations** (Daniel 9:27).

Some have questioned how **Messiah the Prince** could use the Romans to fulfill His word in Matthew 22:7, **He sent forth His armies and destroyed those murderers and burned up their city.** Was it not the Romans that crucified Him? Yes, but remember what He said to Pontius Pilate: **Thou couldest have no power at all against me, except it were given thee from above: therefore he that delivered me unto thee hath the greater sin** (John 19:11). **There is no power but of God: the powers that be are ordained of God** (Romans 13:1). To fulfill His will, God allowed the Judaeans to provoke the Romans into killing their Messiah. That's why Peter said to his fellow Judaeans, **Him being delivered by the determinate counsel and foreknowledge of God, ye have taken, and by wicked hands have crucified and slain** (Acts 2:23).

In like manner, God used the Romans to execute a terminal judgment on the unbelieving Israelites during **the days of vengeance**, 66-70 A.D. In His final word to them, the Messiah said, **Behold, your house is left unto you desolate** (Matthew 23:38); and forty years later He fulfilled the prophecy of Daniel's seventieth week: **For the overspreading of** [the Judaeans'] **abominations, He shall make it** [Israel's house] **desolate, even until the consummation** [God's final judgment upon the rebellious Israelites], **and that determined** [God's judgment] **shall be poured upon the desolate** [Israelites] (Daniel 9:27).

So, to summarize, the prophecy in Daniel foretold a period of **seventy sevens** until the coming of the Messiah, following the command by the king of Persia (including Babylon) to restore Jerusalem. Accepting these to be weeks of years, in sixty-nine weeks, 483 years, the Messiah was announced by John the Baptizer (the last of the Old Testament prophets) as being **Jesus of Nazareth**. Thus began the SEVENTIETH WEEK, in the midst of which Messiah was killed for the sins of others. During His death **the veil of the temple was rent in twain**, signifying that God had **caused the sacrifice and oblation to cease**.

The remaining three-and-a-half years of that SEVENTIETH WEEK was then postponed until 66 A.D. while God called out the **elect remnant (144,000)** from among the Hebrews to give the gospel to other nations. Then came God's closing judgment upon the unfaithful Israelites, resulting in the desolation of Jerusalem and of the Hebrew nation at the end of that final week of seven years.

Chapter 8

The Time is at Hand

In Daniel 9:24-27 we were told that **seventy weeks** (of years) would take place until the coming of **Messiah the Prince**, and that in the midst of the seventieth week Messiah would be killed. A study of history shows that Messiah appeared right on schedule after 483 years, and was crucified after three-and-a-half years.

It was also told to Daniel that, after the Messiah was murdered, His people [meaning the Romans, whom He used to accomplish His purpose] would **destroy the city** [Jerusalem] **and the sanctuary** [the temple]**, and the end thereof shall be with a flood** [of blood]. And our Lord Himself said the same thing, telling His disciples that **there would not be left one stone upon another** of the temple. During a time of **great tribulation** the nation of Israel would be made **desolate**.

But it did not happen immediately. Rather, these cataclysmic events did not occur until almost forty years later. Why the delay? Why was the second half of Daniel's seventieth week postponed until 66-70 A.D.? We will find the answer in the final book of the Bible. Revelation was written to inform the churches that, finally, the time had arrived when God would execute His terminal judgment on the rebellious Israelites to avenge the murder of His Son, and of thousands more who believed on Him. Since it begins, in the first verse, **to show His servants things which must shortly come to pass,** the Apocalypse surely must have been written in the year 66 A.D.

Those who ascribe a later date to the Apocalypse have failed to understand the circumstances under which it was originally written, copied and distributed. Some Second Century church leaders who first saw copies decades after it was written may have presumed that it had been produced recently. Present day scholars cite internal evidence such as the church family at Ephesus who had **left their first love** of Christ (Revelation 2:4). They say the Ephesus congregation had not existed long enough to go through that cycle. But the first church there was probably planted by pilgrims returning to Asia from Jerusalem soon after the **Day of Pentecost** around 31 A.D. When Peter wrote to those **strangers who were scattered abroad** (I Peter 1:1) by the first persecution in Jerusalem, he included those in Asia. And no doubt the church in Ephesus had already been meeting together for years when Paul left Aquila and Priscilla there around 50 A.D. (Acts 18:19).

When John wrote the Apocalypse in the year 66, he didn't send out e-mail copies to other Christians elsewhere. He had no way to make Xerox copies of it for distribution. He didn't even have a mimeograph. Each copy had to be laboriously reproduced by hand on hard-to-get parchment with quills and ink which were also hard to find on the sparsely populated island of Patmos. And the churches which did receive copies would have kept them hidden **for fear of the Judaeans** (John 20:19).

Primarily, Revelation deals with what was foretold 36 years earlier as **the days of vengeance** [when] **there shall be great distress** [tribulation] **in the land** [of Israel] **and wrath upon this people** [the Judaeans]**, and they shall fall by the edge of the sword** (Luke 21:22-24). **The time was at hand** for those horrific events to take place, but, as I have mentioned in previous chapters, Revelation also contains prophecies of events that would occur centuries later. Our ascended Lord appeared to John on the island of Patmos and told him to **Write the things which thou hast seen, and the things which are, and the things which shall be hereafter** (Revelation 1:19). So we should expect that it would be concerned with past, present [66 A.D.] and future events.

Also, it is important to note that parts of the Apocalypse were written in code. With good reason. As one of our Lord's original disciples, John was a hunted man. During the forty year holocaust that followed the crucifixion of their Lord, the disciples and other Hebrew believers were stoned, beaten, imprisoned, tortured and killed by their fellow Judaeans who did not believe. Time after time our Lord warned his followers of what true believers would have to suffer. **They shall put you out of the synagogues,** He said, **yea, the time cometh when whosoever killeth you will think that he doeth God service** (John 16:2). **They will scourge you in their synagogues**, He warned (Matthew 10:17). **In the synagogues ye shall be beaten** (Mark 13:9). **They shall lay hands on you, and persecute you, delivering you up to the synagogues** (Luke 21:12). Hebrew synagogues became death houses and torture chambers for Israelites who believed in Christ during those forty years.

One of the instigators of this tribulation against the Hebrew **remnant (144,000)** of true believers was a Pharisee named Saul of Tarsus who would later confess with shame the evil deeds he had done: **I punished them oft in every synagogue, and compelled them to blaspheme; and being exceeding mad against them, I persecuted them even unto strange cities** (Acts 26:11). Saul began his attacks against his fellow Judaeans who believed in Christ in Jerusalem at first, where the chief priests were leading the assault. It was they who gave Saul authority, he said, **And many of the saints did I shut up in prison . . . and when they were put to death I gave my voice against them** (Acts 26:10).

When the risen, glorified and exalted Christ eventually appeared to Saul (Acts 9:3-6) and stopped the slaughter, Saul became part of the persecuted remnant. He thought he might be spared the trial of fire because he had been a tool of the evil priests. In prayer he said, **Lord, they know that I imprisoned and beat in every synagogue them that believed on thee: and when the blood of thy martyr Stephen was shed, I also was standing by, consenting unto his death** (Acts 22:19). But our Saviour warned him, **Get thee quickly out of Jerusalem: for they will not receive**

thy testimony concerning me (Acts 22:18). And Saul had to flee for his life. But wherever he went his fellow Hebrews were lying in wait to kill him. Five times they beat him with whips, each time one stripe short of the deadly forty; and three times he was beaten with rods. Once they stoned him and left him for dead, but God raised him up (II Corinthians 11:24-25).

During his final visit with the church at Ephesus, Saul (Paul) shared how his life had been in continual jeopardy because of his fellow Judaeans lying in wait to kill him (Acts 20:19). Now, about fifteen years later, the Apostle John had come to Ephesus to minister in the church there, and no doubt some Judaeans in the local synagogue heard that he was in town and began to conceive a plan to kill him. With help from local believers, John escaped to the nearby island of Patmos where there was no synagogue. So there he would be safe from those would-be murderers. That's why he wrote, **I John, who also am your brother, and companion in tribulation, and in the kingdom and patience of Jesus Christ, was in the isle that is called Patmos, for the word of God, and for the testimony of Jesus Christ** (Revelation 1:9).

Our Lord instructed John to address the Apocalypse as a letter **to the seven churches which are in Asia,** and he would have to be careful what was said and how it was worded lest some unbelieving Judaeans should see a copy or hear it read and use it to stir up mob violence against the Christians. But not everything was going to be in code. The message the Lord Jesus sent to the church at Smyrna stated, **I know the blasphemy of them that say they are Judaeans, and are not, but are the synagogue of Satan** (Revelation 2:9). This relates back to what God had revealed to Paul, **He is not a Judaean, which is one outwardly; neither is that circumcision, which is outward in the flesh: but he is a Judaean which is one inwardly; and circumcision is that of the heart** (Romans 2:29). The Judaeans who hated Christ and killed His followers were **broken off the olive tree** of God's covenant and not counted as the seed of Abraham any longer (Romans 11:17-22). That's why those enemies of Christ at Smyrna were called **the synagogue of Satan** as were others in

Philadelphia (Revelation 3:9). So not all denunciations against them were in code.

At the beginning of the coded messages, our Lord used the word "mystery," and then explained the meaning. **Seven golden candlesticks** represented the **seven churches of Asia**, and **seven stars** were the **messengers** of those churches who presumably would be visiting John. The Greek word for "messenger" is *angelos*, which is sometimes translated "angel." Each messenger would carry back a copy of the Book to his respective church (Revelation 1:11, 20). Some other symbols are also explained, but most are left as mysteries to be deciphered by the churches. Another example of the use of code by the Apostles may be found in I Peter 5:13, where the term "Babylon" is used as a code word for "Jerusalem."

Let's look at just one of the coded symbols used in Revelation, the word "sun." In 6:12 it **became black as sackcloth**, but in 8:12 it is shining again and **the third part of the sun was smitten**, while in 9:2 **the sun and the air were darkened.** Obviously, the term "sun" in Revelation denotes something other than the great ball of fire in the sky that heats and illuminates our planet. Further proof of this observation is in 12:1 which speaks of **a woman clothed with the sun**, and 19:17 which speaks of **an angel standing in the sun**. Those teachers who want to take everything in Revelation "literally" will never discern the true meaning of the coded symbols used throughout the Book.

One other thing to note before we go further is that the Apocalypse is not in chronological order. Chapter 14 is a repeat, in part, of Chapter 7. Events in 7:1-8 took place BEFORE those in Chapter 6. Just as the Four Gospels, Matthew, Mark, Luke and John, present separate accounts of the life and ministry of our Lord, so do separate sections of Revelation present various events from differing perspectives. In fact, Chapter 7 deals in part with events that occurred before the Book was written. Which brings us to the subject matter of this chapter of this book: why was the second half of the seventieth week of Daniel postponed for thirty-six years?

The key as to why it was postponed will be found in

Revelation 7:1-10. Just as the heavenly angels were ready to unleash God's final judgment upon the rebellious Judaeans, another angel cried with a loud voice, **Hurt not the land** [Israel]**, neither the sea** [the Romans]**, nor the trees** [believers in Christ]**, till we have sealed the servants of our God in their foreheads. And I heard the number of them which were sealed: and there were sealed an hundred and forty and four thousand of all the tribes of the children of Israel.** Then the tribes are listed, with twelve thousand being sealed from each tribe. By that time the northern-most tribe of **Dan** no longer existed, but the two sons of **Joseph, Manassas and Ephraim**, were each included as separate tribes, as had been done in Old Testament times.

In Revelation 14:4 we are told that the 144,000 **were redeemed from among men, being the FIRSTFRUITS unto God and to the Lamb.** Who were the **FIRSTFRUITS** among the redeemed? They were **Peter and Andrew, James and John, Philip and Bartholomew, Paul and Barnabas**, and **144,000** other Hebrews who came to Christ IN THAT GENERATION. The number includes all those Paul described as **a remnant according to the election of grace** (Romans 11:5). God "elected" 12,000 from each of the Hebrew tribes to be included in His church, and the rest of the Israelites were **blinded**, and **broken off the olive tree** of the seed of Abraham (Romans 11:7-21). We should note also that Paul says the remnant existed **AT THIS PRESENT TIME**, meaning they were his contemporaries. So the final judgment, the flood of blood, was postponed until all of the **firstfruits**, 144,000 Israelites of that generation, were called out and publicly identified with Christ and His churches.

Some teachers have misunderstood one characteristic of the 144,000 mentioned in Revelation 14:4. **These are they which are not defiled with women; for they are virgins.** Thayer's Greek Lexicon states that the Greek word *parthenon* means virgin when applied to women, but regarding men it means those who have abstained from fornication and adultery. **Marriage is honorable, and the bed undefiled** (Hebrews 13:4). So probably a majority of the 144,000 were married men whose lives were undefiled by fornication or adultery. It is not clear in Revelation whether or not the 144,000 included women.

And what was the purpose of the 144,000 being sealed and called forth to be identified with Christ? The answer is in Revelation 14:6 which speaks of **the everlasting gospel to preach to every nation, and kindred, and tongue, and people.** They were to give the gospel to all other nations, as our Lord had told His disciples (who were part of the 144,000) to do. And in Revelation 7:9-10, immediately after the twelve tribes are named, we read of what God would use them to do: **After this I beheld and, lo, a great multitude, which no man could number, of all nations and kindreds, and people, and tongues, stood before the throne, and before the Lamb, clothed with white robes, and palms in their hands; and cried with a loud voice, saying, Salvation to our God which sitteth upon the throne, and unto the Lamb.** God used the 144,000 to begin His objective to have **a people for His name** from every nation.

This all goes back to Genesis 12:1-3 where God called Abram for His purpose to bless all nations. **Neither shall thy name any more be called Abram, but thy name shall be Abraham; for a father of many nations have I made thee** (Genesis 17:5). When the descendants of Noah had gone into idolatry after the flood, God confounded their language at the tower of Babel and scattered them over the face of the earth. **God gave them up** (Romans 1:24, 26, 28), temporarily. For the next 2000 years His witness on earth would be primarily through one nation, the descendants of Abraham, Isaac and Jacob. But when He changed Abram's name to Abraham, God let it be known in no uncertain terms that it was His purpose to eventually bring some from all the nations back to Himself. And He would do it through **the seed of Abraham, our Lord Jesus Christ,** who would use His disciples for that purpose.

God's first promise to Abram, that his seed would become a great nation, was fulfilled during the days of King David and his son, Solomon. The second promise, that "all nations" should be included in God's blessings through Abraham, became effective when the risen Christ, **the son of David, the son of Abraham** (Matthew 1:1), said to His disciples, **All authority is given unto me in heaven and in earth; go ye therefore and teach all nations** (Matthew 28:18-19).

Many Bible teachers have mistakenly said that the Old Testament Israelites were an end in themselves. Rather, they were primarily unregenerate sinners who stoned the prophets whom God sent to preach repentance. God endured them with much longsuffering in order to have **a people for His name** among human beings whom He had created in His own image. In spite of their continual rebellion, and constantly going off into idolatry, God was able to give through the Israelites a revelation of Himself, which we have in the Old Testament, and to prepare the way for the advent of His only begotten Son into the world. Also through them He was able to establish a place on the earth where His name would be made known. **There shall be a place which the Lord your God shall choose to cause His name to dwell there** (Deuteronomy 12:11). This same expression is repeated 18 more times in Deuteronomy alone. But it was not until David reigned as king over all Israel hundreds of years later that Jerusalem was chosen as the place where God's name would be known, and where Solomon the son of David would build the first temple to become a dwelling place, temporarily, for the Living God.

All of those things were temporary. **Behold the days come, saith the Lord, that I will make a new covenant with the house of Israel, and with the house of Judah** (Jeremiah 31:31). When God spoke these words through Jeremiah, the house of Judah (the Jews) had been at war with the other ten tribes of Israel for two hundred years. Few Christians realize that almost a third of the Old Testament concerns those centuries when the Judaeans (Jews) were the bitter enemies of the nation of Israel, which had Samaria as its capital. They were constantly killing each other, thousands at a time. So it's easy to see why a new covenant was needed. **For if the first covenant had been faultless, then should no place have**

**been sought for the second, for finding fault with them . . He
hath made the first** [covenant] **old. Now that which decayeth and
waxeth old is ready to vanish away . . . He taketh away the first,
that He may establish the second** (Hebrews 8:7-8, 13; 10:9). Even
a casual reading of the Epistle to the Hebrews should be enough
to convince anyone that God's dealings with one specific nation
was terminated at the cross of Christ, and that the **new covenant**
was to include believers from **ALL NATIONS**, according to God's
second promise to Abraham, and repeated references through the
Old Testament prophets.

It is important to note also that the great multitude from
among all nations are spoken of as being **they which came out of
great tribulation, and have washed their robes, and made them
white in the blood of the Lamb** (Revelation 7:14). Our Lord said,
In the world ye shall have tribulation (John 16:33). Tribulation
and persecution have been the norm for believers in Christ for
almost 2000 years. First it came from their fellow Judaeans, then
from the Romans, followed by Muslims, which still continues, as
does persecution from the apostate church, although much less than
in previous centuries. Then as the gospel has spread throughout
the world, believers have suffered great tribulation from Hindus,
Buddhists, and hostile governments in many countries, such as Japan
(until the end of World War II) and Burma. Some of the greatest
tribulation of all time was forced upon Christians by atheistic
Communists in the Soviet Union and its satellites for seventy years.
As of this writing, they are still causing great suffering for Christians
in North Korea, China and Vietnam. Many thousands have stood true
through the fires of tribulation, inspired by our Saviour's message to
the church at Smyrna, **Be thou faithful unto death, and I will give
thee a crown of life** (Revelation 2:10).

As mentioned previously, prophecy teachers like John Darby
and C. I. Scofield, who lived sheltered, peaceful lives in Britain and
America a century ago, could not relate to all that the New Testament
says about Christians going through times of great tribulation. So
they invented the fictitious theory about some far-fetched "tribulation

period" that's supposed to come in the future. Such a concept is positively not to be found anywhere in the New Testament. I blindly followed their misguided teachings until I lived in Asia for several years among precious saints who had seen their loved ones tortured and killed, and had themselves barely survived the times of great tribulation which they endured. That **great multitude** which has come through **great tribulation** can signify no other than believers in Christ throughout the past twenty centuries.

Earlier I mentioned how I spent three months trying to give New Testaments to Jewish people in Philadelphia in 1942. My hope was that, after I was caught up to Heaven in the rapture, some of them might be converted through reading those Testaments and would thus become part of the 144,000 Jews who would preach the gospel during the coming tribulation period. Or so I had been taught. Looking back, I think that might have been one of the silliest teachings I ever followed. For one thing, how were all those 144,000 Jewish people going to learn what the gospel of Christ is all about with no Christians there to teach them? Remember, we would all be gone in the rapture. There would be no Bible schools, no Christian colleges, no seminaries, no evangelical churches, no home Bible studies, no Christian broadcasts, no one producing Christian literature: yet I was saying that 144,000 of these largely atheistic Jewish people were going to be transformed into Christian evangelists overnight. And they would lead a great multitude from all the nations of the world to understand what it meant to **wash their robes and make them white in the blood of the Lamb.**

AND ALL THAT WOULD HAPPEN WITHIN A SEVEN YEAR PERIOD, no less. Or so I had been taught by highly esteemed professors of Bible prophecy. Actually, it took 36 years (30 to 66 A.D.) for those original 144,000 to be called out and prepared to evangelize, even though tens of thousands of apostolic Christians were on hand to teach them.

From my studies in years after 1942 I learned from the *Universal Jewish Encyclopedia* (edited by Jewish scholars), *The Thirteenth Tribe* by Arthur Koestler and other sources that my efforts in Philadelphia would have been futile anyway, because virtually all those nice Jewish people were Ashkenazim, known in Europe as "The Yiddish People." Ashkenaz was the son of Gomer and grandson of Japheth (Genesis 10:2-3); also the nephew of Meshech and Tubal (mentioned in Ezekiel 38:2). His descendants eventually settled in the southern part of Russia where they formed a small but powerful empire called Khazaria. They had no religion until the Eighth Century, after which they chose Judaism as a means of remaining neutral in opposition to aggressive Muslims to the east and Roman Catholics on their western borders. In later centuries they were forced to migrate into Russia, Poland and other European countries, and eventually to America, where they were known as Ashkenazi Jews. But since they are not descendents of Abraham, Isaac and Jacob, there is no way they could ever be part of the 144,000 who came from the twelve tribes of Israel. So my motivation during that summer in Philadelphia was based on a teaching that was hopelessly inaccurate, to say the least.

There is another reference to those 144,000 First Century believers in Revelation 6:2 where the Lamb opened one of the seals of the book that was in the right hand of Him that sat on the throne. **When the Lamb opened one of the seals . . . I saw, and behold a white horse, and He that sat on him had a bow; and a crown was given unto Him: and He went forth conquering, and to conquer.** The Greek word translated "conquer" here is "nike," which our Lord had used in His message to each of the seven churches of Asia. Most translations render it "overcome" in those passages, such as, **To him that overcometh will I grant to sit with me in my throne, even as I overcame, and am set down with my Father in His throne** (Revelation 3:21). The white horse represents our Lord's great army of 144,000 Judaean overcomers who gave the gospel to other nations in the First Century.

We know that the white horse represents the Lord Jesus from Revelation 19:11, which depicts His second coming (on a white horse) in power and glory with His holy angels. This first occurrence of the white horse image in Chapter Six depicts the transition from the Old Covenant to the New Covenant. The Old is a continual record of failure, failure, failure. The Israelites could not keep the law of God because they were trying to do it in their own strength. **But what the law could not do, in that it was weak through the flesh, God sending His own Son in the likeness of sinful flesh, and for sin, condemned sin in the flesh: that the righteousness of the law might be fulfilled in us, who walk not after the flesh, but after the Spirit** (Romans 8:4-5). Life under the New Covenant is a record of victory, victory, victory. **We are more than conquerors through Him that loved us** (Romans 8:37). **Thanks be unto God, who always causeth us to triumph in Christ** (II Corinthians 2:14). So the white horse depicts the victorious army of 144,000 Hebrew believers in Christ who went forth in His power after the day of Pentecost, sharing the gospel of salvation with multitudes of people from their own and other nations.

As the rider on the white horse, our Lord is depicted as having been given a crown. After He died for our sins and rose again, He ascended into the heavens where His Father crowned Him **king of all kings,** and **put all things under His feet, and gave Him to be head over all things to the church, which is His body** (Ephesians 1:22-23). Having thus been highly exalted and **given all authority in Heaven and in earth,** our Saviour first demonstrated His glorious might on the Day of Pentecost when He poured out His Holy Spirit upon His disciples and **endued them with power from on high**. They then went forth in His name, **conquering and to conquer,** and so as His body are aptly represented by the white horse figure in Revelation 6:2.

Most of my teachers attributed the white horse figure to the fictitious "antichrist" character which they thought was coming sometime in the future. It seems obvious to me that it depicts rather the mighty overcoming power of true believers whom our Lord has anointed with His Holy Spirit.

One of the pleasant memories of my childhood is when we would go door to door in Charlottesville selling apples, tomatoes and other farm produce, proceeds from which my Dad would let me and my brothers keep ten cents each for admission to the Lafayette theater where, every Saturday evening, they showed a "cowboy movie." And one thing we knew for sure, the man on the white horse was always the good guy. When he came riding to the rescue we would applaud and cheer. They never showed a bad man riding a white horse. This imagery goes far back into human history. It was said of Napoleon that only he was allowed to appear on the battlefield riding a white horse. And the appearance of that distinguished steed was said to be the equivalent of adding a hundred thousand men to the French forces because the presence of the emperor himself so inspired his troops to valor. So the white horse in Revelation Chapter Six can surely represent no other than the soul-winning forces of the King of Kings during those forty years following the Day of Pentecost.

God held back the execution of the second half of Daniel's seventieth week, which had foretold His final judgment upon the Hebrew nation, for 36 years (30-66 A.D.) while he called out, prepared and anointed twelve thousand **chosen vessels** from each of the Hebrew tribes. It was they who would, in turn, give the gospel of Christ to other nations. **Other sheep I have,** our Saviour had said, **which are not of this fold: them also I must bring, and they shall hear my voice; and there shall be one fold and one shepherd** (John 10:16). **Neither pray I for these alone, but for them also which shall believe on me through their word** (John 17:20). And in answer to that prayer, the Word of God has been spreading to all nations throughout the world ever since those original 144,000 Hebrew believers first began to share the message of salvation in Christ with people of other tribes and nations.

Fulfillment of the second half of Daniel's seventieth week was held back until the 144,000 were called out and commissioned to give the gospel to other nations. The Apocalypse announced the completion of this objective, and that **THE TIME WAS AT HAND** for execution of God's conclusive judgment upon the rebellious, unfaithful Israelites, other than **the elect remnant (144,000)** who alone were recognized as being **the Israel of God** (Galatians 6:16).

Chapter 9

The Wrath of the Lamb

Mine eyes have seen the glory of the coming of the Lord;
He is trampling out the vintage where the grapes of wrath
are stored;
He hath loosed the fateful lightning of His terrible swift
sword . . .

Once I heard a choral group from Jerry Falwell's Liberty University singing that song, and I wondered whether they had any idea of its origin, or what the words really meant. Julia Ward Howe, a Unitarian abolitionist (regarding slavery) composed the poem in 1862 to encourage Yankee soldiers to kill the Confederates, and suggested that their actions were "the coming of the Lord" to loose "His terrible swift sword." The actual meaning of poetic imagery is not always understood by those who appreciate its beauty.

So it is with the Apocalypse of John which begins (1:7) **Behold He cometh with clouds; and every eye shall see Him, and they also which pierced Him: and all the [Hebrew] tribes of the land [Palestine] shall wail because of Him.** Note carefully that it does not say that He is coming **IN** the clouds, which is the wording that would be used if this were speaking of His second coming. Here He is said to be coming **WITH CLOUDS.** In the original Greek this is a military term, the same as in Hebrews 12:1, which speaks of us being **compassed about with a great CLOUD of witnesses.**

A Roman army on the march in those days would in itself appear as a cloud of creatures moving over the countryside. Large ranks of mounted cavalry would lead the way, followed by thousands of foot soldiers with shields reflecting the sunlight. These would be followed by hundreds of support personnel with carts hauling equipment and provisions, all pulled by mules or oxen. And as the procession moved along dirt roads it would stir up huge clouds of dust. That's why a moving military force was said to be "coming with clouds." Every eye in Palestine would have seen a military column during the three-and-a-half years of war from 66 to 70 A.D. as Roman armies subdued the rebellious Israelites throughout Galilee, Samaria and Judaea.

Knowing that He was going to be killed by His fellow Judaeans, our Lord had said that He was going **to send His armies to destroy those murderers and burn up their city** (Matthew 22:7). When He was rejected by His fellow Israelites in Jerusalem, the Lord wept over the city, saying that the days were coming when **thine enemies shall cast a trench about thee, and compass thee round, and keep thee in on every side, and lay thee even with the ground, and thy children within thee** (Luke 19:43-44). My liberal professors at the University of Chicago used to say that our Lord's description of the impending destruction of Jerusalem must have been written "after 70 A.D. because there was no way Christ could have known it was coming?" In so saying they revealed their pitiful ignorance of the fact that our Lord and Saviour was God Almighty living on earth in a human body, the One who **knows the end from the beginning**.

I have mentioned previously how, when the disciples heard the Lord speak of the impending destruction of Jerusalem, they asked, **When shall THESE THINGS be?** They confused it with Christ's second coming, so He made very clear to them that the two events were completely separate. His second coming would not take place until He had a witness for Himself, a people for His name, among all the nations of the world.

When we sing *Battle Hymn of the Republic*, we know full well

104

that Julia Ward Howe did not mean that God Himself, in person, was leading those Yankee troops into battle against the Confederates. When she said "mine eyes have seen," she was obviously referring to an invisible presence which people like her could visualize. So it was with Judaeans in Palestine who wailed because of the "terrible swift sword" being wielded by armies sent by the Son of God during the three-and-a-half years of vengeance from 66 to 70 A.D.

Repeatedly in the Old Testament the prophets said it was God who used the Assyrians to lead captive the ten idolatrous tribes of Israel; and that Nebuchadnezzar, king of Babylon, was God's servant to execute judgment on the idolatrous tribes of Judah and Benjamin and take them captive. So, likewise, He used the Romans to carry out His conclusive retribution on the Judaeans of Christ's generation. And every eye saw Him coming, just as Julia Ward Howe thought she saw the hand of God in the abolitionist movement and the bloody Civil War which it brought forth in the United States.

In seems to have been a supernatural act of God that a Judaean named Flavius Josephus should have been miraculously kept alive by the Romans, and lived to record in a book of horrors the carnage that took place during **the days of vengeance**. He served as interpreter for Titus, the Roman commander, who had hoped it would not be necessary to destroy the city of Jerusalem. Josephus went inside the walls to talk with John of Gischala, leader of a Judaean faction that was killing and plundering inside the besieged city, and begged him to stop the slaughter of his fellow Judaeans, in exchange for which Titus would spare the temple and the city. John cursed Josephus repeatedly, and said he (John) was not afraid of the Romans because Jerusalem was God's city. In reply to his fellow Judaean, Josephus said, "It is God Himself who is using the Romans to purge His temple with fire and exterminate this city because it is so choked with pollution." Then, as the Messiah had done some 39 years earlier, Josephus wept over the city, contemplating its inevitable destruction. He probably didn't realize that an angel had said to Daniel, **For the overspreading of their abominations, He** [the Messiah] **will make it desolate** (Daniel 9:27).

After the Romans had destroyed the city, Josephus wrote of the terrible corruption, intrigue, murder, struggles for power and desecration of the temple area which he had witnessed there before the conflict with Rome had even begun. "This is why," he wrote, "it is my opinion that God turned Himself away from our city and brought the Romans upon us."

When our Lord went forth, bearing His cross, to be crucified, some faithful women stood weeping as they watched. His word to them was, **Daughters of Jerusalem, weep not for me, but weep for yourselves, and for your children. For, behold, the days are coming in which they shall say, Blessed are the barren and the wombs that never bare, and the breasts which never nursed a baby. Then shall they begin to say to the mountains, Fall on us, and to the hills, Cover us** (Luke 23:28-30). That the time had arrived for the fulfillment of these words is evident from Revelation 6:15-17, where we read: **And the kings of the earth** [Israel]**, and the great men, and the rich men, and the chief captains, and the mighty men, and every bondman, and every free man, hid themselves in the dens and in the rocks of the mountains; and said to the mountains and rocks, Fall on us, and hide us from the face of Him that sitteth on the throne, and from THE WRATH OF THE LAMB: for the great day of His wrath is come; and who shall be able to stand?**

Some say it is not in keeping with the character of "lowly Jesus, meek and mild" to take vengeance. To them the Apostle Paul asks, **Is God unrighteous who taketh vengeance?** (Romans 3:5). Then, later, he quotes Deuteronomy 32:35, **Vengeance is mine; I will repay, saith the Lord** (Romans 12:19). God would not be holy, just and righteous if He failed to judge the wicked. And our Lord Jesus would not be God if He failed to do likewise. To those women who wept for Him as He bore His cross to Golgotha, He was saying, **Vengeance is mine, I will repay,** and thus demonstrated His deity as the Son of God. **The wrath of God is revealed from Heaven against all ungodliness and unrighteousness of men** (Romans 1:18).

Some say that Revelation 6:12-17 refers to the second coming of our Lord, but I disagree. Rather, it is a flashback to that fateful day 36 years earlier when **there was a great earthquake, and the sun was darkened and the earth did quake and the rocks rent** as the Son of God went into the outer darkness for our sins. No doubt the stars (angels) of Heaven swept down from the heights and the whole universe trembled, as the Creator **spared not His own Son but delivered Him up for us all** (Romans 8:32). Remember, Revelation is a book of coded symbols and mysteries which God has challenged us to decipher. The very fact that Revelation 6:17 says that **the great day of the wrath of the Lamb had come** indicates that it is the same as **the days of vengeance and wrath upon this people** (Luke 21:22-23).

As mentioned in the previous chapter, Revelation Chapter Six begins with the symbol of the rider on a **white horse**, which represents the risen, exalted, conquering Christ working through His chosen 144,000 Hebrew disciples, beginning on the Day of Pentecost when the first 3000 believed. Shortly thereafter the number had grown to 5000 (Acts 4:4). When, after thirty-six years, the number had grown to 144,000 the time had come to unleash **the wrath of the Lamb** on His fellow Judaeans who had been killing those who believed in Him. The beginning of this judgment is symbolized by the rider on the **red horse** (Revelation 6:4) who would **take peace from the land** [Palestine], **that they should kill one another: and there was given unto him a great sword.**

The Romans had been in control of Palestine for ninety years when our Lord began His public ministry. In 63 B.C. General Pompey had subdued conflicting parties among the Judaeans, and stopped them from killing one another in horrible civil wars that often resulted in the slaughter of thousands. After the legions of Rome had imposed peace by force upon the warring Israelites, King Herod the Great rebuilt the temple in Jerusalem and allowed the Judaeans to practice their religion as in times past. The ensuing period of relative peace and prosperity provided an environment in which the gospel could spread and churches multiply rapidly throughout the empire. But wherever believers went, they faced continual harassment, opposition, persecution and violence from jealous Judaeans who hated Christ.

That's why John was given a vision **of the souls of them that were slain for the word of God, and for the testimony which they held: and they cried with a loud voice, saying, How long, O Lord, holy and true, dost thou not judge and avenge our blood on them that dwell in the land** [Palestine] . . . **and it was said unto them that they should rest yet for a little season, until their fellow servants** [of the 144,000] **also and their brethren, that should be killed as they were, should be fulfilled** (Revelation 6:9-11). Remembering that Revelation is not chronological, the prayer of these martyrs would have occurred during the ride of the **white horse**, and before the **red horse** indicated that the time had come for God to avenge the death of those Hebrew believers who had been killed by their fellow Judaeans.

So, finally, in the year 66, God said that **THE TIME WAS AT HAND** to end this holocaust, which had its origins from synagogues in Palestine. As the **red horse** symbolized, the peace that had been imposed on the Judaeans in Palestine by the Romans for 128 years was coming to an end. The most terrible time of carnage and suffering that the Israelites had ever known was about to break forth upon them.

The trouble began in the year 64 when Emperor Nero appointed Gessius Florus as procurator of Judaea. At that time marauding gangs of Judaean brigands were plundering the population in many places, but rather than arrest them, Florus joined in league with them in exchange for a share of the loot. Josephus reported his corruption by saying that he "stripped whole cities and ruined entire populations."

In the year 66 some Judaeans wanted to enlarge a synagogue in Caesarea, but the neighbor refused to sell the space they needed. So the Judaeans gave a bribe of eight talents of silver (equivalent to many thousands of dollars) to Florus in exchange for his promise to force the issue. But Florus kept their money and did nothing. A riot broke out in Caesarea related to the problem, and when the Judaeans sent a delegation to negotiate with Florus regarding the matter, he put the delegation in prison. When protests erupted, Florus dispatched troops to punish those who were disrespectful toward him, and 3000 men, women and children were killed.

Soon afterwards King Agrippa visited Jerusalem where he heard from a delegation which complained about the misuse of power by Florus. The king urged them to be patient until Nero could appoint a replacement for Florus. In response, some Judaeans rioted and threw stones at Agrippa.

At that time it was customary for the Romans to present an annual gift to the temple treasury in honor of the emperor, but the high priest in Jerusalem ordered that no more gifts should be accepted from the Romans. This insult to the emperor infuriated the Romans.

Meanwhile, Judaeans were becoming sharply divided by zealous leaders of revolutionary parties which wanted to expel the Romans altogether. Moderates who preferred to live in peace under Roman protection sent a delegation to King Agrippa urging him to send troops to Jerusalem to crush the revolutionaries. He sent 2000 soldiers but they were defeated by the rebels, as were the Judaean moderates who had fought on the side of the Romans. The rebels were led by Menahem, son of Judas of Galilee. When the high priest fled from the city, Menahem burned his house. Next, his rebel forces overcame the Roman stronghold at Masada and made off with a huge supply of arms and military equipment. Emboldened by the victory, Menahem said that Judaeans should obey God only, not the Romans. He returned to Jerusalem where he killed Ananias, the high priest, who favored living at peace with Rome. The revolutionary forces then expelled all but one garrison of the Romans from the city of Jerusalem.

As revealed by the **red horse** (Revelation 6:4) which John had seen in his vision on the isle of Patmos, **peace was taken from the land** [of Palestine].

With most Romans out of the city, Judaeans in Jerusalem

were left to fight among themselves. Menahem, his ego inflated by success, became a tyrant and set himself up as being king of the Judaeans. But when he arrayed himself in royal robes and went into the temple, a rival faction led by a man named Eleazar captured him and put him to death with horrible torture. Eleazar and his gang then attacked the one remaining Roman garrison. Metilius, commander of the garrison, realized there was no escape, so he offered to exchange arms for the safe release of his men. Eleazar accepted the agreement with an oath, but as soon as the Romans laid down their arms and marched out of the garrison they were brutally massacred. This horrible treachery made war an unavoidable certainty.

Roman residents of Caesarea rose up and slaughtered about 20,000 Judaeans living there. In retaliation, Judaeans attacked neighboring Syrian towns, killing many of the residents, which provoked the Syrians to kill all the Judaeans in nearby towns and villages. When bands of Judaean rebels invaded the city of Scythopolis, they found only fellow Hebrews living there. But the Judaeans of Sythopolis wanted no part of the rebellion, so they rose up and killed 13,000 of their fellow Israelites.

A Roman fortress called Cypros, near Jericho, was taken by Judaean rebels and the troops there were massacred. Realizing that full scale war was now in progress, King Agrippa sent a large force from Antioch under General Cestius to stamp out the insurrection. With skirmishes along the way, his army marched to Jerusalem and attacked the city for five days. But zealous Judaeans fought back so furiously that the Roman forces retreated on the sixth day. Inspired by their apparent victory, the Judaeans pursued after the Romans and seized many of the weapons and provisions which were abandoned by the fleeing army.

Upon their return to Jerusalem, the victorious rebels convened a conference in hopes of uniting the opposing factions which had been fighting among themselves. Commanders were then appointed to lead military forces throughout all Palestine. Flavius Josephus, who would later write a history of the conflict, was made commander of Galilee. Finally, it seemed, the Judaeans might stop killing each other and unite to fight the Romans.

Josephus recruited an army of 100,000 volunteers willing to sacrifice their lives to drive the occupation forces out of Galilee. But they were no match for the well trained, highly disciplined, fully equipped soldiers of the Roman army. Nero had sent his top general, Flavius Vespasian, to crush the rebellion in Palestine. His first encounter with the motly ranks assembled by Josephus caused the Judaeans to flee in disarray. Josephus retreated to the walled city of Jopatata where he and his remaining troops withstood Vespasian's assault for forty-seven days. But, finally, the Romans breached the walls and slaughtered more than 40,000 inhabitants. Josephus, because of his rank and valor, was taken alive as a prisoner. In a private interview with Vespasian, Josephus spoke of God and foretold that Vespasian would soon replace Nero as emperor. After asking other Judaeans about him, Vespasian came to believe that Josephus might indeed be a prophet of the God of the Hebrews.

With his son, Titus, in charge of cavalry forces, Vespasian and his troops conquered all of Galilee, killing hundreds of thousands of Judaeans as they subdued city after city. They continued the slaughter as the Roman forces moved on through Samaria and then overran all of Judaea. Finally, they reached the gates of Jerusalem.

In the wake of Roman conquests, marauding bands of thieves and robbers, all Judaeans, raided every city and town, looting, plundering and killing. Helpless women were assaulted, raped and murdered. These renegade natives were said to be more merciless and harmful than the Roman foreigners as they increased the horrors of that time of **great tribulation.**

While he was gathering his forces outside Jerusalem, where over three million Judaeans had taken refuge inside its massive walls, Vespasian's spies reported that mass killings were taking place inside the city. Leaders of a party known as the Zealots were killing thousands of other Judaeans in a power struggle for control. Vespasian then told his officers that to invade the city was premature; rather, he said, give them enough time and those Judaeans would all kill each other. Instead, he marched his army from place to place in Judaea to slaughter the inhabitants. They overran the cities of Gadara, Bethennabris, Lydda, Emmaus, Jericho and others.

At about this time Vespasian received word that Nero had died, and had been succeeded by Galba, who was promptly assassinated. With the government in such a state of confusion, Vespasian withdrew his forces from Jerusalem and left them in Caesarea.

It has been reported that, during this lull in the war, many believers in Christ who were still in Jerusalem fled the city and took refuge in remote mountain areas of Judaea, Samaria and Lebanon. They were prompted by the words of Christ, who said, **When ye shall see Jerusalem compassed with armies, then know that the desolation thereof is nigh. Then let them which are in Judaea flee to the mountains; and let them which are in the midst of it depart out; and let not them that are in the country enter thereinto** (Luke 21:20-21).

Even before he could return to Rome, Vespasian was proclaimed emperor. So he commissioned his son, Titus, to take charge of the war in Palestine and finish off the Judaean rebels, while he, Vespasian, proceeded to Rome to take over the government.

While the Romans were withdrawn, horrendous civil war raged inside the walls of Jerusalem, and bands of Judean outlaws ravaged what was left of cities and towns throughout Judaea, Samaria and Galilee. Some of the criminal bands then entered Jerusalem where they continued to plunder the population. They joined up with the Zealots who had taken control of the city and killed hundreds of residents, casting their dead bodies over the walls to be eaten by dogs and vultures. They even appointed one of their own to be a false high priest so they could give religious sanction to their murderous plundering. Ananus II, the legitimate high priest, gathered a group to oppose them, and a fierce battle raged within the temple area. Outnumbered by the traditional majority, the Zealots convinced a group from Idumea (southern Judaea) to come and help them. To win their support, the Zealots falsely accused the traditionalists of collusion with the Romans. Some 20,000 men marched to Jerusalem from Idumea, and joined with the Zealots in slaughtering 8500 persons the first night, including Ananus II, and threw their corpses out of the city without burial. Next day they continued to butcher the people, and tossed 12,000 more bodies over the walls into gullies and ravines below.

Later, Josephus would write that it was his belief that the ancient Hebrew prophets had foretold how the temple would be burned to the ground and the city destroyed if the place was defiled by evil men such as the Zealots. He also said that the warring factions of rival Judaeans within Jerusalem did as much to destroy the city as the Romans did.

As the struggle for power continued, the Holy Place within the temple was repeatedly defiled with the blood of those who were slaughtered, while outside the formidable walls of the city Roman forces under the command of Titus, son of Emperor Vespasian, prepared for a siege.

Within a few months the food supply inside the city was completely exhausted, and the rider on the **black horse** of the Apocalypse appeared (Revelation 6:3-6). Starvation drove the people to madness, as leaders of rebel factions sent their men from house to house inside the city, searching for any scrap of food that might be hidden. Family members would fight each other over any edible item that could be found. About 500 persons daily slipped over the walls to search for food outside, and most were captured by the Romans. Titus ordered his soldiers to crucify many of them in sight of those inside the city looking over the ramparts. His purpose was to convince the occupants of the city to surrender so he wouldn't have to destroy it and the temple. But when he sent Josephus to the foot of the wall where he could speak to them in their own language, they cursed him and tried to kill him with stones and arrows.

Since the total length of the wall around the city was about five miles, it was difficult for the Romans to guard every exit day and night. So Titus ordered additional barriers constructed which would block every exit, and prevent any possibility of food being smuggled in. So thousands died of starvation. Josephus said that he received a report of 115,800 corpses being thrown over the walls within eleven weeks, and a total of more than 600,000 since the famine began. Every ravine and gully along the walls contained dead bodies. The rebels killed everyone who suggested making a deal with the Roman commander. The stench of decaying flesh was so horrible that even the mighty Roman legions had to withdraw because of it.

Still the rebel factions within the city refused to surrender. False prophets among them began to spread rumors that the Messiah was going to burst on the scene at any moment to deliver them. This was in direct fulfillment of the words of the true Messiah whom they had delivered to death thirty-nine years earlier: **Then if any man shall say unto you, Lo, here is Christ, or there; believe it not . . . if they say unto you, Behold, He is in the desert, go not forth; behold, He is in the secret chambers, believe it not** (Matthew 24:23, 26).

As the horrors of the famine continued to increase, reports of cannibalism were circulated widely. One concerned a woman named Mary who came from a wealthy family in Bethezuba. She had fled to Jerusalem for safety, taking along her infant child. But she could not bear to see it starve to death, so she cooked it to end its misery. After she had eaten half of it, others, who had been attracted by the odor, discovered what she had done; so she offered to share the remaining portion of her child's body with them.

Titus wanted to spare the temple from destruction. As the future Caesar he had high respect for magnificent buildings. But the angel Gabriel had said to Daniel, **For the overspreading of** [their] **abominations he shall make it desolate** (Daniel 9:27). The Zealots had fought their most bloody conflicts against rival factions within the temple itself. The holy place had been repeatedly desecrated with the blood of their murdered victims. There could be no greater abomination in the sight of God. So God's fateful prediction was going to be fulfilled, as the true Messiah had said earlier, **Behold your house is left unto you desolate** (Matthew 23:38). Titus had no other choice, even as the foolish Zealots clung to their false hope that the Messiah was going to appear at the last moment to save them.

Prophecy teachers today who promulgate the fictitious fantasy of a coming Antichrist during an equally fictitious yet future "tribulation period" are eerily reminiscent of those Zealots in Jerusalem so long ago.

One terrible tragedy of **the days of vengeance** occurred when a false prophet said people would be safe if they gathered in a certain portico of the temple. A huge group crowded into the space on the same day that Romans troops set fire to the wooden gates in the temple area. Flames spread to that fateful portico, and 6000 women and children were burned alive, their screams causing even the Roman soldiers to weep. Titus was alarmed by the tragedy. He went into the temple himself and ordered his men to extinguish the flames. But it was too late. The temple was destroyed.

Thus appeared the **fourth horse** of the Apocalypse, the **pale horse ridden by Death and Hell. Power was given unto them over the fourth part of the land** [Palestine], **to kill with the sword, and with hunger, and with death, and with the beasts of the earth** (Revelation 6:8). The entire Hebrew population of Palestine suffered during the last half of Daniel's seventieth week, the three-and-a-half years from 66 to 70 A.D. Titus estimated that two million seven hundred thousand still remained bottled up inside the walls of Jerusalem without food or water during the siege, and very few of them survived. And at least half a million (some say one million) Israelites also died in fighting elsewhere in Judaea, Samaria and Galilee.

The Messiah had said, **Except those days should be shortened, there should no flesh be saved: but for the elect's sake those days shall be shortened** (Matthew 24:22). The "elect" were the 144,000 remnant of true believers whom God had chosen from among the Hebrew tribes (Romans 11:5). And no doubt some of them were still inside Jerusalem during the last days of God's retribution against those who killed the Messiah and His disciples. But they would surely have kept to themselves and had no part in the heinous deeds of the fighting factions within the city. Nevertheless, unless the Romans had succeeded in breaking through the gates and entering the city, every living person there would have been dead within two or three weeks, since there was not a scrap of food left anywhere within the walls. God providentially intervened by allowing the Romans to break in and save the remaining survivors who were still alive.

Able-bodied Hebrew men who were still walking were sold into slavery or used to entertain crowds by being forced to face lions and tigers in Roman outdoor theaters. Over 2000 were killed in one day in Caesarea to celebrate the birthday of Domitian, brother of Titus. That's the meaning of Revelation 6:8 where it says they were killed **with the beasts of the earth.**

Perhaps the greatest **overspreading of abominations** for which Jerusalem was laid desolate had to do with the obsession of the priests for hoarding material wealth. Secret treasury chambers within the temple were stashed with tons of gold. Our Lord had said to the money grabbers who **devoured widows' houses** that **God's house shall be a house of prayer, but ye have made it a den of thieves** (Luke 19:46). And He drove the money changers out of the temple. But of course they came right back, until the final judgment that permanently ended their abominations.

Jerusalem was the financial hub of the world in those days, as New York is today. Thousands of bankers, money lenders and businessmen there were extremely wealthy. And the priests were the ultimate fund raisers. They extracted tithes, plus additional gifts and offerings, from every person. In addition, they received enormous gifts of gold and jewels presented by visiting dignitaries from other countries. In violation of the laws of Moses they excused successful men from caring for their elderly parents by giving their money to the priests instead (Mark 7:9-13). And rather than use their accumulated hoard of wealth to help the poor, the priests piled it up, heaps upon heaps. Inner rooms of the temple in Jerusalem were so sacrosanct that every foreigner or Judaean non-priest who visited the area respected the restrictions imposed by the priests. So there was no way that anyone could know of the billions of dollars worth of gold, silver and jewels which were hidden there. Even the ornate display of walls and ceilings of the inner sanctuaries being overlaid with pure gold had been visible only to the priests who were allowed access to these secluded areas. So no one really knew of how much wealth was there.

During the Roman assault on the city, the Zealots who seized control inside the walls used the Holy Place of the temple as a combat area where they killed the rival priests, but there was no way they could touch the treasury because they had no other place to hide it. And they could not take it outside the city walls because of the Romans. So Titus found the entire hoard intact. As might be expected, he took it all to Rome as a trophy of his victory over the rebellious Judaeans who had disrupted the peace of the empire. Gold worth billions of dollars, most of it given as offerings to the God of Israel, was then used to pay for construction of the mighty Colosseum in Rome, which still stands today as a tragic reminder of God's conclusive judgment on the Israelites, of whom He said, with great sorrow, **I have spread out my hands unto a rebellious people . . . a people that provoketh me to anger continually to my face . . . I will not keep silence, but will recompense** (Isaiah 65:2-6).

Also standing in Rome today is the Arch of Titus which commemorates his subjugation of the rebellious nation that disrupted the *Pax Romana*, the peace of Rome. That period had brought prosperity and international cooperation to the Mediterranean world for more than a century. Inscribed on the inside wall of the Arch is a copy of the golden Menorah, a candelabrum with seven branches, which was taken from inside the sanctuary of the temple in Jerusalem; another reminder of God's judgment.

Much of Jerusalem, including most of the temple area, was made level with the ground by the Romans. Not by choice, however. Titus continually tried to persuade the rebellious Judaeans to surrender so the city and temple could be preserved. But the murderous Zealots who had taken control inside the city refused to compromise, foolishly hanging on to the false hope that the Messiah promised in the Old Testament would miraculously appear to rescue them. Little did they realize that, as Peter had said on the day of Pentecost, **Let all the house of Israel know assuredly, that God hath made that same Jesus, whom ye have crucified, both Lord and Messiah** (Acts 2:36). The Messiah had come already, and they had killed Him. Now He had come again with His armies to execute vengeance on those who were responsible for His murder.

Among the writings of Josephus are statements saying that never in the history of the world had there been such a time of anguish and suffering as was experienced by that pitiful multitude compressed like **grapes in a winepress** inside the walls of Jerusalem. That's what the Greek word *thlipsis*, translated *tribulation*, means in the New Testament. Speaking of that awful time, our Lord said, **Then shall be great tribulation, such as was not since the beginning of the world to this time, no, nor ever shall be** (Matthew 24:21).

Chapter 10

Babylon the Great is Fallen, is Fallen

And he cried mightily with a strong voice, saying, Babylon the great is fallen, is fallen, and is become the habitation of devils, and the hold of every foul spirit, and a cage of every unclean and hateful bird (Revelation 18:2). **And there followed another angel, saying, Babylon is fallen, is fallen, that great city, because she made all nations drink of the wine of the wrath of her fornication** (Revelation 14:8).

We remember from the Old Testament how the upper classes of Judaea were taken captive to Babylon by King Nebuchadnezzar and held there for seventy years. So the term "Babylon" was in common usage in New Testament times to connote a place where bad things happened.

The first church, which began on the Day of Pentecost in Jerusalem, was something new in human history. It was a congregation of five thousand Judaeans (Acts 4:4) who **were of one heart and of one soul: neither said any of them that aught of the things which he possessed was his own; but they had all things common . . . and great grace was upon them all** (Acts 4:32-33). Nearly all were from faraway places: Parthia, Media, Mesopotamia, Cappadocia, Phrygia, Pamphylia, Pontus, Crete, Arabia, Rome,

Asia and elsewhere (Acts 2:9-11). The Greek word for "visitors" is usually translated into English as "strangers," as used regarding these Hebrew pilgrims who had come to Jerusalem for the fifty-day celebration from Passover to Pentecost.

As their numbers grew, bitter opposition came from the chief priests, scribes and Pharisees. The apostles were beaten and imprisoned. Steven was murdered by stoning. And then, finally, **There was a great persecution against the church which was at Jerusalem; and they were all scattered abroad . . . except the apostles** (Acts 8:1). The apostles didn't have to leave because they were natives of Palestine, but all those pilgrims had to go back where they came from. This experience was reminiscent of the "Babylonian captivity" of the Old Testament, so "Babylon" became a nickname for Jerusalem. Soon after they were dispersed, Peter wrote a letter of encouragement to all those **strangers** who had been **scattered abroad** (I Peter 1:1). He ended it by saying, **The church that is at Babylon, elected together with you, saluteth you** (I Peter 5:13). Obviously, he was referring to the native Hebrew believers who were still left in Jerusalem, all part of the elect **remnant of 144,000**.

There are many parallels between the Old Testament Babylonian captivity of the residents of Judaea and the expulsion of five thousand new believers in Christ from Jerusalem. The Babylonian captives would have been forced into slave labor with lashes from whips. Many of those new believers in Jerusalem would have been beaten while there, and upon returning to their homes would have been beaten more by relatives, then dragged into synagogues for still more beatings. The Old Testament captives lost all of their property in Judaea, and the pilgrims who returned home from Jerusalem as believers in Christ would have had all their property confiscated by Hebrew relatives. **Ye endured a great fight of afflictions . . . ye were made a gazingstock by reproaches and tribulations** [Greek, *thlipsis*] . . . **and took joyfully the stealing of your property** (Hebrews 10:33-34). That's why when Peter wrote a letter to these **strangers scattered abroad** from Jerusalem, he said, **Think it not strange concerning the fiery trial which is to try**

120

you . . . that the trial of your faith, being much more precious than of gold that perisheth, though it be tried with fire, might be found unto praise and honor and glory at the appearing of Jesus Christ (I Peter 1:7, 4:12).

While in Jerusalem, these 5000 new believers had enjoyed the fellowship and moral support of the family of God to sustain and strengthen them. But when they were **scattered abroad** back to their original homes, they were virtually alone among hostile relatives who would want to kill them for breaking with legalistic Hebrew traditions. Just as those taken captive in Babylon were torn from their families, the Christians who were expelled from Jerusalem were torn from the new family of God of which they had become a part. And upon return to their original homes they would have been shunned and excluded by their original Hebrew families. Mock funerals would have been conducted for them while they were still alive. And in many cases, those who were killed had no funerals at all. Their bodies were cast out to be eaten by maggots, dogs and vultures.

So when Peter concluded his letter to those former members of the church in Jerusalem, we can readily understand why he would conclude it by saying, **The church that is at Babylon [Jerusalem], elected [being part of the 144,000 elect remnant of Israel] together with you, saluteth you** (I Peter 5:13). And it therefore should come as no surprise that the Apostle John used the term **Babylon** in Revelation to connote the unbelieving Israelites who were not part of the **remnant (144,000)** of true believers, **the Israel of God** (Galatians 6:16), but rather were their persecutors. In Chapter 14 we read of the **144,000** being **the FIRSTFRUITS to God and to the Lamb . . . having the everlasting gospel to preach to them that dwell in the land** [to the Judaeans first], **and to every nation, kindred, tongue and people.** Then immediately afterwards we read, **Babylon is fallen, is fallen, because she made all nations drink of the wine of the wrath of her fornication** (verse 8). The **remnant, 144,000** faithful Israelites, were called out during the 40 years following the Day of Pentecost, and then **BABYLON**

(Jerusalem) was destroyed.

We also know that the term **BABYLON** in Revelation refers to the disobedient Israelites (controlled from Jerusalem) of that day because included in the judgment upon them was divine retribution to avenge the blood of the Old Testament prophets. **They have shed the blood of saints and prophets, and thou hast given them blood to drink** (Revelation 16:6). **Rejoice over her . . . ye holy apostles and prophets, for God hath avenged you on her** (Revelation 18:20). **In her was found the blood of prophets, and of saints, and of all that were slain upon the land** [of Palestine] (Revelation 18:24). There is no way that avenging the murder of Old Testament prophets could apply to any other people than the unbelieving Judaeans of that day. As the Messiah said, after He wept over the city, **Woe unto you, scribes and Pharisees, hypocrites . . . ye are the children of them which killed the prophets. Fill ye up then the measure of your fathers. You snakes, you generation of vipers, how can you escape the damnation of hell? Behold I send unto you prophets, and wise men and scribes: and some of them you shall kill and crucify; and some of them you shall scourge in your synagogues, and persecute them from city to city: that upon you may come all the righteous blood shed upon the land, from the blood of righteous Abel unto the blood of Zacharias son of Barachias, whom you slew between the temple and the altar. Verily I say unto you, all these things shall come upon this generation** (Matthew 23:29-36).

Another proof that Babylon in Revelation refers to Jerusalem of that day was that the city is accused of spiritual fornication and spiritual whoredom. These expressions are direct quotes from the Old Testament, beginning with Moses, where instead of being like a faithful wife to God, the unfaithful Israelites committed spiritual adultery by idolatry and materialism. Instead of standing apart from others as a "holy nation," the Hebrews compromised with their neighbors and rulers, and thus failed to be a witness for the Living God.

The Old Testament prophet Hosea put it this way: **The land**

hath committed great whoredom, departing from the Lord . . . I will no more have mercy upon the house of Israel; but I will utterly take them away . . . for ye are not my people and I will not be your God . . . she [Israel] is not my wife, neither am I her husband . . . for she hath played the harlot . . . they have committed whoredom continually (Hosea 1:2, 6, 9, 2:2, 5, 4:18).

God wanted "Israel" to be the **apple of His eye**, as a loving and faithful wife is to her husband. Instead, she became a spiritual whore: **How is the faithful city become an harlot** (Isaiah 1:21). **They went a-whoring after other gods** (Judges 2:17). **Jehoram . . . made high places in the mountains of Judah, and caused the inhabitants of Jerusalem to commit fornication . . . and has made Judah and the inhabitants of Jerusalem to go a-whoring, like the whoredoms of the house of Ahab** [king of Israel] (II Chronicles 21:11-13). **Thou hast polluted the land with thy whoredom** (Jeremiah 3:2). **Judah . . . played the harlot, and . . . through her whoredom defiled the land, and committed adultery** (Jeremiah 3:8-9). **Thou hast multiplied thy whoredoms, thou hast committed fornication with the Egyptians; and hast increased thy whoredoms to provoke me to anger. Thou hast played the whore also with the Assyrians, because thou wast unsatiable; yea, thou hast played the harlot with them, and yet couldst not be satisfied . . . how weak is thine heart, saith the Lord God, seeing thou doest all these things, the work of an imperious whorish woman** (Ezekiel 16:25-26, 28, 30).

Because of the unfaithfulness of the Israelites, the Old Testament prophets also used the figure of divorce to indicate their rejection by God. **Thus saith the Lord, where is the bill of your mother's divorcement, whom I have put away? . . . for your transgressions is your mother put away** (Isaiah 50:1). **For all the causes whereby backsliding Israel committed adultery, I had put her way, and given her a bill of divorce; yet her treacherous sister Judah feared not, but went and played the harlot also, and through her whoredom she defiled the land** (Jeremiah 3:8-9).

Through the Old Testament prophets, God continually

repeated His longing to be reconciled to the Israelites, with promises of great blessings if they returned to Him in repentance and obedience to His law. He wanted the Israelites to be **the apple of His eye** (Deuteronomy 32:10), but instead He had to say, **Because thou hast defiled my sanctuary with all thy detestable things, and with all thine abominations, therefore will I diminish thee; neither shall mine eye spare, neither will I have any pity. A third part of thee will die with pestilence and with famine; and a third part of thee shall fall by the sword; and I will scatter a third part of thee into all the winds** (Ezekiel 5:11-12).

Of course, looking back from the New Covenant perspective, we know what the problem was. Instead of being **the apple of His eye**, the Judaeans failed to measure up to God's expectations because **by one man sin entered into the world, and death by sin; so death passed upon all men, for that all have sinned** (Romans 5:12). All men are born **dead in trespasses and sins** (Ephesians 2:1). And there was no way that the Israelites could be any different. That's why a new covenant was necessary. When our Saviour died to make atonement for our sins, those who believed could be counted righteous before God through faith in His blood. The Holy Spirit of God could then come into human hearts and transform lives so that we become **new creatures; old things will then pass away and all things will become new** (II Corinthians 5:17). It did not happen sooner because **the Holy Spirit was not given until our Lord Jesus was glorified** (John 7:39). The Hebrews, living in sin under the Old Covenant, did not realize what their problem was. So when the prophets repeatedly foretold that the Messiah was coming, the Israelites foolishly thought that He would take over with political and military control so they could go on sinning with no one to stop them. They failed to listen when God warned that Messiah would bring judgment instead.

The Lord, whom ye seek, shall suddenly come to His temple . . . behold He shall come, saith the Lord of hosts; but who may abide the day of His coming? And who shall stand when He appeareth? For He is like a refiner's fire, and like a

fuller's soap: and He shall sit as a refiner and purifier of silver" (Malachi 3:1-3).

We all know what happened. When the promised Messiah came He found the conduct of Judaeans as bad as ever. **He came unto His own, and His own received Him not** (John 1:11). **Woe unto you, scribes and Pharisees, hypocrites,** He thundered, **for you shut up the kingdom of God against men: ye neither go in yourselves, neither suffer ye them that are entering to go in** (Matthew 23:13). There in that Twenty-third Chapter of Matthew our Lord spelled out some of the abominations of the religious leaders of His fellow Judaeans. The prophet Ezekiel had used the word **abominations** forty-six times to describe the sins of his fellow Israelites. He was hopeful that change would come, that the Hebrew people might eventually make themselves acceptable to God, but they never did.

From events that took place at that time, it is easy to see why the term **Babylon** was used as a code word or nickname for Jerusalem by our Lord's disciples, who were victims of great persecution which He had said was coming upon them from their fellow Judaeans. And that's why in the Apocalypse, right after the elect **remnant (144,000)** are called out from among the twelve tribes of Israel to give the gospel to other nations, we read, **Babylon is fallen, is fallen, that great city, because she made all nations drink of the wine of the wrath of her fornication** (Revelation 14:8). The context clearly indicates that the destruction of Jerusalem by the Judaean Zealots and Roman armies would take place as soon as the Hebrew **remnant (144,000)** had all been brought into the family of Christ. And then the angel said, **Come hither; I will show unto thee the** [final] **judgment of the great whore . . . with whom the kings of the earth have committed fornication, and the inhabitants of the land** [of Palestine] **have been made drunk with the wine of her fornication** (Revelation 17:1-2).

I saw a woman sit upon a scarlet colored beast, full of names of blasphemy . . . decked with gold and precious stones and pearls, having a golden cup in her hand full of abominations and

filthiness of her fornication: and upon her forehead was a name written, MYSTERY, BABYLON THE GREAT, THE MOTHER OF HARLOTS AND ABOMINATIONS OF THE LAND. And I saw the woman drunken with the blood of saints, and with the blood of the martyrs of Jesus (Revelation 17:3-6). These verses sound like quotations from the Old Testament prophets, from whom we can easily find a solution to the mystery. The **great whore** which was about to suffer God's terminal judgment was collective Israel centered in Jerusalem.

Now, before we go any further, we must emphasize again that in no way whatsoever should the spiritual whore of 2000 years ago be associated or identified with the State of Israel or other Jewish people of today. To do so is as ridiculous as the motivation of teenage gangs of Roman Catholic boys in New York City a century ago who beat up Jewish boys, calling them "Christ killers." Those Ashkenazi Jewish boys were not biologically related to the ancient Judaeans who killed their Messiah, so the accusations against them had no basis in fact.

There is no Saul of Tarsus in any synagogue today who would confess with shame, **Many of the saints did I shut up in prison . . . and when they were put to death I gave my voice against them. And I punished them oft in every synagogue, and compelled them to blaspheme** (Acts 26:10-11). I have been given a friendly welcome in every synagogue I have visited in the past sixty years, and I am sure other believers in Christ would likewise be received with cordiality. Nor are there evil priests who **devour widows' houses**. Rather, thousands of Jewish attorneys and judges labor diligently to protect the rights of widows and orphans today. In synagogues now we do not find unscrupulous religious leaders who extract money from any and all to hoard it away as thieves. Instead, we see thousands of Jewish philanthropists, charities and foundations which donate billions of dollars for medical care, orphanages, education, and other human needs around the world.

Jewish people today are in the forefront of activities that benefit mankind: scientific research, new products development, defense of human rights, labor relations, retail trade, democratic government, finance, journalism, medicine and every other enterprise that makes our world a better place for all who live here. So we must be very careful that we never forge any link between the Jerusalem that God destroyed in 66-70 A.D. and the State of Israel or other Jewish people of today.

Having again made that emphasis, and we cannot do so too strongly, let's go back to the judgment of the **great whore** which killed the prophets and stoned the messengers which God had sent during the thousand years in which He was trying to win her allegiance and devotion. In fulfillment of earlier prophecies, most of the Judaeans had returned from captivity in Babylon during the days of Ezra, Nehemiah, Haggai and Zechariah. Some of the other tribes also returned from captivity in Assyria during that time. The rest returned during the CENTURY OF RESTORATION that began around 165 B.C. when Judas Maccabeus and his brothers liberated the country, restored the temple and returned the nation to its former glory. Through the prophets, God had given great promises of how a united Israel could be His peculiar treasure on the earth, but it never happened. Instead, there was continual fighting, killing, and struggles for power. So when the Roman general Pompey came in 63 B.C. and put an end to the civil war by imposing Roman rule over all of Palestine, many Judaeans and Israelites considered it to be a mixed blessing.

Thus began a century-long love affair between a people who had once been called **the wife of Jehovah, the apple of His eye,** and the polytheistic pagans of Rome whose gods were idols of their own creation. "Peace at any price" became the order of the day. If marriage to the Romans brought an end to civil war, then that would be their choice. Herod the Great was appointed king of the Judaeans in 40 B.C. and promptly married a Judaean lady, perhaps to help gain the loyalty of her relatives, and his son and heir would then be a native-born Israelite. He built a new temple in Jerusalem, gave religious freedom to all, and ushered in an era of peace and prosperity that was without precedent. The Judaeans loved it.

So much so that they became obsessed with materialism. Caesarea became the busiest commercial center in the world while under Roman rule. The magnificent port constructed there by King Herod exceeded any that had ever existed anywhere, with its technology for the protection of ships and cargo, and the efficiency with which they could be handled. Commerce from and to India, Persia and other Eastern countries moved overland as far as Caesarea, then by sea to and from Rome, Greece and other countries to the West. Jerusalem then became the financial capital of the Roman world, much as New York is today. Among the Hebrews in Palestine, love of money replaced love of God. And those who were most successful in raking it in were the priests of the temple, together with their followers, the scribes and Pharisees. **They bind heavy burdens . . . and lay them on men's shoulders, but they themselves will not move them with one of their fingers. All their works they do to be seen of men . . . outwardly appear righteous but within are full of hypocrisy** (Matthew 23:4-5, 28).

Into this environment was born Jesus the Christ, the Son of the Living God. He remained out of public view for thirty years, during which time he had ample opportunity to learn what was going on. Once each year He left his home town of Nazareth to visit Jerusalem for a few days, and what he saw in the temple must have been disgusting. Finally, when His hour was come, He went into the temple and **overthrew the tables of the money changers**; then **made a whip of small cords** and drove all the business people out of the building. Instead of it being **a house of prayer**, He said it had become **a den of thieves** (Matthew 21:13) and **a house of merchandise** (John 2:16). From that time forth **the chief priests and scribes sought how they might kill Him** (Luke 22:2); and **after these things Jesus stayed in Galilee: He could not go into Judaea, because the Judaeans sought to kill Him** (John 7:1).

When He finally did make His last visit to Jerusalem, the temple priests gathered a mob which dragged the Son of God before the Roman governor. They falsely accused Him of saying they shouldn't pay taxes to the Romans. Because He had preached the kingdom of God, they lied again, saying that He had spoken against Caesar. They further convinced Pilate by saying, **If you let this man go, you are not Caesar's friend** (John 19:15). Then to show where their loyalty really lay, they said, **We have no king but Caesar** (John 19:15). That's why the woman in the Apocalypse is depicted as **sitting upon a beast**. Obviously, that beast was Rome.

The beast was said to have had seven heads (also called mountain peaks), which are identified as seven kings or rulers, of which **five are fallen, one is; and the other is not yet come . . . and the beast that was, and is not, even he is the eighth, and is of the seven** (Revelation 17:9-11). At first, this passage seems puzzling. How could "the eighth" be one of the seven kings? And in Verse 8 we are told that the eighth (or seventh) king **was, and is not, and yet is**. Actually, this enigmatic passage reveals to us when the Apocalypse was written. The seven kings are Roman emperors.

While serving as president of the Roman Senate, Julius Caesar became, to all intents and purposes, *pontifex maximus* of the empire until his assassination in 44 B.C. Henceforth, the title of *Caesar* would be assumed by major European potentates for 1900 years, ending with the last *Tzar* of Russia and *Kaiser* Wilhelm of Germany. Following Julius there was Augustus (Octavian) (31 B.C.-14 A.D.), followed by Tiberius (14-37), Caligula (37-41), Claudius (41-54), and Nero (54-68). When we read **five are fallen, and one is, and the other is not yet come** (Revelation 17:10), we know the Book was written in 65 or 66 A.D. because King Number Six (Nero) was still alive. Who, then, is the mysterious "eighth," who is **one of the seven**?

This eighth king is "now you see him, now you don't." He **was, and is not, and yet is, even he is the eighth, and is one of the seven** (Revelation 17:8, 11). This has to be Vespasian, who surrounded Jerusalem with his armies and then disappeared. In fact, he never came back, but rather was proclaimed Emperor and returned to Rome. Was he the successor to Nero? Yes and no. There was another in between who would **continue a short space** (Revelation 17:10). In fact, very short. Following Nero's death, Galba was proclaimed the new emperor, but he was promptly murdered, and succeeded by Otho; but legions in Germany chose Vitellius instead. When Vitellius marched on Rome with his superior forces, Otho committed suicide. But Vitellius proved to be an incompetent, drunken glutton and was killed by a mob only eight months after his appointment. He was never a true emperor. Meanwhile, Vespasian had moved on to Egypt, and while there was proclaimed by his troops and many others to be the true emperor or Rome.

He, then, was the mysterious King Number Eight, who was **one of the seven**, the one whom, as far as Jerusalem was concerned, **was and is not, yet is**. And when Vespasian became emperor he returned to Rome and dispatched his son, Titus, to finish off the rebels in Palestine.

The ten horns which thou sawest are ten kings which have received no kingdom as yet; but receive power as kings one hour [term] with the beast . . . these shall make war with the Lamb, and the Lamb shall overcome them: for He is Lord of lords and King of kings (Revelation 17:14). This is an obvious reference to Roman emperors that would come after Vespasian, and who would instigate systematic persecution of Christians. The first was Vespasian's son, Titus, who had destroyed Jerusalem. He lived only about two years (79-81) after succeeding his father, and in turn, was succeeded by his brother, Domitian (81-96), who launched a vicious persecution against the Christians.

Persecution of the elect **remnant (144,000)** of the Israelites from their fellow Judaeans was greatly diminished after the destruction of Jerusalem, so the believers came out of hiding and boldly proclaimed salvation by faith in Christ in every synagogue of the Judaeans, as well as to the Greeks and Romans. Many synagogues became churches and rabbis preached Christ. So the number of Christians exploded throughout the empire, and included among their numbers were many of the aristocracy, the ruling class and intelligentsia of Greece and Rome. Alarmed at this growing movement within the population, Domitian and his successors **made war with the Lamb** for more than 200 years, but the Lamb won in the end for **they that are with Him are called, and chosen and faithful** (Revelation 17:15).

The rest of the **ten kings** were Nerva (96-98), Trajan (98-117), Hadrian (117-138), Antonius (138-161), Marcus Aurelius (161-180), Commodus (180-193), Septimus (193-211), and Aurelius Antonius (211-217). These all **made war with the Lamb**. And as the angel had said to John, **The ten kings shall hate the whore, and shall make her desolate and naked, and shall eat her flesh and burn her with fire** (Revelation 17:16). Of course, the first to do so was Titus, who made a total **desolation** of the city of Jerusalem. His brother, Domitian, continued the Roman assault against the Judaeans, as well as the Christians. He tended to associate the two groups together, because so many of the Christians were of Hebrew ancestry.

The climax of continued assaults against the Judaeans came under Hadrian in 129 when he himself visited Syria and was confronted by Judaean forces which had regrouped under a false messiah named Bar Kokba and a rabbi name Akiba. They gathered a huge following and foolishly tried to expel the Romans from Judaea. The result was a lesser repeat of the siege by Titus, and in 132 Jerusalem was destroyed again. Judaeans were thereafter forbidden to enter what was left of the city. Rather, Hadrian had the survivors scattered far and wide, and the able-bodied men sold into slavery. The ten emperors who followed Vespasian all made Jerusalem **desolate and naked**, as the Apocalypse had foretold.

Another indication that **the great whore** in Revelation refers to Jerusalem may be found in this verse, which in the original Greek says: **The woman which you saw is that great city which lords itself over the kings of the earth** (Revelation 17:18).

Earlier it is written that Christ had made those who believed in Him to be **kings and priests unto God and His Father** (Revelation 1:6), and that He is therefore **the prince of the kings of the earth** (Revelation 1:5). Then later it is revealed that **the kings of the earth bring their glory and honor into the holy Jerusalem,** which is **the bride, the Lamb's wife (Revelation 21:10, 24).**

A record of how religious leaders of Jerusalem began to **lord themselves over the kings of the earth** begins in Acts Chapter Four, when the apostles were first arrested and threatened, then released. But soon they were arrested again and this time they were beaten (Acts 5:40). Then Stephen was murdered by stoning (Acts 7:59) under the oversight of Saul of Tarsus.

And at that time there was a great persecution [by the Hebrew leaders] **against the church which was at Jerusalem, and they were all scattered abroad, except the apostles** (Acts 8:1).

The worst of all persecutors was Saul of Tarsus, whose murderous rampage is recorded in Acts 9:1-2 and repeated by Saul (Paul) when he gave his testimony to the Hebrew mob that attacked him in Jerusalem (Acts 22:1-21). He further described his attacks against **the kings of the land [earth]** before the governor, Felix, then two years later before Governor Festus and King Agrippa (Acts 26:1-29).

Until his conversion to faith in Christ, Saul of Tarsus was a major figure in **that great city** [of Jerusalem] **which lorded itself over the kings of the land** [of Palestine].

I remind you again that the Apocalypse is not chronological. The entire Eighteenth Chapter is a prophetic lamentation over the city of Jerusalem which was destined for imminent destruction. Often I have heard liberal teachers of religion cite this chapter as proof that the Apocalypse had to have been written after 70 A.D.; otherwise, they say, there is no way John could have known what was coming. I disagree. The Apocalypse is a supernatural revelation from God concerning **"things that must shortly come to pass."** God revealed in advance the mourning that would take place after the city was destroyed, just as the prophet Jeremiah wrote his book of **LAMENTATIONS** concerning the conquest of Jerusalem and captivity of its inhabitants by the Babylonians in his day. In fact, there are many parallels between **LAMENTATIONS** and **REVELATION** 18. A careful reading of the two together will reveal these similarities. Here are some verses from Lamentations:

Jerusalem hath grievously sinned, therefore she is

removed . . . her filthiness is in her skirts [whore] . . . among her lovers [fornication] she hath none to comfort her . . . the Lord hath afflicted me in the day of His fierce anger . . . I called for my lovers [whore] but they deceived me . . . the Lord was as an enemy: He hath swallowed up Israel . . . women eat the fruit of their own bodies [cannibalism] . . . the pitiful women have boiled their own children: they were their food in the great destruction . . . greater than the punishment of the sin of Sodom, that was overthrown in a moment . . . for the sins of her priests that have shed the blood of the just in the midst of her . . . thou hast utterly rejected us; thou art very wroth against us.

Now note some things that were said about Jerusalem in Revelation 18: **The habitation of devils, the hold of every foul spirit, a cage of every unclean bird . . . the merchants of the earth are waxed rich through her . . . her sins have reached unto heaven . . . her plagues shall come in one day: death and mourning and famine; and she shall be utterly burned with fire . . . the merchants of the earth shall mourn over her; for no man buyeth their merchandise any more: gold, and silver, and precious stones, and pearls, and fine linen, and silk, and ivory, and marble, and wine, and oil, and fine flour and slaves, and souls of men . . . alas, alas, that great city wherein were made rich all that had ships in the sea by reason of her costliness! For in one hour she is made desolate. Rejoice over her, ye holy apostles and prophets; for God hath avenged her on you . . . in her were found the blood of** [Old Testament] **prophets, and of saints, and of all that were slain upon the land** [of Israel].

Finally, I must repeat once again, just as we say "Motown" for Detroit, "Big Apple" for New York, and "Sin City" to mean Las Vegas, so "Babylon" was a nickname for Jerusalem among the true Israelites, the elect **remnant** of **144,000** whom God called out to know Christ, between 30 A.D. and 70 A.D. The primary message of the Apocalypse of John was to report that **THE TIME WAS AT HAND** for God's terminal judgment on that wicked city which had stoned His prophets and coveted gold, silver and precious stones rather than serving the Living God. Almost half of Revelation is devoted to that conclusive judgment.

The term "Babylon" could not possibly apply to any city other than Jerusalem of that generation because only they had killed God's **holy apostles**, which must certainly refer to the original eleven chosen by the Messiah. And it was to that generation that the Messiah had said, **O Jerusalem, Jerusalem, thou that killest the prophets, and stonest them which are sent unto thee . . . upon you will come all the righteous blood shed upon the land, from the blood of righteous Abel unto the blood of Zacharias son of Bacharias, whom ye slew between the temple and the altar. Verily I say unto you, all these things shall come upon this generation** (Matthew 23:37,35).

The judgment upon "Babylon" in Revelation was to avenge the killing of Old Testament prophets by the religious hypocrites who controlled Jerusalem. And the Messiah said their blood would be required **OF THAT GENERATION**. There is no way, therefore, that God's judgment upon "Babylon" could possibly apply to any persons or places other than Jerusalem which existed at that time.

Thou are righteous, O Lord, which art and wast, and shalt be, because thou hast judged thus; for they have shed the blood of saints and prophets, and thou hast given them blood to drink . . . even so, Lord God Almighty, true and righteous are thy judgments (Revelation 16:5-7).

Chapter 11

What is Replacement Theology?

It is not theology at all. It is an erroneous teaching which suggests that "The Church" REPLACED "Israel" after Christ came. I cannot see anything theological about this dubious concept. It stems from a failure to understand what is meant by "the church" and what is meant by "Israel" in the Scriptures.

I have found about two hundred times in the Old Testament where collective Israel is referred to as a metaphorical HARLOT engaged in spiritual WHOREDOM. The only way she could be replaced by "the church" is if we would interpret Revelation 17:1 to mean that the **great whore** mentioned there refers to the apostate Roman Catholic Church of the dark ages. Many prophecy teachers have held this position, but, as I have already explained, the **whore** in Revelation 17 refers to apostate Israel. So the "church" did not replace "Israel" in that category.

There was no way the "church" could replace "Israel" when only a few of the Hebrews were recognized by God as being His people, and only **born again** believers in the churches are said to be children of God. In the days of Elijah the number which God recognized was down to a total of **seven thousand** (I Kings 19:18), less than 2% of the total population of Israel and Judah at that time.

Except the Lord of hosts had left us a very small remnant, we should have been as Sodom, and like unto Gomorrah [Isaiah 1:9]. A majority of the Israelites are said to be equivalent to Sodom in God's sight. **Hear the word of the Lord, ye rulers of Sodom; give ear unto the law of our God, ye people of Gomorrah** [Isaiah 1:10]. The number of Hebrews whom God recognized as being His people is referred to as a **remnant** more than sixty times by the Old Testament prophets. And at the end of the old covenant period, the Apostle Paul states **at this present time also there is a remnant according to the election of grace** [Romans 11:5]. The number of that elect remnant is given in Revelation as being **144,000** from the twelve tribes of Israel, again, less than 2% of the total number of Israelites living at that time.

They are not all Israel which are of Israel: neither because they are the seed of Abraham are they all children [Romans 9:6-7]. As I have already stated, among the Israelites, only those who were **circumcised in heart** were recognized by our God as being His people (Romans 2:28-29).

Likewise, in the churches God recognizes only those who have been **born again** as being His children. Most church congregations have some **sheep** and some **goats**, some **wheat** and some **tares**, some who have been quickened by the Spirit and others who are still dead in sins. The church at Corinth had some true believers (**gold, silver, precious stones**) and others who were called **wood, hay and stubble**, awaiting the **consuming fire** of God's judgment (I Corinthians 3:12).

There is no "replacement" teaching in the Word of God. There are only those who are God's true children, both under the Old Covenant and under the New Covenant, as contrasted with other Israelites or other professing Christians who were still dead to God. Whether they were Hebrews or church members made no difference in His sight. **Man looketh on the outward appearance, but the Lord looketh on the heart** (I Samuel 16:7).

Water baptism of new believers was not a REPLACEMENT for circumcision. In fact, the first 3000 who were baptized (Acts 2:41) were all men who had been circumcised. When **Abraham believed God and it was counted unto him for righteousness** (Romans 4:3), **he received the sign of circumcision** (Romans 4:11) as a mark of identification for his posterity. But water baptism in the New Testament had nothing to do with a person's heredity. It was a public testimony by which a new believer let everyone know that he had been **buried with Him** [Christ] **by baptism into death: that like as Christ was raised up from the dead . . . even so we also should walk in newness of life** (Romans 6:4). During the past 2000 years, millions of newly converted Christians have been alienated from their own unconverted family members by being baptized. Circumcision, on the other hand, served to identify the recipients with their earthly families.

It was only after the **falling away** that baptism came to be considered as a REPLACEMENT for circumcision. Apostate church leaders failed to comprehend that all men are born dead to God [Romans 5:12] and **must be born again** in order to be made spiritually alive. Instead, they returned to the Old Testament in their thinking and began to teach that babies born of Christian parents were *ipso facto* children of God. Thus began the silly practice of baptizing babies, as a REPLACEMENT for the Old Testament custom of circumcision. And when the Anabaptist movement developed during the Reformation period, those who knew the truth of God were persecuted by church clergy who were still holding on to Old Testament traditions.

God's promise to Abraham that his posterity would include ALL NATIONS did not REPLACE the previous promise that his descendants would become a great nation. Rather, the promises were always given together, by which God showed that the two combined were actually one. The growth and development of the one nation was preliminary and in preparation for the inclusion of all other nations into the family of God after redemption was purchased by the Messiah.

King David did not REPLACE King Saul; rather he succeeded him, and greatly enlarged his kingdom. In like manner, the Lord Jesus SUCCEEDED His father David, and enlarged the kingdom to include ALL NATIONS, as God had promised Abraham. No longer would it be known as the **kingdom of Israel**, but from that time forth it was enlarged to be the **kingdom of God. The law and the prophets were until John: since that time, the kingdom of God is preached** (Luke 16:16). True believers who were received into the **kingdom of God** under the New Covenant were then added to members of God's family under the Old Covenant who were **circumcised in heart**, and all together formed the great company of His people.

Sarah did not "replace" Hagar as the mother of Abraham's posterity. Rather, God had planned all along that through the son of Sarah, Isaac, **would his seed be called**. The **son of the bondwoman** was a temporary arrangement to be terminated at the birth of Isaac. God allowed these developments to take place to create an allegory of the events that would follow, just as He later arranged for the Israelites to be held in Egyptian bondage. Their coming out of Egypt is an excellent picture of how believers in Christ come out of spiritual death into eternal life. Even so, God revealed the meaning of another allegory to Isaiah, from whom it was quoted by the Apostle Paul in his epistle to the Galatians. Let's look at what God revealed through Isaiah and Paul. Remember, the prophecy in Isaiah 54 is immediately following the marvelous revelation in Isaiah 53 regarding how Christ would die for our sins and thus reconcile us unto God.

Sing, O barren, that did not bear . . . for more are the children of the desolate than the children of the married wife, saith the Lord (Isaiah 54:1). Paul quotes this verse in Galatians 4:27 as being an allegory based on the story of Sarah, the barren wife of Abram. Since Sarah gave him no children, Abram mated with the slave-girl Hagar, who bore him Ishmael. Paul says that Hagar is a picture of the Israelites, whose relationship to God was equivalent to that of a bondwoman because of the Law. But this arrangement was temporary. God planned all along that His children among other nations would be far greater than those He had temporarily among the Israelites. His promise to Abraham regarding ALL NATIONS reveals this fact.

Enlarge the place of thy tent . . . lengthen thy cords and

strengthen thy stakes; for thou shalt break forth on the right hand and on the left; and thy seed shall inherit the nations (Isaiah 54:2-3). This is a prophecy of how the people of God among OTHER NATIONS would eventually far outnumber the true believers among the Israelites, just as the descendants of Sarah (**the desolate**) eventually exceeded in number the descendants of Hagar, **the married wife**.

Here we must pause to define what constituted marriage in biblical times. **Rebekah** became the wife of **Isaac** when **he brought her into his tent** (Genesis 24:67). Abraham had a **concubine** named Keturah (I Chronicles 1:32) but she was also called his **wife** (Genesis 25:1). Marriage in the sight of God has nothing to do with getting a license and having a ceremony as we do today. These things are recent traditions. When I was a child I went to school with numerous children from the Blue Ridge mountains whose parents had never obtained a marriage license or had a wedding ceremony. When they started living together it was called "common-law" marriage. The Apostle Paul said that when a man visits a prostitute he is married to her in the sight of God: **Know ye not that he which is joined to an harlot is one body? For two, saith He, shall be one flesh** (I Corinthians 6:16). When a man and a woman join their bodies in a sexual union, they are then married in the sight of God. The modern belief that couples can live together without being married is nonsense. It's "common law" marriage.

Hagar was therefore the **married wife** of Abraham that illustrates the allegory mentioned in Isaiah 54 and Galatians 4:27. Sarah was **the barren that did not bear**. During the Old Testament period, the family of God was more or less limited to believers among the Israelites, represented by Hagar. Other nations, represented by Sarah, were left outside the fold. But even though it covered 2000 years, that was a short time in God's sight, to whom **a thousand years are but as yesterday when it is past** (Psalm 90:4). So when He speaks of regathering a people from among the nations, as He promised Abram, God says, **For a small moment have I forsaken thee; but with great mercies will I gather thee.**

139

In a little wrath I hid my face from thee for a moment; but with everlasting kindness will I have mercy on thee, saith the Lord thy redeemer . . . THE GOD OF THE WHOLE EARTH SHALL HE BE CALLED (Isaiah 54:5,7-8).

Abraham had two sons, one by a bondmaid, the other by a freewoman. The one who was of the bondwoman was born after the flesh; but he of the freewoman was by promise. Which things are an allegory: for these are two covenants, one from Mount Sinai, which gendereth to bondage, which is Hagar, and answereth to Jerusalem which now is, and is in bondage with her children. But Jerusalem which is above is free, which is the mother of us all. As it is written, Rejoice thou barren that bearest not; for the desolate [Sarah, meaning OTHER NATIONS] hath many more children than she which hath an husband [Hagar, meaning collective Israel]. Now we, brethren, as Isaac was, are the children of promise. And, as then, he that was born after the flesh persecuted him that was born after the spirit, even so it is now. Nevertheless, what saith the Scripture? Cast out the bondwoman and her son: for the son of the bondwoman shall not be heir with the son of the freewoman. So then, brethren, we are not children of the bondwoman, but of the free (Galatians 4:22-31). Unbelieving Israelites were **cast out** as far as being recognized as the people of God after the Messiah came.

Sarah did not REPLACE Hagar; rather, she was the one whom God had planned all along should be the mother of His Old Covenant people. The episode with Hagar and Ishmael was a temporary arrangement until Isaac, the one God had originally planned, should come along. Likewise, God planned all along that ALL NATIONS should be included among His covenant people (represented by Isaac). The Old Testament episode with the Israelites was a temporary arrangement until **the seed should come** (Galatians 3:19) through whom God's promise to Abraham would be fulfilled. **And the Scripture, foreseeing that God would justify the nations through faith, preached before the gospel unto Abraham, saying, in thee shall ALL NATIONS be blessed** (Galatians 3:8).

Those who speak of REPLACEMENT THEOLOGY have failed to fully comprehend what the Scripture teaches regarding differences between **the Israel of God** and **the synagogue of Satan**. They have not rightly divided the word of truth concerning **the body of Christ** and the paganized church **which has two horns like the Lamb but speaks** [with the voice of] **the dragon** (Revelation 13:11). Which REPLACEMENT are they speaking of, the evil church replacing evil Israel or the true church replacing those few Israelites who were **circumcised in heart**?

This whole subject has no relevance for Christians who know their Bibles and who know the facts of history. For the past four thousand years our God has had a personal relationship with a tiny minority of human beings who are justified by their faith in Him, even as **Abraham believed God, and it was counted unto him for righteousness** (Romans 4:3). **How was it then reckoned? Not when he was in circumcision, but in uncircumcision** (Romans 4:10). **He is not a Judaean who is one outwardly, neither is that circumcision which is outward in the flesh: but he is a Judaean who is one inwardly, and circumcision is that of the heart** (Romans 2:28-29). No doubt Paul, in writing those verses, had in mind numerous Old Testament references which speak of **circumcision of the heart** as being that which makes a person right with God and being one of His people. Likewise the New Testament teaches that only those who are **justified by faith in Christ** and **born again by His Spirit** are included among God's people. Unbelieving collective "Israel" and unregenerate members of hundreds of different kinds of apostate "churches" collectively have no place in God's reckoning.

Those who were **circumcised in heart** under the Old Covenant, and **born again** believers under the New Covenant are ALL ONE IN CHRIST JESUS, and are so portrayed in Revelation 21 as making up **the bride, the Lamb's wife, the holy city, the new Jerusalem**. Our Saviour gave His life, not that some should REPLACE others, but to make us all a part of His eternal heavenly family of true believers.

Chapter 12

The Church Age is the Main Event, not a Parenthesis

Although it was sixty-nine years ago (in 1940), I still clearly recall Dr. Harry Thompson frequently repeating, "The Church Parenthesis." While I was greatly blessed by some of his other teachings, I'm afraid that dear man of God was made spiritually poor by his obsession with the "Israel" of the Old Testament. I never heard him speak of the urgency of planting a witness for our Lord within unreached nations. To him, the present "church age" was a temporary parenthesis inserted, as if it were an afterthought, between other ages involving "Israel."

Then in 1945 I met Hubert Mitchell, formerly the song leader for Paul Rader's evangelistic crusades in Chicago and elsewhere. Hubert was obsessed with planting a witness for our Lord among those people and in those places where as yet He had no people for his name. So once he was married he asked Dr. Rader to send him and his bride off to the island of Sumatra, part of what is now called Indonesia. There in the jungles they shared the message of salvation in Christ with a primitive tribe that had no written language, and which had never heard the name of Christ Jesus our Lord.

Several years and four children later, Hubert buried the lifeless body of his precious wife there in the rain forest, and providentially returned to the USA with his four youngsters just before the invading Japanese occupied Sumatra. When I met him in 1945 he was director of Youth for Christ in Los Angeles and still very much obsessed with foreign missions. His younger sister, Jean, was serving as a missionary to India along with Rachel Edwardson from Norway. Jean acted as matchmaker, and arranged for Hubert and Rachel to be married. Then in 1947 they were off to India to continue the work together, along with their children.

I share this to emphasize a contrast I observed between evangelicals like Dr. Thompson, who have returned to the Old Testament as their major emphasis, and those with "missionary eschatology," like Hubert Mitchell, whose driving force in life is to "bring back the King" (Matthew 24:14) by reaching every tribe and nation with the gospel.

Then I worked with the Inter-Varsity Christian Fellowship for four years, and was in continual partnership with other staff who had strong missionary vision. They made me a vice president of the Student Foreign Missions Fellowship, in which our objective was to motivate Christian students toward foreign missionary service. Our mentor was Dr. Robert McQuilken of Columbia (S.C.) Bible College. I never heard him mention "Israel" as being relevant today; his total emphasis was in spreading the kingdom of God among unreached peoples. In December 1946 I shared in a big missionary conference which IVCF conducted in Toronto where, again, I never heard "Israel" mentioned even once. Our focus was on taking the gospel of Christ to the ends of the earth. And, thankfully, that emphasis continued as similar conferences were conducted by IVCF in Urbana, Illinois, every three years thereafter.

When I first started to work with Youth for Christ, our main concern was to win the young people of America to our Saviour, but very quickly our vision reached out to **the regions beyond**, and YFC became YFC INTERNATIONAL. Bob Pierce, Director of YFC in Seattle, went to China in 1947, and then he and I were together in Korea in 1950. After the Korean war broke out, Bob returned there as a news correspondent, which resulted in his starting World

Vision, with help from Frank Phillips, who had been Director of YFC in Portland, Oregon. When Billy Graham moved on from YFC to establish his own evangelistic association, he included a strong foreign missionary outreach as part of his ministry, and provided my personal support for missionary service in Asia. Billy's wife, Ruth, who grew up in China as the daughter of missionary parents, helped keep him focused on foreign fields.

One precious brother whom God used to direct my life toward foreign fields was J. Christy Wilson, Jr. whose parents were missionaries in Iran. He learned some Persian while attending a school in Teheran. Years later he went to Afghanistan as a "tent maker" and taught English in a high school. Dari, a dialect of Persian, was the major language there. Afghan students who came to America told me he was "the kindest man they ever met." He was pressured to leave that country because the government at that time was clamping down on "faith based" NGO's. While we were traveling together overseas in 1948, Christy helped me to draw up a plan for International Students, Inc. and Overseas Students Mission, the first foreign missionary ministries aimed at reaching foreign students for Christ while they are here and sending them home as missionaries among their own people.

Meanwhile, at every opportunity I was attending conferences on prophecy where the emphasis was very different from those concerned with foreign missions. One held in Chicago in 1945 had as its theme: WILL RUSSIA SEIZE THE MANDATE FOR PALESTINE FROM GREAT BRITAIN. The major concern of those people was political, rather than winning lost souls to Christ. A lady in Pennsylvania told me she had lost interest in foreign missions since she started attending a study group on Bible prophecy. While conducting special meetings in a Baptist church in Minnesota around 1955, I stayed in the home of a successful young businessman who was especially enthusiastic about the spread of the gospel among unreached people. But when I returned to that church two years later he had lost interest. Why? He had made a trip to the "Holy Land" and now he had switched his focus to "Israel," and what he called "the end times."

During the past fifty years God's people have become sharply divided between two kinds of eschatology, or "end times" teachings. One is "missionary eschatology," which focuses on our Lord's great commission to take out a people for His name from among every tribe and nation. The other concentrates on the state of Israel as being the key to God's purpose for the end of the age. Mark Hanna, who worked with me in International Students, Inc. before he went on to get his Ph.D. and serve on the faculty of Talbot School of Theology in California, is outspoken in his criticism of unconditional support of Israel by evangelicals. Dr. Hanna gave a series of lectures at Dallas Theological Seminary and had a feature article on "Israel in Prophecy" published in *Christianity Today*. He maintains that some present day "worship" (unconditional endorsement) of Israel is a form of idolatry. And the growing obsession with political Zionism by evangelical Christians has become a major distraction in competition with the completion of our Lord's eternal purpose to plant His church within every nation (people group) on earth.

Samuel E. Waldron wrote a book titled THE END TIMES MADE SIMPLE that was published by Calvary Press in Amityville, N.Y. in 2003. He says (on Page 10), *The popular eschatology widely taught in our day in evangelical churches really does have comparatively little to do with the gospel of Christ. Prophecy was often taught in the evangelical church in which I was raised. One of the things I keenly remember being taught was that the church age in which we live was a great parenthesis in biblical prophecy, a mystery unforeseen by biblical prophecy. It would end with the rapture of the church by the secret coming of Christ in the air before the tribulation period . . . it would not be preceded by any prophetic events. Only with this secret rapture would the prophetic clock start ticking again . . . all having to do with God's other, earthly people, the Jewish nation, not His heavenly people, the church. I remember feeling disappointed that I lived in such a blank or vacant period with regard to biblical prophecy.*

During the years I worked with Youth for Christ, my home

base was in Chicago where I rented a guest room at Moody Bible Institute. If ever I was free at church time (usually midweek) I attended anything that might be happening at nearby Moody Memorial Church. The senior pastor, Harry Ironside, was a dear man of God who blessed me often with his excellent teaching of God's Word. Except when he got off on the subject of prophecy. He taught that the present (church) age, "from the cross to the rapture," was "a dateless parenthesis in God's great plan." No wonder he personally had such a weak emphasis on foreign missions. I continually resisted the urge to scream at him that he had it backwards. The Old Testament period, from Abraham to John the Baptizer, was like a parenthesis. How could Dr. Ironside be pastor of that great church and fail to recognize that God had not one servant under the Old Covenant who even came close to the marvelous ministry of Dwight L. Moody? The only one that was even slightly similar was Jonah, and his was a one-time revival which he led reluctantly. God used Moody to rescue hundreds of thousands of lost souls from eternal death, and bring them into the glorious victory of eternal life. During the temporary Old Covenant "parenthesis," most of God's servants, even Moses and Elijah, included mass killings among their activities. They were more involved in killing people than saving them. The New Covenant (which was God's main purpose revealed to Abraham in the beginning), on the other hand, is redemptive. Our Saviour came **not to destroy men's lives but to save them**. And Moody was just one among thousands whom God has used for the salvation of others.

The temporary Old Testament period was necessary to show us that all men are sinners who need a saviour. It demonstrated that even if God Himself appeared to people as a visible presence, which He did to the Israelites, they would still turn against Him and go into idolatry. It revealed that no matter how much God begged them to keep His laws, they would still go on killing one another, and killing their neighbors. God's prophetic clock with the Israelites ended with the calling out of an **elect remnant (144,000)**, called **ALL ISRAEL**, from among the twelve tribes during a forty year period, 30-70 A.D. He then used that remnant to give the gospel to other nations at that time. His terminal judgment upon the other Hebrews who lived in Palestine took place 66-70 A.D. After those events, there is only one further prophecy regarding the Israelites as a distinct and separate nation to be found anywhere in the Word of God. That's in Revelation 17:16 which foretells how ten Roman emperors would continue to carry out God's judgment upon some of the Judaeans after 70 A.D.

But much is said regarding **that great multitude which no man can number from all peoples and kindreds and tongues and tribes and nations** for whom and concerning whom **the ends of the ages have come** (I Corinthians 10:11). If only we realized who we are and what we mean in God's plan, we would never again tolerate the nonsensical notion that what has been happening for the last 2000 years is only "a dateless parentheses in God's great plan." Rather, we would realize that it is THE MAIN EVENT. It includes the major purpose for which this planet exists. As I wrote in an earlier book (*The Future of Foreign Missions*), what happened before Christ came was a PRELUDE TO HIS COMING. The 2000 years from Abraham to the advent of our Saviour was in PREPARATION FOR HIS COMING. Things that have happened since He came are an unfolding of THE PURPOSE OF HIS COMING. Events of the church age are far more important because they include the redemption of lost souls from ALL NATIONS, not just twelve tribes that spent most of their time killing one another or trying to kill their surrounding neighbors.

One of the more serious errors that some teachers have made is to say that THE CHURCH IS NOT REVEALED IN THE OLD TESTAMENT. I clearly recall Clifton Fowler saying those very words to me 69 years ago. Many others have said the same thing.

Most of them base their conclusions on the Apostle Paul's words regarding **the mystery of Christ which in other ages was not made known unto the sons of men as it is now revealed unto His holy apostles and prophets by the Spirit** (Ephesians 3:4-5). Paul never said that his Lord failed to foretell that ALL NATIONS were to be included among His people. He well knew that God had said just the opposite throughout the Old Testament. Almost immediately after He created the nations at the tower of Babel, God called out Abram and told him that through him **ALL NATIONS WOULD BE BLESSED**. Then God changed Abram's name to Abraham, meaning father of nations.

The Hebrews, Abraham's descendants, eventually became obsessed with themselves and, instead of thinking about blessing other nations, thought only about killing them or ruling over them. Tragically, present-day evangelicals who have returned to the Old Testament in their thinking still talk of the Israelites ruling other nations. They have failed to understand what God's word reveals, and say that the idea of the church was a **mystery which from the beginning has been hid in God** (Ephesians 3:9). The fact that **ALL NATIONS** would be included within God's family was not hidden. The mystery which was not revealed in the Old Testament was how it would take place.

The **hidden mystery** during the Old Covenant period was that in due time **other nations would be fellowheirs, and of the same body, and partakers of His promise** (Ephesians 3:6). Whereas under the Old Covenant there was a political kingdom made up primarily of Israelites, God planned that when the Messiah came He would bring a spiritual kingdom in which both the Hebrew remnant and believers from other nations would be **one body in Christ and every one members one of another** (Romans 12:5).

God's word to Abraham that in due time He intended to include **ALL NATIONS** within the scope of His blessings was repeated to Isaac (Genesis 26:4) and also to Jacob [Israel] (Genesis 28:14). Throughout writings of the Old Testament prophets there is constant repetition of God's purpose to include **ALL NATIONS** among His people, although the way it would be done remained a **mystery** until the Redeemer came. For example, in the great prophetic Psalm which foretold Christ upon the cross we read **All the ends of the earth shall remember and turn unto the Lord: and all the kindreds of the nations shall worship before** thee (Psalm 22:27). Another, **Thou art my Son, this day have I begotten thee. Ask of me and I shall give thee the nations for thine inheritance** (Psalm 2:7-8). Both of these Messianic Psalms foretell how that when the Messiah came, **ALL NATIONS** would be numbered among His people.

God's intended purpose for the Hebrews under the Old Covenant was that they should **Declare His glory among the nations, His wonders among all people** (Psalm 96:3), but they miserably failed because they could not do it in the strength of their own sinful selves. It was not until the Messiah died for their sins that any could have peace with God and thus receive the power of His Holy Spirit to enable them to be His witnesses to the nations. Until that time, the people of God were in a holding pattern (parenthesis) as far as bearing witness to the nations was concerned. My point is, God planned all along that **ALL NATIONS** should be included among His people, and that plan was fulfilled under the New Covenant. **God be merciful unto us, that thy way may be known upon the earth, thy saving health among ALL NATIONS** (Psalm 67:1-2). **ALL NATIONS shall come and worship before thee, O Lord; and shall glorify thy name** (Psalm 86:9).

The prophet Isaiah mentions the inclusion of **ALL NATIONS (the CHURCH)** into God's earthly family over and over, climaxed by the marvelous prophecy in Chapter 54 which explains how the children of **the desolate** (other nations) would eventually outnumber the children of **the married wife** (the Israelites). After He came, Messiah's seed would **inherit the nations** (verse 3) and **the God of the whole earth shall He be called** (verse 5). Some say that these Old Testament prophecies are looking forward to the millennium age, but the Apostle Paul quoted Isaiah and applied it specifically to the church age (Galatians 4:22-31). There is no other alternative because Chapter 53 describes Christ's sacrificial death which made the church possible.

Lo, I come, and I will dwell in the midst of thee, saith the Lord. And MANY NATIONS shall be joined to the Lord in that day, and shall be my people (Zechariah 2:10-11). That this is a prophecy of the day when Messiah would come and begin His church is crystal clear. It was to Zechariah that God revealed how He would do it: **Not by might, nor by power, but by my Spirit saith the Lord** (Zechariah 4:6). Because of the sinfulness of their flesh, the political kingdom of Israel had been an utter failure as God's witness to the nations. That's why He foretold how He would dissolve it and raise up instead the **KINGDOM OF GOD** which would be spiritual rather than under the political control of human flesh. **And He shall bring forth the headstone** [chief corner stone] **thereof crying, Grace, grace unto it** (Zechariah 4:7). The gospel of grace had to supersede the Old Covenant law, **For the law made nothing perfect, but the bringing in of a better hope did** (Hebrews 7:19).

It was God's plan all along, revealed as a mystery in **the law and the prophets**, to phase out the hopeless agenda of having one particular ethnic group as His witness on earth, and to have instead a great company of regenerated saints from among **ALL NATIONS**, including the Hebrews. What took place was explained by the Apostle Paul: **He is our peace, who has made both one, and has broken down the middle wall of partition between us . . . to make in Himself one new man, that He might reconcile both unto God in one body by the cross . . . that OTHER NATIONS should be fellow-heirs, and of the same body, and partakers of His promise in Christ by the gospel** (Ephesians 2:14-16, 3:6).

It is only when we come to the "church age" in human history that we learn what life on this earth is all about. God's plan and purpose for this planet is centered not in a "chosen people" but a CHOSEN PERSON. He **is the image of the invisible God, the firstborn** [heir] **of all creation, for on account of him were all things created that are in heaven, and that are in earth, visible and invisible, whether they be thrones, or dominions, or principalities, or powers: all things were created because of Him and for Him, and He is before all things, and by Him all things consist . . . that in all things He might have the preeminence** (Colossians 1:15-18). **We see Jesus crowned with glory and honor . . . for whom are all things and on account of whom are**

all things (Hebrews 2:9-10).

The primary purpose for the existence of the universe, especially our planet and human beings, centers in the Person of the Son of God. His Father wanted to have a Son in whom He could be well pleased. Not one who would grow up and have everything pleasant in the garden of Eden, but one who would be tested and tried by things that build character: hard work, opposition, persecution and, ultimately, by death itself. One who was so totally unselfish that he gave His life to redeem His enemies from the eternal punishment we all deserve. He was **the Lamb slain before the foundation of the world** (Revelation 13:8).

It is only in Christ that we see why God placed this planet in its present orbit with a marvelous balance of time and temperature, of atmosphere, land and water; then created man in His own image. It was essentially in preparation for the day when His only begotten Son would be conceived by His Holy Spirit and born of Mary, His virgin mother. God had a plan when He allowed the first man He had created to rebel against Him and plunge the human family into violence, wars, diseases, poverty, suffering and physical death. He was preparing the way for His only Son to come on the scene and be tested in every way, yet to come through each trial triumphantly.

The 4000 years before our Saviour came were essentially a time of preparation for His coming. The designation of a remnant of the descendants of Abraham to be God's witnesses for 2000 years was a temporary "parenthesis." They were not an end in themselves but instruments which God used to prepare the way for the birth, life, death, resurrection and exaltation of His only Son; to be followed by the extension of His kingdom into every tribe and nation.

As part of that exaltation, the God and Father of our Lord Jesus Christ turned everything over to His Son after His resurrection and ascension. I am reminded of the founder and major shareholder of a billion dollar manufacturing company who became a good friend of mine and a generous contributor to Christian Aid. During my first visit with him he took me on a personal tour of the factory and introduced me to a perspiring young worker in sawdust-covered overalls who, to my great surprise, turned out to be his son. Later that same son visited our mission headquarters while he was in Washington on company business. Now he was being tested in the sales division. Later I visited the factory again and found this bright young fellow being tested and prepared in the administrative offices, serving as a vice president. Then when I returned again I found him in the office of the chief executive. His father had made him president, and turned the entire company over to him.

This weak illustration gives us a picture of what has happened. After the Son of God had passed every test, His Father **put all things under His feet** (I Corinthians 15:27, Ephesians 1:22, Hebrews 2:8), and proclaimed Him Lord of the universe. In fact, God's Word declares, **He left nothing that is not put under Him** (Hebrews 2:8). In due time **He will show who is that blessed and only Potentate, the King of Kings and Lord of Lords** (I Timothy 6:15) and **At the name of Jesus every knee shall bow . . . and every tongue confess that Jesus Christ is Lord** (Philippians 2:10-11).

So what is He waiting for? Just this. The eternal purpose of His Father is now being continued by the Son. Included in that purpose are two essential things. One, as I have already mentioned, is that looking down from the heavens our God may find faithful followers bearing witness for Him on the earth. Just as Solomon's temple in Jerusalem was a witness to the nations that the living God was present there, so today He has ten million temples made up of **living stones**. Where true believers **gather in His name, our Lord is present with them** (Matthew 18:20), even as the Spirit of God appeared as a shining glory in the holy of holies when Solomon dedicated the temple in Jerusalem.

While on earth our Lord said, **Destroy this temple, and in three days I will raise it up** (John 2:19). **But He spoke of the temple of His body** (John 2:21). That's why the term **body** is used in the epistles of Paul to denote a local group of believers in Christ who constitute the **temple of God** in their locality (I Corinthians 3:16). And the primary thing our Sovereign Lord is doing in this world today is to plant His temple among those people and in those places where heretofore He has had no witness for His name.

Each local temple (body of believers in whom Christ dwells) constitutes a "church," which in the New Testament means a group of believers who meet together in the name of Christ. Each is **the body of Christ** in that locality (I Corinthians 12:27). But there is a universal sense in which true believers among all of these local groups are looked upon by the Lord as being one body also (Colossians 1:24). And the Lord Jesus is head of that body. As part of turning everything over to Him, His Father **gave Him to be the head over all things to the church, which is His body** (Ephesians 1:22-23).

Perhaps that's why believers in New Testament times addressed their prayers to our Lord BY His name (rather than adding on at the end "in His name"). When Stephen was stoned he prayed, **Lord Jesus, receive my spirit** (Acts 7:59). Writing to the Romans Paul said [in the original Greek] **If you will confess with your mouth "Lord Jesus" and believe in your heart . . . you shall be saved** (Romans 10:9). **For whosoever shall call upon the name of the Lord** [Jesus] **shall be saved** (Romans 10:13). The Apostle John concluded Revelation with the prayer, **Lord Jesus, come quickly**. Our Saviour never used the term "Lord" when addressing His Father, even though it was the title most generally used by the Hebrews at that time. In the New Testament the term "Lord" is reserved exclusively as a title for the One whom Thomas called, **My Lord and my God** (John 20:28).

Yes, God's primary purpose today is to build His house (temple) in every place in every nation. But there is more to it than that. I have mentioned how God wanted to have an only Son in whom He would be well pleased. He also wants His Son to have His own family as well. Or perhaps we should say, the Son wants sons of His own. He speaks of **bringing many sons unto glory** (Hebrews 2:10). **As many as received Him he gave power** [the right] **to become sons of God, even to them that believe on His name** (John 1:2). **Beloved, now are we the sons of God, and it doth not yet appear what we shall be: but we know that when He shall appear we shall be like Him** (I John 3:2).

The term "sons" is used to designate both men and women believers because when we are with the Lord there will be no differentiation between male and female. So our Lord's eternal purpose is not only to have a witness for His name within every tribe and nation on earth, but also to gather out for Himself one great big wonderful heavenly family. Included in it He wants **some from every tribe and nation**. So whereas His Father had just one **only begotten Son**, our Lord Jesus has millions of sons and daughters in His family. That doesn't mean we are God as He is, but we are nevertheless members of His family in a special way, being **born of God** (John 1:13).

The great master plan of our Lord and Saviour to have sons and daughters from among all the nations began at the tower of Babel. The Israelite "parenthesis" of the Old Testament period was temporary, as God indicated to Abram when He changed the patriarch's name to Abraham, meaning **father of nations.** It's that second covenant promise alone which is valid today.

That's why our Lord is not in a big hurry to come back again. When some of His children who had been beheaded for their faith prayed, **How long, O Lord, holy and true**, He told them to just be patient for a while because there were other believers **yet to be killed as they were** (Revelation 6:11).

One of them was a British missionary named Thomas who was working in China more than a century ago. His heart was burdened for the closed land of Korea where at that time there was no witness for the Lord. Determined to be the first apostle to go there, he packed up some Bibles in Chinese characters, which literate Koreans could read, and paid for passage on a merchant sailer that was going to Pyongyang. As he was unloading his Bibles after arrival, the local Buddhists took one look at him and decided he must be a devil from hell. So they cut his head off. But some of them took the Bibles out of curiosity and became believers as a result of reading them. In Korea in 1950 I met a gospel preacher who told me, "My grandfather was among the assassins who found faith in Christ through reading one of those Bibles." If our Lord had returned before that time, that missionary martyr would not have been in His heavenly family.

Or if He had returned even earlier there would have been no Martin Luther or John Wesley or William Carey or Dwight L. Moody. Had He come a century ago His family would not have included Billy Sunday or Billy Graham or Bakht Singh of India or Prem Pradhan of Nepal or the great Zulu apostle Nicholas Bhengu or John Sung, "father of 10,000 churches" in China. It's easy to see why He is not in a hurry. He wants millions more in that **great multitude which no man can number from every people, tongue and nation who have washed their robes and made them white in His blood that He shed for us** (Revelation 7:9 & 14).

The MAIN EVENT which our Lord has planned for the human race is to complete His body, the true church, which He also calls His **bride**. Remember, all these metaphors are just pictures to help us visualize what He is doing. He calls us His **children**; also **His body, His building, His harvest crop, the sheep of His pasture and branches on His vine**.

When He comes again He will **change our vile body, that it may be fashioned like unto His glorious body** (Philippians 3:31). We will be caught up to meet Him as He comes in the clouds of heaven (I Thessalonians 4:17) and there above the atmosphere will take place **the marriage supper of the Lamb** (Revelation 19:7-9). The holy city described in Revelation 21 is what the Scripture says it is: **the bride, the Lamb's wife**. I am frequently disappointed when I hear otherwise intelligent Bible teachers speak of the **bride coming down from the heavens** as though it were composed of inanimate materials such as gold or emeralds or pearls. Haven't they read the third chapter of First Corinthians where the Apostle says that a local church should be made up of **gold, silver and precious stones**, which signify the building materials of God's temple? These are metaphors which help us visualize what our Lord is doing on earth today. Several times in the Gospels He is quoted as calling Himself the bridegroom and his redeemed saints as virgins that make up His bride.

When our Lord comes again He will **bring with Him** the

spirits of those whom He has redeemed from every nation, and each will be **clothed upon** (II Corinthians 5:4) with a new body resurrected from the dust of the earth or the depths of the sea. These are the jewels of the New Jerusalem. Those who will shine the brightest are the ones who have become **gold tried in the fire** (Revelation 3:18), **the trial of whose faith, being much more precious than gold,** has purified them until they are **found unto praise and honor and glory at our Lord's appearing** (I Peter 1:7). That's why He promises in Revelation 21 to **wipe away all tears from the eyes** of those who have suffered for His sake **when I make up my jewels** (Malachi 3:17).

That the term **holy city** refers to the body and bride of Christ should have been clear to every Bible teacher who has ever taught Galatians. In Chapter Four the Apostle speaks of two Jerusalems: the one in Palestine which was at that time, he says, **in bondage with her children**, and the other is the heavenly Jerusalem which is the bride of Christ **and mother of us all**, meaning all true believers. It is in this context that he quotes Isaiah 54, **Rejoice thou barren that bearest not . . . for the desolate hath many more children than the married wife**. Paul draws an allegory for us here, saying that the natural descendants of Abraham in Old Testament times are equivalent to Hagar, Abraham's slave by whom he had his first son. Sarah (**the barren that did not bear**), on the other hand, represents the body of believers redeemed from among other nations, and who will make up most of the jewels in our Saviour's bride, the New Jerusalem.

But the Old Testament saints are also there, the remnant of true believers who were **circumcised in heart** and not **blotted out of the Book of Life** because of sin and unbelief. In fact, the names of the twelve tribes of Israel are pictured as pearls, while each one of the twelve Apostles is pictured individually as a distinctive precious stone.

Gleaming brightly among the pearls will be the 144,000 Hebrews whom God elected between 30 and 70 A.D. to give His gospel to other nations. These were **the first fruits unto God and to the Lamb** (Revelation 14:4) who for their witness paid a terrible price of persecution and suffering at the hands of their fellow Judaeans at that time.

The **holy city** of Revelation 21 illustrates why the church age is God's MAIN EVENT. Our Saviour is **making up His jewels** from within every tribe and nation. He is building His permanent temple in the heavens. On this earth He is cutting the stones of which it is being built. When Solomon constructed the original temple in Jerusalem, no hammer or chisel was heard within it. Each stone was cut in the quarry to fit perfectly in its appointed place. So today, our Lord uses tribulation and persecution for cutting the stones on this earth to make up His heavenly bride, **the holy city, the new Jerusalem**. There He will **wipe away all tears from our eyes and there shall be no more death, neither sorrow nor crying, neither shall there be any more pain, for the former things are passed away** (Revelation 21:4).

I will never forget the words of a precious saint in Korea who had been horribly beaten and tortured by the Japanese because he would not bow to their idols or deny his allegiance to Christ. His body was scarred and disfigured by what he suffered. But as he gave his personal testimony at a meeting I attended, his eyes sparkled with the fire of faith. "A diamond has no beauty," he said, "until it is cut and polished. I rejoice to have been counted worthy to suffer for my Saviour, because it has served to make me more like Him."

In the first chapter of Revelation we are told that our Lord has made us **kings and priests**, and that He is **the Prince of the kings of the earth**. Then Chapter 21 tells us that these same **kings of the earth will bring their glory and honor into the New Jerusalem** and in verses 24 and 26 it is revealed that **the nations** will bring their glory and honor into it. When we combine this vision with God's second promise to Abraham, and our Lord's words about **all nations**, we begin to get the completed picture. And we see how pioneer foreign missions is the most important activity taking place on this planet today. It is the MAIN EVENT of human history for which the Old Testament "parenthesis" was only a prelude.

Chapter 13

Who then is "That Man of Sin"?

During the Reformation Period (A.D. 1500-1700) in Europe, the Reformers were generally agreed that the Vatican dynasty was a fulfillment of the prophecy concerning **that man of sin** given by the Apostle Paul in his Second Epistle to the Thessalonians.

In his first Epistle to the church at Thessalonica, Paul had said, **The Lord Himself shall descend from heaven with a shout, with the voice of the Archangel, and with the trump of God: and the dead in Christ shall rise first; then we which are alive and remain shall be caught up together with them in the clouds, to meet the Lord in the air.** This event is what we evangelicals today call "the rapture of the church."

But apparently some Thessalonian believers took it too literally and gave up working, expecting that the Lord would come at any moment. In his second, follow-up letter Paul dealt very sternly with those who had quit working (see Chapter 3, verses 5-12), while he also informed the whole church that the return of the Lord would be delayed until certain other events took place. He discussed these in the first 12 verses of Chapter 2.

Now we beseech you, brethren, by the coming of our Lord Jesus Christ, and by our gathering together unto him, That ye be not soon shaken in mind, or be troubled, neither by spirit, nor by word, nor by letter as from us, as that the day of Christ is at hand. Let no man deceive you by any means: for that day shall

not come, except there come a falling away first, and that man of sin be revealed, the son of perdition; who opposeth and exalteth himself above all that is called God, or that is worshipped; so that he as [a] god sitteth in the temple of God, showing himself off like a god. Remember ye not, that, when I was yet with you, I told you these things? And now ye know what withholdeth that he might be revealed in his time. For the mystery of iniquity doth already work: only [that which] now hinders will hinder, until [it] be taken out of the way. And then shall that wicked one be revealed, whom the Lord shall consume with the spirit of His mouth, and shall destroy with the brightness of His coming: even him, whose coming is after the working of Satan with all power and signs and lying wonders, and with all deceivableness of unrighteousness in them that perish; because they received not the love of the truth, that they might be saved. And for this cause God shall send them strong delusion, that they should believe a lie: that they all might be damned who believed not the truth, but had pleasure in unrighteousness.**

So Paul said that the Lord Jesus was not going to come back to earth right away; many other events were going to take place first. One major event on the list was the "falling away," the seeds of which were already being sown in Paul's time. That's why he wrote, **The mystery of iniquity doth already work**. Paul spent three years building up the church at Ephesus, but within about 20 years thereafter the Spirit of God would say through John, **I have somewhat against you, because you have left your first love. Remember therefore from whence you are fallen, and repent . . .** (Revelation 2:4-5).

Another church in which Paul likely had a part was the one at Thyatira. He had won a Thyatira woman named Lydia to the Lord while she was in Philippi on business (Acts 16:14). No doubt she was active in the church in Thyatira after her return, but it was also infiltrated by a "Jezebel" that advocated sexual promiscuity (Revelation 3:20-23). Then there were the "Nicolaitans" (Revelation 2:15) who were active in the church at Pergamos, and whom God hated. Their definition is a combination of two Greek words: *nico* or *nike*, meaning "to overcome, conquer or rule," and *laos* meaning "the people," and from which we get the word "laity." Even then, in Paul's time, there were carnal, ambitious churchmen who wanted to rule over others, and divide church congregations into "clergy" and "laity."

These are some of the reasons why Paul said, **The mystery of iniquity doth already work**. The falling away was coming, he said, but something was hindering its full development until that something would be taken out of the way. There can be no doubt but that he was speaking of the imperial Roman government. The very fact that Paul said **You know what it is** should be a clear indication of his meaning, because Paul was very careful never to mention the Roman government in any of his epistles. Instead, he reminds the Thessalonians that he had told them these things when he was there with them.

Roman government oversight, opposition and persecution prevented would-be "Nicolaitans" from rising to power in the churches. Carnal Christians were envious of the pagans who enjoyed favor from the government for lavish weddings, funerals and holiday celebrations, while Christians continued to be held down as a minority religion. Persecution tended to purify the churches, and delayed the foretold "falling away."

But everything changed in the year 312 when the emperor Constantine professed to have accepted "the Christian religion" and granted toleration to all who practiced it. **That which hindered** the apostasy was then **taken out of the way**.

There was almost universal euphoria among Christians throughout the empire when Constantine professed conversion, and few realized how destructive this event would eventually prove to be within the churches. What actually happened was a gradual merger of "Christianity" with the pagan religions of Greece and Rome. Roman temples became Christian temples. Roman priests became Christian priests. And Christian names were given to Roman gods and goddesses.

The chief goddess of the empire was the *Parthenon* (Greek

for *Virgin*), in whose honor a temple still partially stands in Athens as one of the most magnificent structures ever built. The Virgin goddess was universal, known as *Notre Dame* (*Our Lady*) with a thousand names, one for each locality. Priests sprinkled "holy water" on thousands of statues and christened them as "Our Lady of Ephesus" or "Our Lady of Milan," or Our Lady of wherever. In so doing they identified them with the blessed mother of our Lord and thus attributed virtual deity to her, which I believe has deeply grieved her Son.

Constantine called a conference of church leaders, held in Nicaea in 325, to end divisions and establish "one universal (Latin: *catholic*) church." Thereafter, over time, local assemblies lost their autonomy and all congregations were forced into the monstrous state church of the empire, with the Bishop of Rome as absolute, infallible dictator. Eventually he was elevated to the position of "Vicar of Christ," which came to be recognized as the equivalent of "God on earth."

Never in human history has such worship been accorded to a mere man as was given to the Medieval popes. When a new one was crowned, all the cardinals were required to wiggle on their bellies across the Temple called St. Peter's Cathedral in Rome and kiss his toe. Neither the Kings of Nepal, the Lamas of Tibet, the Manchus of China, Mikados of Japan and certainly not the mighty Caesars of Rome were more highly deified and venerated than were the popes of Rome for 12 centuries.

And it is still going on to a lesser extent. Unless you have seen for yourself, it is difficult to imagine how the popes developed into exact opposites of what our Lord said His disciples should be. I was in the Temple called Saint Peter's Cathedral one day in 1951 when Pope Pius XII made a personal appearance. The place was packed with people except for a center aisle which was roped off for "His Holiness" to use.

In due time a procession appeared, led by Swiss guards in fancy uniforms. The pope was riding high above everyone else in a combination chair and throne borne on the shoulders of his attendants. As the procession moved slowly down the center aisle of the cathedral, the assembled crowd continually shouted with one voice, "Viva il Papa! Viva il Papa!"

Such adoration of a mere man who professes to represent Christ on earth borders on blasphemy. God alone is worthy of our worship. He has said, **Why should my name be polluted? I will not give my glory to another** (Isaiah 48:11).

At that time (1951) I had been working with Billy Graham for five years. He had been preaching almost daily to greater audiences than any man in human history. Yet I never once saw any of those throngs offer any sign of praise or adulation toward Billy Graham as a person. Even if someone had tried to do so, he would never have allowed it. He pointed people to Christ, not to himself. But the **MAN OF SIN** whose coming was foretold by the Apostle Paul **exalted HIMSELF above all that is called God, or that is worshipped; so that he sits in the temple of God showing himself off like a god** (II Thessalonians 2:4).

Here we must pause to define what is meant by the term **TEMPLE**. Under the Old Covenant it was the place which God chose **TO PUT HIS NAME THERE** (Deuteronomy 12:5,11,14,21), and even though it became **a den of thieves** it was still recognized as being the house of God. That's why the Son of God drove the **money changers** out of it with a whip.

Under the New Covenant the temple of God is a place where Christ is named. When believers **gather in His Name, He is present in their midst** (Matthew 18:20). Paul called the assembly at Corinth **the TEMPLE of God** even though some who met there were guilty of fornication and other sins. So when the Apostle wrote of **that man of sin sitting in the temple of God showing himself off like a god,** he was looking forward prophetically to the time when a pope would parade through a church building in the name of Christ.

Another man of God with whom I worked for many years was Bakht Singh of India. He was from a Sikh family in what is now Punjab state, and came to Christ while an engineering student in Canada. He returned to India as an anointed apostle of Christ.

There God used him to become the spiritual father of more than 2000 assemblies of believers. Each year these churches conducted several "Holy Convocations" in various parts of India. Attendance was often in excess of 25,000 believers at these joyful celebrations. But never was there any adulation or praise of Bakht Singh. On the contrary, each gathering displayed a huge banner saying **THE LORD ALONE SHALL BE EXALTED**, a quotation from Scripture. When Bakht Singh **departed to be with Christ** at the age of 97, an estimated 600,000 people gathered in Hyderabad for his funeral. They did not come to honor Bakht Singh; but rather they came to glorify our Lord Jesus Christ, for whom Bakht Singh was an ambassador.

I mention these things to emphasize what happened as a result of the **FALLING AWAY** when **THAT MAN OF SIN** arose, calling himself "the Vicar of Christ" and claiming infallibility. The medieval popes of Rome were the exact opposite of what our Lord said His disciples should be. Their pomp and self-glorification were in stark contrast to true believers such as Billy Graham and Bakht Singh. So I believe that Martin Luther, John Calvin, John Knox and a host of other reformers got it right when they concluded that the **falling away** was the paganization of the churches which began in the Fourth Century, and that the **man of sin** represented the corrupt Papal Dynasty which controlled Europe for more than a thousand years. In fact, Paul's language so closely parallels the facts of history that the interpretation should be obvious to anyone and everyone who has studied the subject seriously.

The peak of Papal power was around 1300 when Pope Innocent III used "the Inquisition" to torture and murder any and all who would not submit to his absolute authority by acceptance of the idolatrous doctrines and practices of Medieval Catholicism. Throughout the centuries of those dark ages, many thousands were killed by the priests of the **false prophet** (Revelation 15:13) who revived the fallen empire which had been **wounded unto death** and called it the Holy Roman Empire.

In II Thessalonians 2:8 we are told that this **man of sin** would continue until our Lord consumed him with **the spirit** [Greek: breath] **of His mouth**. Our Lord is presented in Revelation as having a **sharp, two-edged sword** proceeding out of His mouth. In Ephesians 6:17 and Hebrews 4:12 we are told that the **sword of the Spirit** is the **Word of God**. And it was that Word which ultimately shattered the yoke of Papal power over the minds of men.

The turning point began around 1450 when Johann Gutenberg invented the printing press and the first Bibles were printed in Latin, and then in other languages. John Wycliffe had completed an English translation of the New Testament in 1380 and William Tyndale published an even better one in 1526. Wycliffe's influence reached all the way to Bohemia where his disciple, John Huss, began to preach the Word of God rather than papal heresy. For so doing he was burned alive by evil Roman priests on July 6, 1415. Some of his disciples were also burned, including Jerome of Prague. So furious was the Pope's hatred of God's Word that he ordered his henchmen to dig up the remains of John Wycliffe, who had died in 1384, and burn his bones. Tyndale was burned on October 6, 1536. His disciple, John Frith, had already been burned alive in 1533. Four others: Thomas Cranmer, Nicholas Ridley, Hugh Latimer and John Hooper were burned in 1555.

As everyone knows, the most significant of all the reformers during that heroic era was Martin Luther. While living as a cloistered Augustinian monk he read the New Testament and discovered that peace with God comes by faith alone. God gave him the courage to declare that faith and he was promptly condemned by the Vatican. But his life was spared as a result of being kidnapped and protected by Prince Fredrick, and while hidden away in Wartburg castle he translated the New Testament into the German language. After it was published in September 1522 its message spread like wildfire throughout much of Germany and other parts of Europe. And even though thousands of new believers were murdered by agents of the **Man of Sin** in Rome, God's Word proved to be **living and powerful and sharper than a two-edged sword**.

Once Bibles were printed in quantity, the collapse of the

pseudo-Christian religion of Rome was inevitable. Wherever the Bible was distributed in Northern Europe, the power of the Papacy was broken. Not only was Catholicism replaced by Protestant, and eventually evangelical, churches but also was itself dramatically reformed. Comparing Pope John Paul II with the murderous mastermind of the Inquisition, Pope Innocent III (1198-1216), would be somewhat like comparing Mahatma Gandhi with Leon Trotsky.

God's Word says, **In the mouth of two or three witnesses shall every word be established** (II Corinthians 13:1). That's why we have Four Gospels. And why various events are repeated several times in Old Testament books. And why prophecies are often repeated in different books of the New Testament. I believe that several things mentioned in the Second Chapter of II Thessalonians are repeated in Revelation. Which leads us to the two "beasts" of Revelation 13.

The first rose up out of the sea, a symbol for pagan nations. The fact that it had seven heads [rulers] and ten horns [provinces, with sub-rulers] means that it had to be a dynasty, or political empire, covering many years if not centuries. Prophecy teachers make a big mistake when they say "the beast" represents a single individual.

There are many similarities between the prophecies in Revelation and those of the prophet Daniel in the Old Testament. In Chapter Seven of Daniel the prophet speaks of a vision in which he saw four beasts come up from the sea, and was told that they represent **four kings** [or kingdoms] **which shall arise** (Daniel 7:17). A careful study of that chapter will reveal that the fourth beast which Daniel saw was the yet-to-come Roman Empire.

And there should be no doubt that the **beast out of the sea** in Revelation 13 also represents the Roman Empire which, when John wrote this book, was soon to begin a reign of terror against the rapidly growing minority group called "Christians." The fact that **the dragon** [Satan] **gave him** [it] **power and seat and great authority** should in itself be indication enough that this is a symbol of the Roman Empire. There had never been anything like it before, and nothing quite like it since.

In the Book of Acts the Roman authorities are generally presented as being protective of the Christians, who for the first 40 years of their existence suffered horrendous atrocities at the hands of their fellow Judaeans [Jews]. Many, including Paul several times, were rescued from beatings and murder by Roman magistrates. But when war broke out in Palestine in the year 66 and the Romans became embroiled in conflict with the Judaeans there, it changed the situation. According to Revelation Chapters Seven and Fourteen, 144,000 of the first Christians were Israelites, so they came under suspicion during the Palestinian war, just as most Japanese-Americans were rounded up and imprisoned by the U.S. Government after the Japanese attack on Pearl Harbor in Hawaii on December 7, 1941. The Romans would not have understood that when Hebrews accepted Christ they ceased to be Judaeans in the Old Testament sense. Anyway, it is reported that when the Emperor Nero dispatched General Vespasian to put down the rebellion in Palestine, he, Nero, also took punitive measures against the Judaeans in Rome, including many of those who believed in Christ.

Later emperors were said to be worse, mounting waves of terror and bloodshed against the rapidly growing number of Christians throughout the empire. For the next 240 years they **made war against the saints**, and crushed them under the bloody boots of persecution. Greek and Roman priests of pagan temples often directed the holocaust, as hundreds of thousands of believers in Christ went through the fires of persecution to prove their willingness to be **faithful unto death**. Two famous sayings have come down to us from that frightful period. One is that "the blood of martyrs is the seed of the church"; and the second is "Adeste fideles" which means "Come all ye faithful." Traditions say that when groups of Christians faced torture and death in Roman arenas, they would shout "Adeste fidelis" to the throng of spectators, and hitherto secret believers would climb down to die with them in the pit.

Power was given him [the Beast, Rome] **over all kindreds, and tongues, and nations. And all who dwell upon the earth shall worship him** [i.e., Rome], **whose names are not written in the**

167

· **Book of Life of the Lamb** (Revelation 13:7-8). The first beast of Revelation Chapter Thirteen has to be the Roman Empire. But then that Beast was **as it were, wounded unto death** (Revelation 13:3).

Obviously, this is a reference to the collapse of the Roman Empire. Many historians have written voluminous books entitled THE FALL OF ROME. The greatest empire of ancient times collapsed, and beginning in the Fifth Century was overrun by barbarians, such as the Visigoths and Vandals.

But prior to the final "wounding unto death" a different type of wound had stabbed at the heart of the Beast that was killing Christians by the thousands. In the year 312 the emperor Constantine came to realize that for every Christian the Romans killed, God would raise up two to take his place. Making war against the saints only produced more saints. And true believers often did not make good soldiers when conscripted into brutal Roman armies. And so began the saying, "If you can't lick them, join them." Constantine professed conversion to "the Christian religion." So persecution of believers by "the [first] Beast" gradually ceased throughout the empire after the Beast [Rome] was **wounded unto death**.

But then, **the deadly wound was healed** (Revelation 13:3). The Beast would live again. It was to be resurrected by a second beast which would **have two horns like a lamb** (Verse 11) but **speak like a dragon** (the Devil). This second Beast was to rise "up out of the earth." Before 70 A.D. the term "earth" in Revelation refers to Israelites in Palestine, but thereafter to "Christendom." This second beast would come from the churches, with two horns like the Lamb of God and professing to be the "vicar of Christ." Obviously, this prophecy of a second Beast, which would resurrect the first one, refers to the papal dynasty, which eventually was almost as powerful politically as were the Caesars that preceded it.

The second Beast did not emerge immediately. So-called "Christian" emperors such as Theodosius (379-395) and Justinian (527-565) not only proclaimed "Christianity" to be the official religion of the Empire, but also demanded, on pain of death, that all people adhere to it. Justinian attempted to revive the already wounded empire, and was partially successful. But at the height of his reign the bubonic plague was brought into Europe by rats on board ships from Asia. Nearly half the population of the empire was wiped out by this scourge, and the "wounding unto death" was completed. So the empire was not revived at that time. It never recovered from that frightful plague.

When Barbarians overran the Empire after the plague, the power of emperors declined and disappeared, but gradually they were succeeded in power by consecutive Bishops of Rome, who would soon be regarded as *Pontifex Maximus*, the supreme head of the church; and, eventually, the supreme head of everything else. They revived the Roman Empire, calling it the Holy Roman Empire. And essentially, the official religion of the Empire was similar to pagan times, except that the idols of Roman gods and goddesses had been given Christian names. And acceptance of this revived Roman religion was required of everyone, often enforced by horrible tortures. I would urge all Christians today to read Foxe's BOOK OF MARTYRS which documents the persecution of true believers by the Second Beast of Rome. And one of the most precious books I have ever owned is MARTYR'S MIRROR, a huge volume first published by Mennonites of Holland in 1659. It chronicles thousands of cases of true believers who died at the hands of the Second Beast and his followers in medieval Catholicism.

In my early years as a new Christian I heard numerous prophecy speakers talk about a soon coming "revived Roman empire." But they didn't know church history. When I studied medieval history as an undergraduate and graduate student in two major universities, I learned that the Roman Empire had been revived 1144 years earlier. At the Vatican on December 25, 800, Pope Leo III placed a crown on the head of Charles the Great (Charlemagne) of France and proclaimed him "Emperor Augustus [Caesar] of the Romans." The official proclamation stated: "To Charles, Augustus, crowned of God, great and pacific Emperor of the Romans, be life and victory." Since it was the Pope who crowned him, were they not saying that the Pope was a god? Anyway, that was the official beginning of what was to be called "The Holy Roman Empire." And from that time forth, the Popes controlled Europe. The emperors were forced to be obedient and subservient to the Popes that crowned them. When one of them knelt before him, the Pope placed the crown on the emperor's head with his feet. Then, before the new sovereign could arise, the Pope kicked the crown off his head. "Let that be a lesson to you," the Pope said. "Just as I have the power to crown you, so also I have power to remove that crown from your head."

It was while doing research in medieval history that I began to doubt seriously whether contemporary prophecy teachers had ever studied history. If so, how could they continue to teach and write about the future coming of a so-called "revived Roman empire" when it had already happened? I cannot find any shred of evidence in God's Word about a revived Roman empire beyond that which began to take place 1200 years ago.

The **second beast** (Revelation 13:12), the Vatican dynasty, would **exercise all the power of the first beast**, and **cause the earth and them that dwell therein to worship the first beast** [the religion of the Roman Empire] **whose deadly wound was healed**. The first task assigned to Charlemagne by Pope Leo III was that he should deploy his armies in an attempt to drive the Muslims out of Spain. All people in Western Europe would henceforth be forced to accept the official Roman religion, which now had Christian names for its gods and idols, even if they were fictitious. The Popes couldn't come up with a Christian name for Mercury, the god of travel, so they invented one. Only recently did the Vatican acknowledge publicly that Saint Christopher never existed. Yet millions of Roman Catholics have carried an idol image of this substitution for Mercury to insure good luck when they travel.

While visiting Jerusalem 57 years ago, I witnessed a repetition of the **fire come down from heaven** miracle which the religious beast was foretold to perform. A great number of pilgrim priests had gathered at the so-called "Church of the Holy Sepulchre," each bearing an unlighted torch. Then a special priest appeared, also holding high before him an unlighted torch. As we watched in awe, the torch of that special priest burst into flames, and was used to light all the others. We were told then that each of those pilgrim priests would walk all the way back to the place from which he had come, carrying the flame which had "miraculously appeared" in Jerusalem.

As foretold in Revelation 13:14, miracles in Catholicism have been commonplace throughout the centuries, and are still being reported today. Many miracles have been attributed to Roman images, icons and idols, as was foretold in Verse 15 of Revelation 13. Millions of pilgrims go to shrines that venerate supposed apparitions of heavenly beings or relics of deified "saints" that are said to have magical powers.

Also fulfilled was Verse 17 of Revelation 13 that no man might buy or sell unless he bore **the mark of the beast**. During the horrible days of the Inquisition, economic discrimination was universal against all persons who failed to acknowledge belief in and worship of what the Pope dictated. Any failure to go along completely with the Pope's dictates resulted in deprivation, torture and even death. On Ash Wednesday every person was required to have a mark on his forehead signifying conformity. Among Egyptian and Eastern churches, a permanent tattoo on the right hand was required. Without these marks a person could not buy or sell, transact business, own property or be legally married.

Another significant prophecy regarding the resurrected Roman beast was that it would continue "forty and two months" (Revelation 13:5). This time frame is repeated elsewhere in Revelation as well. But each mention refers to the same thing. For example, in Chapter Eleven, Verse Two we are told **the holy city shall they tread under foot forty and two months**. In Chapter 21 we are told that **the holy city** is **the bride, the Lamb's wife**, meaning the true church composed of all born again believers. Put these all together and we get the picture: the true church would be trodden under foot by the pagan church for forty-two months. But in prophecy, God says, **I have appointed thee each day for a year** (Ezekiel 4:6). So if we use the figure of 30 years for each month, we come up with 1260 years.

If we add 1260 years to the time of the falling away, beginning with the professed conversion of Constantine, we come up with the time of the Reformation around the latter half of the Sixteenth Century. That's when the power of the Roman Beast was broken, and the holy city began to emerge from underneath the heel of the tyrant.

Another prophetic reference to this 1260 year period is in Revelation 12:6, where the true church is depicted as **a woman clothed with the sun, and the moon under her feet, and upon her head a crown of twelve stars**. The editors of the Scofield Reference Bible and other prophecy writers say that this woman is symbolic of "Israel," but they don't say which "Israel." There was **the Israel of God** (Galatians 6:16) and also **the synagogue of Satan** (Revelation 2:9, 3:9). There were the **stiffnecked and uncircumcised in heart** (Acts 7:51) as opposed to those who were **a chosen generation, a royal priesthood, an holy nation** (I Peter 2:9). There was the "Israel" made up of **snakes, a generation of vipers** (Matthew 4:7, 22:33) in contrast to those who had **put off the old man with his deeds; and had put on the new man which is renewed after the image of Him that created him** (Colossians 3:9-10). **Though the number of the children of Israel be as the sand of the sea,** [only] **a remnant shall be saved** (Isaiah 10:22, Romans 9:27). Most of the Israelites in both the Old Testament and New Testament periods were wicked sinners in rebellion against God, whom the prophets from Moses onward repeatedly called a spiritual whore. There is no way that the saintly woman mentioned in Revelation Twelve could be unregenerate Israel.

Rather, she is the **elect REMNANT** of Israel (Romans 11:5), the **144,000** who alone were recognized by God as being His people, and who at that time constituted **ALL ISRAEL** (Romans 9:6-7) in His sight. All other Hebrews had been **broken off the olive tree** (Romans 11:17) and were not recognized as the seed of Abraham any longer (Romans 9:8).

But the **elect remnant** alone did not make up the godly

woman of Revelation 12:1. She also included those **who sometimes were far off are made nigh by the blood of Christ, who hath made both one, and hath broken down the middle wall of partition between us . . . to make in Himself of twain one new man** (Ephesians 2:13-15). By His sacrificial death on the cross, our Saviour eliminated forever any distinction between Judaean believers and those who were not Israelites; but rather, **that those of other nations should be fellow-heirs, and of the same body and partakers of His promise** (Ephesians 3:6). **Now therefore they are no more strangers and foreigners, but fellow-citizens, and of the household of God** (Ephesians 2:19).

So the saintly woman in Revelation 12 is **the Israel of God** (144,000) combined with believers from other nations. She is the **Lamb's wife** and mother of His children (Galatians 4:26), who are collectively called **His body, His flesh and His bones** (Ephesians 5:30). The metaphor of the church giving birth to Christ is used in Galatians 4:19 where the Apostle says, **My little children, of whom I travail in birth again until Christ be formed in you**. We use it in the Christmas carol: "O holy child of Bethlehem, descend to us we pray; cast out our sin and enter in, be born in us today." The Woman in Revelation 12 is the heavenly Jerusalem, **the mother of us all** (Galatians 4:26), and the child she brought forth was the **body of Christ**, which in I Corinthians 12:12 is also called Christ. Our Lord Jesus was God living on earth in a human body. The church He brought forth at Corinth (and other places) was God living on earth in a body of humans. When our Lord spoke to Saul of Tarsus on the road to Damascus, he asked, **Why do you persecute ME?**

The great dragon first used blood-thirsty Judaean priests and Pharisees like Saul of Tarsus in Palestine. Then, after 70 A.D., Romans throughout the empire devoured many of the children of the Lamb's wife as soon as they were born. Beginning around 312 there was respite for a century or two and then the holocaust began again, with the Bishop of Rome as the chief executioner. Surviving true believers had to go underground, and exercise their faith as secret believers. That's what is meant in Revelation 12 about the woman being hidden in a wilderness for 1260 days (years).

One key to understanding this figure is the use of the word **remnant**, which identifies true believers in contrast with other Israelites, or other professing Christians who have not been reconciled to God. **The dragon was wroth with the woman, and went to make war with the REMNANT OF HER SEED, which keep the commandments of God, and have the testimony of Jesus Christ** (Revelation 12:17).

The fact that a **REMNANT OF HER SEED** remained after the woman gave birth, and also after her offspring **was caught up unto God**, indicates that her offspring included many persons, not just one single child. Those who were **caught up** were the martyrs from among the 144,000 who were killed by their fellow Judaeans. **I saw under the altar the souls of them that were slain for the word of God, and for the testimony which they held; and they cried with a loud voice, saying, How long, O Lord, holy and true, dost thou not judge and avenge our blood on them that dwell on the earth** (Revelation 6:9-10). The continued slaughter of her children, and the hiding of the true church in the wilderness of obscurity, went on for 1260 years: from the falling away beginning in the Fourth Century until the time of the Reformation in the Sixteenth Century.

So, to summarize this chapter, we must conclude that the two "beasts" in Revelation 13 refer to religio-political dynasties. The first beast **out of the sea** (pagan nations) is a prophecy of the holocaust that would come, especially during the Second and Third Centuries, when the Roman Empire would persecute Christians unmercifully. Then, the fall of Rome is foretold as that first beast being **wounded unto death**. The second beast **out of the earth** (Christendom), with **two horns** that mimic the **Lamb of God**, foretells the emergence of the Papal dynasty which would resurrect the Roman Empire and persecute true believers. This second beast, called **the false prophet**, is the same personage as the **man of sin** foretold in II Thessalonians 2:3-4 who was predicted to set himself up as a god on the earth. So God's Word foretold the **falling away** of His people that would last 42 months of years until the printing press was invented and the availability of printed Bibles produced the Reformation. Finally, then, after hiding in the wilderness for 1260 years, **the Bride, the Lamb's wife** (Revelation 19:7-8, 21:9) emerged as was foretold, and began to **make herself ready** for her wedding day when our Saviour returns in glory.

Chapter 14

The Beginning of the End

I have already mentioned that the Book of Revelation is not chronological, and how events are repeated in different chapters from various perspectives. But Chapter Fourteen is unique. It presents a panorama of the present age, from the first coming of Christ Jesus our Lord until His second coming, with a brief mention and emphasis of the high points of history during the past 2000 years.

It begins with the redeemed **remnant**, **ALL ISRAEL**, the **144,000** who were the **firstfruits unto God and to the Lamb**. These were called out during a forty year period 30-70 A.D.

Next, in Verse Six, there is a mention of **the everlasting gospel** being preached by **the 144,000** and their successors to **all nations**, beginning with those who **dwell in the land** (the Israelites) and then **to every kindred, tongue and people**. This is still going on today.

Then in Verses Seven and Eight we are told that **the hour of His judgment** [upon His fellow Israelites who killed Him] **has come**, which took place 66-70 A.D. Included in that judgment is the fall of **Babylon, because she made all nations drink of the wine of the wrath of her fornication**. As I mentioned earlier, **Babylon** was a code word for Jerusalem among the Judaean believers (I Peter 5:13).

Verses Nine through Twelve cover almost fifteen hundred years, as we are given a vision of those who were **faithful unto death** during those terrible centuries of persecution from leaders of the Roman Empire, followed by the Holy Roman Empire, which in some ways was even worse, during the centuries of the Inquisition implemented by the papal dynasty. Verse Thirteen is a tribute to the martyrs of faith during both of those times of tribulation, at the hands of the original Romans and then during the centuries of the (revived) Holy Roman Empire when the Popes controlled the rulers of Europe. During these centuries the believers also suffered persecution from the followers of the Antichrist, Muhammad, in places where Muslims gained political control.

In Verse Fourteen we see our King, wearing His crown as He sits upon a white cloud in glory, and in His hand is a sharp sickle. This image relates to John 4:35-36: **Lift up your eyes and look on the fields, for they are white already to harvest. He that reapeth receiveth wages, and gathereth fruit unto life eternal.** As head of His church, our Lord is addressed by an angel: **Thrust in thy sickle and reap, for the time is come for thee to reap; for the harvest of the earth is ripe. And He that sat on the cloud thrust in His sickle and the earth was reaped.** This prophecy foretold the events of world evangelization that were to take place before the second coming of our Saviour. They began about two hundred years after the Reformation. The reformers (Luther, Calvin, Knox, etc.) were not evangelistic. In fact, most of them retained the dead form of the state church, including professional clergy aligned with political rulers. Those with more biblical church life (Anabaptists, Mennonites, etc.) tended to be separatists who kept to themselves and did not aggressively reach out to evangelize the nations which were without Christ.

Our Lord thrust in His sickle and began to reap around the middle of the Eighteenth Century when Count Ludwig von Zinzendorf and his fellow Moravians became the first evangelistic foreign missionaries since the First Century. Through them John Wesley, an unconverted Anglican priest, was born again, and together with his brother Charles conducted huge evangelistic campaigns throughout the British Isles. When he was forbidden to preach in Anglican churches, Wesley preached to large audiences out-of-doors for half a century. His highly disciplined, methodical followers called themselves "Methodists." They sent Francis Asbury to evangelize the colonies in America, and he reaped a great harvest. Though not a Methodist, George Whitefield was an even more effective reaper at that time, throughout the colonies as well as in Britain.

During the Nineteenth Century the Lord of the Harvest sent reapers to all the world, beginning with William Carey going to India (in 1792), Adoniram Judson to Burma (1812), Robert Morrison to China (1807) and hundreds more from Europe and America going to Asia and Africa. Great emphasis was given to worldwide evangelistic harvest by the ministry of Dwight L. Moody whose mass evangelism meetings brought tens of thousands to faith in Christ. Moody's foreign missions vision inspired many of his converts to go out to foreign fields. The Student Volunteer Movement was a step-child of Moody's ministry. Most Protestant churches began to implement foreign mission boards as part of their outreach in the latter half of the century. At the beginning of the Twentieth Century there was great enthusiasm for overseas missions within the Protestant churches of America and Western Europe. Outstanding leaders such as Robert E. Speer and John R. Mott conducted numerous international conferences to inspire the churches in world evangelism.

Then the enemy counter-attacked. Liberalism permeated the churches. Evangelism and soul winning were replaced with the "social gospel," which focused on trying to save society rather than the individual. Belief in the Bible was discredited by "modernists" in the churches. And those who still believed were sidetracked by campaigns for prohibition (of alcohol), women's suffrage and other causes.

A great rebirth of our Saviour's final harvest began during World War II and greatly increased from that time forward as evangelistic ministries began to proliferate and new means of communication developed. Evangelist Charles E. Fuller's Old Fashioned Revival Hour was heard on more radio stations than any other program, secular or religious. The Gideons, Pocket Testament League and other ministries began widespread Scripture distribution.

Child Evangelism ministries were winning children to Christ at an early age. Youth for Christ was winning thousands of high school students. The Navigators were winning men and women in military service. Inter-Varsity and Campus Crusade were reaching the college crowd. ISI and OSM were reaching foreign students and sending them home as missionaries to their own people. Christian Women's Clubs were evangelizing older women. Christian Business Men's Committee and the Full Gospel Business Men's Fellowship brought many thousands of men into the kingdom of God. The harvest was being reaped, especially in America. And almost all of these evangelistic ministries contributed to the worldwide spread of the gospel through hundreds of foreign missionary agencies.

Especially significant were the tremendous evangelistic crusades conducted by gifted men such as Billy Graham and Oral Roberts. Millions of lost souls were harvested by these men of God in America, while at the same time our Lord was using the great Zulu apostle, Nicholas Bhengu, to reach hundreds of thousands in Africa, and Bakht Singh to reap a similar harvest in a dozen states of India. Meanwhile, John Sung accepted Christ as a foreign student in America and was known as "the father of ten thousand churches" after he returned to China as a flaming evangelist. Hundreds more were similarly used on every continent. After the collapse of Communism, gifted preachers such as Slavik Radchuk were free to preach openly to an average audience of more than 10,000 daily in most Soviet countries, and thousands of new churches emerged from the ashes of Marxist repression.

Perhaps the greatest ingathering of lost souls in all of church history has taken place in South Korea and China during the past 60 years. An estimated 40% of the population of South Korea had become evangelical Christians by 2008, a higher percentage than any other country. Numerous gatherings there have been attended by more than one million believers. In China, the percentage is much smaller, but the numbers are astronomical. In spite of repression and opposition from Communist bureaucrats, house church groups have grown and multiplied by tens of thousands. When I left China in

1949, we estimated that evangelical Christians there numbered about half a million, and many of those were killed by the Communists. But today, even prejudiced government officials estimate that the number is sixty million or more.

Numerous new developments have contributed to the tremendous increase in the number of born again Christians throughout the world during the past seventy years. Bible institutes and Christian colleges were used of God to guide many into unshakable faith in the Bible as the Word of God. A proliferation of new evangelistic organizations aimed at specific groups such as children, teenagers, college students, businessmen, etc. served to make millions aware of the gospel. The availability of huge auditoriums and stadiums enabled gifted evangelists to reach multitudes at once, especially after the development of public address systems and other technologies that have made mass communication practical. Dissemination of the gospel by radio, television, print media and the internet has also added immeasurably to the end-time harvest.

Two other developments during the last half of the Twentieth Century also made a massive impact on the great ingathering of human souls into the kingdom of God. One was the emergence of interdenominational and nondenominational ministries that brought evangelicals together in united efforts of evangelism and foreign missionary outreach. Thousands of these organizations (about 4000 in India alone, and even more in Africa) were used of God to gather into His family a great multitude of new believers from hundreds of tribes and nations.

The other new development was the broadening of the Pentecostal movement, which had begun around 1900, into the "charismatic movement" beginning around 1950. The original Pentecostals tended to be somewhat sectarian and divisive, which caused their worldwide influence to be rather negligible. But around mid-century the Pentecostal movement moved into the mainstream, and barriers between "charismatics" and other evangelicals tended to fade away. The result has been a dynamic explosion of evangelism by Pentecostals, especially in Africa, India and Latin

America. Multiplied millions of new believers have been brought into the kingdom of God by them, and thus hastened the day when our Lord shall have accomplished His purpose and will be married to His bride, **a great multitude which no man can number, of all nations, and kindreds, and people, and tongues . . . saying, Salvation to our God which sitteth upon the throne, and unto the Lamb** (Revelation 7:9-10).

Another thrilling development during the past half-century has been the emphasis by evangelistic missions of planting a witness for our Saviour among UNREACHED PEOPLE GROUPS. I am confident that it was the Holy Spirit Himself who moved me to make this objective a priority in my own ministry beginning in 1953. Likewise I have seen evidence of His working similarly in hearts of the leaders of hundreds of other missionary ministries during this period. Christian Aid Mission has made contact with more than two thousand indigenous ministries in Asia, Africa and Latin America which make the evangelization of unreached nations their number one priority. Tens of thousands of native missionaries are taking the gospel to hundreds of tribes and nations which had never heard it before. And numerous missions based in Canada, the USA, Korea and other industrialized countries have been led of the Spirit to concentrate their efforts on planting a witness for our exalted Redeemer in every place where His name is as yet unknown.

A century ago more than twenty countries were totally closed to Christian witness. The largest of these were Afghanistan, Mongolia, Saudi Arabia, Nepal and Tibet. They had never knowingly admitted a Christian missionary, or had any kind of church within their borders. Today, believers gather in all of these countries except one.

Due to the Soviet invasion, and harsh rule by the Taliban sect, hundreds of thousands of Afghans fled into neighboring Pakistan. There they were befriended and assisted by local Christians and many came to know Christ. After the Taliban regime was decimated by U.S. forces, many refugee believers returned and now bear witness for Christ in that closed land.

Mongolia was closed off by Lama Buddhism, imported from

Tibet. But the Communist "religion" took over and broke the stranglehold of the lamas upon the population. Then after the Communist regime collapsed, a vacuum was created and Christian missionaries moved in. Many churches are thriving in Mongolia today.

Nepal, a country of more than sixty different nations, was isolated by the highest mountains in the world. Its borders were tightly guarded by the Hindu king who was worshipped as a god and ruled as absolute dictator. But many Nepalese crossed the border into India to serve as mercenary soldiers. One of them, Prem Pradhan, found Christ as Saviour through a local Christian assembly started by Bakht Singh. After three years as a believer, Prem returned to Nepal and traveled from village to village preaching Christ among his people. Because he dared to baptize new believers publically he was incarcerated within fourteen different dungeons, but conducted Bible classes among his fellow inmates in each one. From those small beginnings around 1965 the number of Christians in Nepal grew to almost one million within forty years.

Perhaps the most autocratic dictator in the world a century ago was the Dalai Lama of Tibet. He was worshipped as a god, and the region was tightly controlled by tens of thousands of Buddhist monks who were in total subservience to the Dalai Lama. Any foreigner who dared to enter their territory with a different religion was killed immediately. The only Christian who ever went in and came out alive was Sadhu Sundar Singh, a former Sikh who became a mighty apostle for Christ in India. He learned the Tibetan language, wore a saffron robe like the monks, and made twelve successful journeys into that forbidden land in the 1920s. He was apparently killed by the Lamas on his thirteenth trip. But then, later, the Chinese Communists invaded and destroyed hundreds of monasteries; the monks were scattered, and the Dalai Lama fled to India. Since then, hundreds of Christians have moved in from China and started assemblies of believers.

When God arose to judgment . . . the wrath of man shall praise thee (Psalm 76:9-10). **If Satan cast out Satan, he is divided against himself; then how shall his kingdom stand** (Matthew

12:26). God has allowed atheistic Communists and other pagan forces to break down the walls of several closed lands, and now He has a witness for Christ within each one. Only Saudi Arabia, homeland of the Antichrist Muhammad, remains as a major country where no native believers gather in the name of our Lord. But many Saudis have accepted Christ while away from home. I have had fellowship in His name with several of them. It is only a matter of time until our Lord has **a people for His name** in that forbidden land also.

All of these developments point toward the consummation, when God's promise to Abraham about **ALL NATIONS** being blessed, and our Lord's promise that He would come again when **ALL NATIONS** have been reached with His gospel, will be fulfilled. **Be ye also patient; stablish your hearts: for the coming of the Lord draweth nigh** (James 5:8).

Sadly, one activity by certain evangelical leaders has, I fear, delayed our Lord's return. It has to do with the many unreached nations which are located within Islamic countries. Great progress was being made toward planting a witness for Christ among them sixty years ago, but the situation has changed drastically as a result of what I believe are misguided actions by many of my brothers and sisters in Christ. And it has brought untold suffering to our fellow believers in many lands that are closed to foreign missionaries. During the years I lived in Asia I met hundreds of former Muslims who had accepted Christ and were witnessing for Him among their own people. Christian Aid Mission has sent financial help to at least a dozen indigenous evangelistic ministries which were led by former Muslims who had given their lives to Christ. I have been personally involved in the baptism of many Muslims who accepted Christ, including several from Afghanistan.

The gospel of Christ is much more powerful than Islam. Muslims are universally concerned with the final judgment when, they believe, God will send them either to the fires of hell or to the bliss of paradise. There are no atheists among Muslims. And their only hope of salvation is based on their earthly works. They have no assurance of having already received eternal life as a free gift from God which is the "blessed assurance" of born again Christians. Our acceptance before God has been provided by the sacrifice of Christ for our sins. So the gospel of salvation by grace is a powerful message to Muslims, plus we have the indwelling presence of the Holy Spirit to make it real in our lives.

When Muslims have seen lives transformed by the saving grace of our risen Saviour, many have expressed admiration. Except for angered family members, and those in extreme countries like Afghanistan and Saudi Arabia, most Muslims showed a remarkable tolerance toward any of their people who gave up Islam to become Christians half a century ago. But beginning around 1967 there was a gradual change in the attitude of Muslims toward Christians in most Islamic countries. It stems from the conflict between Israelis and Palestinians, and the almost universal backing of Israel, and hostility toward the Palestinians, by a large number of evangelical Christians.

During World War I British forces defeated the Ottoman Turks and occupied Palestine. In 1917 British Foreign Secretary James Balfour declared that Palestine should be a "national home" for Jewish people, providing that NOTHING SHALL BE DONE WHICH MAY PREJUDICE THE CIVIL AND RELIGIOUS RIGHTS OF EXISTING NON-JEWISH COMMUNITIES IN PALESTINE.

At that time, this arrangement seemed acceptable to the original residents of Palestine, 40% of whom were nominal Christians and 60% were nominal Muslims. No doubt a majority of both groups were descendants of the ancient Hebrews, many of whom had accepted Christianity between 30 and 630 A.D., and the rest melted into Islam beginning around 630. All were Semitic people, and certainly a majority were descendants of Abraham, Isaac and Jacob. Many present-day Palestinians believe, therefore, that their ancestral homeland of Palestine is theirs by right because God gave it to their father Abraham.

Following the Balfour Declaration of 1917, small numbers of Jewish people began to immigrate peacefully into Palestine. Most were from among the poorer classes, and their motivation was to search for a better life. Wealthy, successful Jews in Europe and

America showed little interest. To Jewish millionaires for whom I worked in Miami Beach in 1940, the idea of emigrating to Palestine made no sense at all. The same was true of my wealthy Jewish classmates at the University of Virginia in 1941-44 and at the University of Chicago in 1946-47.

Contributions from the Rothschild family of European bankers and other Jewish sympathizers enabled some immigrants to buy land, build homes and start businesses in Palestine for a while, but after 15 years of struggling, many were ready to give up. Then in 1933 help came from an unexpected source -- Adolph Hitler.

What happened has been documented by the award-winning Jewish reporter, Edwin Black, in his 1984 book, *The Transfer Agreement.* A later edition, published in 2001, has an afterword by Abraham Foxman, national director of the [Jewish] Anti-Defamation League of Bnai Brith.

Edwin Black tells how when the November 1932 elections proved to be indecisive, President Paul von Hindenburg appointed Hitler as interim chancellor of Germany on January 30, 1933. Successful Jewish merchants and businessmen in Germany were generally supportive of Hitler in the beginning, but not so the Jewish activists in America. Led by Rabbi Stephen Wise, they began massive protests against the new Nazi regime, and called for a boycott against purchase of any product made in Germany. They persuaded members of labor unions to refuse to unload German products from ships arriving at U.S. ports. The intensive campaign was so successful that it could have toppled Hitler in his first year as he and his associates struggled to pull their country out of economic depression.

Hitler retaliated by calling for a boycott against doing business with Jewish merchants and professionals inside Germany. This action caused many of these professionals to be infuriated against the American activists whose prejudiced interference had brought undue hardship upon successful Jews in Germany. The German economy as a whole was made to suffer, but many of the Jews in Germany suffered even more.

Then came the Zionists in Palestine to the rescue of both

parties. They concluded what was called the "Transfer Agreement" with the Third Reich. In summary, Zionists in Palestine would use their influence to persuade Jewish activists in America to call off the boycott in exchange for Hitler sending 60,000 Jews as immigrants from Germany to Palestine, along with the transfer of $100,000,000 to the Zionists there. Adjusted for inflation that would be over two billion dollars today. When Edwin Black published *The Transfer Agreement*, documenting these dramatic events, it was generally received by his Jewish contemporaries as being a painful but, in retrospect, providential chapter in Jewish history.

In any case, this huge infusion of cash and new immigrants saved the fledgling Zionist colony in Palestine from extinction, and the Nazi regime was spared economic collapse in its first year of power.

When the Zionist population in Palestine virtually doubled in so short a time, it brought about a hubbub of excitement among evangelical teachers of Bible prophecy. The chorus echoed around the world, "The Jews are going back to Palestine." Never mind that the ancestors of those "going back" had never lived there in the first place. Or if no hint or suggestion of such an event is mentioned in the New Testament. Old Testament prophecies of "the return" were all fulfilled beginning with Ezra and Nehemiah and reached completion in the era of the Maccabees beginning around 165 B.C. As a result of the victories of the Maccabean brothers, Judaea became an independent country again, larger and more powerful than in the days of Kings David and Solomon. Exiles from all of the 12 tribes returned, the temple was restored, and temple worship was resumed again. During that 160 year period all things were made ready for the coming of the Messiah, our Lord and Saviour. The Encyclopedia Britannica called this era "without a doubt the most stirring chapter in Jewish history." Still today Jewish people commemorate it in December as Hanukkah, the eight day Feast of Dedication.

Following the influx from Germany starting in 1933, a new element known as "militant Zionists" began to appear. Most were not religious at all. Many claimed to be atheistic disciples of Karl Marx. Not content with the peaceful development of a Jewish community in Palestine, the militants wanted to drive out the natives and take over by force. The infamous *Stern Gang* and the *Irgun,* led by such men as Menachem Begin and Yishak Shamir, conducted a reign of terror against Palestinian natives, driving them out of their homes and taking their property. Begin has been quoted as calling himself "the father of terrorism." The Palestinians retaliated in like manner, and there has been no peace there since 1933.

Many of the Jewish people who had emigrated to Palestine before 1933 were the Sephardim, or "real Jews" as they call themselves, mainly from Spain, Portugal and Morocco. Some of them may possibly be biologically related to the ancient Hebrews. The new arrivals from Germany were Yiddish-speaking Ashkenazim. Those who were Communistic disciples of Karl Marx, a fellow Ashkenazi, wanted to do in Palestine what Leon Trotsky had done in Russia. The Sephardic immigrants generally favored living peacefully among the original residents of Palestine, and were not at all pleased with the aggressive conduct of the new arrivals.

The problem was exacerbated by the flood of new Ashkenazim immigrants that poured into Palestine as a result of Nazi persecution during World War II. In the aftermath of the war many displaced Ashkenazim from Europe chose Palestine as a safe haven to relocate. Among them were militant Zionists who began to attack the British occupation forces. In 1946 they bombed the King David Hotel which served as British headquarters. Around that time I saw a news article which said that moderate Sephardic Jews were protesting against belligerent acts of the new immigrants. The article contained a photo of these Jewish demonstrators carrying a huge placard inscribed "Ashke**NAZI**." Peaceful Sephardic Jews were accusing the new immigrants of imitating Hitler. Even today hundreds of thousands of conscientious Jews are outspoken in their denunciation of the way Palestinians have been treated by the Zionists for 70 years. Also, many Israeli soldiers have refused to carry out orders to shoot unarmed Palestinians, and some Israeli Air Force pilots have refused to bomb and strafe women and children in the refugee camps. However, the government has justified these actions as necessary retaliation for Palestinian attacks against Israelis.

Certain evangelical Christians tend to be very outspoken in their praise and support of everything the Zionists have done. Any conscientious Christian who dares to speak out in confirmation of objections raised by Jewish opposition parties in Israel or elsewhere may be savagely attacked and denounced by evangelical Zionists.

On December 9, 2001, over two hundred Jewish citizens of South Africa jointly published a "Declaration of Conscience" titled *NOT IN MY NAME* in which they said that the establishment of segregated "settlements" and the treatment of Palestinians by Zionists in the territories occupied since 1967 was equivalent to earlier apartheid policies of white minority rulers in South Africa. But I never heard or read one word of praise or objection to their opinions being expressed by an evangelical Christian. Apparently, it was considered okay for Jewish people to speak out against the misdeeds of their fellow Jews. Yet when President Jimmy Carter published *PALESTINE PEACE NOT APARTHEID* in 2006, he was bitterly denounced by many of his fellow evangelicals.

When nominal Christians were driven out of their ancestral homes in Palestine, they tended to suffer in silence, even sometimes turning the other cheek. But not so the Muslims. They followed the Old Testament precept of **an eye for an eye and a tooth for a tooth**. Retaliation in kind became the order of the day. And each time the Muslims retaliated, the militant Zionists responded in turn, and so the cycle was repeated continually. The result has been 70 years of war and bloodshed. I remember reading an article in *Collier's* magazine around 1938 entitled *Hell in the Holy Land*. The chaos has continued since that date.

Evangelicals, fundamentalists and Pentecostals in America have almost universally sided with the Zionists and opposed the Palestinians in this conflict. Most do so because they believe that when the state of Israel was set up in 1948 it was the fulfillment of some prophecies they had read in the Old Testament. I am deeply concerned as to how these beliefs have impacted the cause of Christ in Islamic countries.

Since Muslims tend to identify every country with its major

religion, they speak of the USA as being a Christian country. So when America began to give billions of dollars to finance Israeli economic development, it led to the conclusion that Christians were supporters of Zionism. And as billions of dollars worth of U.S. equipment built up Israel to become a military superpower, it was deemed as a potential act of war by Christians against Islamic countries.

Muslims say that it was superior arms provided by U.S. "Christians" which enabled the Israeli juggernaut to destroy opposing forces in less than a week in the 1967 war. Territories conquered and taken away from Egypt, Jordan and Syria during that war are regarded as proof that the Zionists are bent on conquering and controlling the entire Middle East.

So-called "settlements" in Palestine are places where Israelis have gone into conquered territories and erected new houses and apartments to be occupied by Jews only. Muslims often quote the Jewish leaders in South Africa who have said this practice is equivalent to the apartheid system which was formerly practiced there. Muslims also say that the more than 300,000 Zionists living in the settlements, with their checkpoints, military guards, private highways, roadblocks, monopolized utilities, public services and segregated water supply, are really advanced outposts strategically placed for eventually taking over the remainder of Palestine not yet officially incorporated into the state of Israel. Many American evangelicals have enthusiastically endorsed these settlement projects, and assisted them financially. And when Ariel Sharon dismantled the settlements which he had initially helped to establish in Gaza, Muslims noticed that many outstanding evangelicals were among those who most vehemently opposed the pull-out. My long-time friend Pat Robertson even went so far as to say that the debilitating stroke which Sharon suffered was God's judgment upon him for "giving up the land."

When Palestinians had no arms capable of resisting Israeli tanks, they began to sacrifice their lives as suicide bombers in retaliation for injuries inflicted upon their countrymen. While we regard these zealots as terrorists, Muslims praise them as patriotic, unselfish martyrs.

In many Islamic countries, the Arabs who sacrificed their lives to retaliate against America on 9-11-01 are also regarded as patriotic heroes and martyrs. They point out that the American lives lost were far less than what the Palestinians have suffered from American arms supplied to the Israelis during the past 60 years.

Many Muslims accuse American evangelicals of persuading President Bush to launch the unprovoked war on Iraq. Bible prophecy teachers have quoted Genesis 15:18 to insist that God gave Abraham's descendants all the land **from the river of Egypt to the great river Euphrates**. The problem is that a majority of the Israelis are the Ashkenazim, or Yiddish people, who originally came from the region of Khazaria in southern Russia. Semitic Palestinians are more likely to be descendants of Abraham, Isaac and Jacob than are Japhethite Jewish immigrants. Palestinian Christians say there is no sensible way that God's promise to Abraham 4000 years ago could be construed to apply to the Yiddish people whose ancestors are said to have been the original residents of Khazaria.

Muslims have seen political statements published in Christian magazines (and reproduced on websites to be viewed by millions) that declare "Israel's sovereignty over the Holy Land, including Judea and Samaria," meaning all of what is now called the "West Bank," or Palestine. Full page ads signed by prominent evangelicals such as Jerry Falwell, Kay Arthur, John Hagee, Jack Hayford and Thomas Trask pledged to help bring this about, even though these occupied territories, conquered in 1967, are still outside the official borders of the state of Israel. Do they not realize that the inflammatory rhetoric they are using is looked upon as a declaration of war, not only by four million Muslims living in greater Palestine, but also by Muslim sympathizers in other countries all over the world? When evangelical Zionists voice these threats against the residents of Palestine, they are perceived to be enemies of Islam.

Zionist conquests in Palestine are generally considered to have been the catalyst that triggered Islamic copycat actions in other countries. "If Christians help Zionists to drive out the inhabitants of Palestine and make it a Jewish state," the Muslims ask, "then why should we not drive out the Christians from other places and make them Islamic states?" As a result of this idea spreading in Asia and Africa, we have seen assaults on Christians by Muslims in many countries. After living together peacefully for a century or more, Christians in the Philippines and Indonesia have been attacked by Muslims who want to drive them out of certain islands and make those territories purely Islamic. Since 1967 numerous unprecedented attacks upon Christians by Muslims have also taken place in Pakistan, Nigeria and many other countries of Asia and Africa. These moves are believed to be the result of endorsement of and support for political Zionism by evangelical Christians.

When I first came to Christ 68 years ago, I fully expected His return within my lifetime. The reason I became a missionary is because He said, regarding His return, **The gospel must first be published among all nations** (Mark 13:10). But there are still more than 1000 "nations" where as yet our Lord has no people for His name. And many of them are located within Islamic countries.

Has our pro-Zionist involvement as evangelicals with the Israeli/Palestinian conflict, and its extension into Iraq, delayed our Lord's return? Has our preoccupation with Zionistic interpretations of Biblical prophecy unwittingly caused us to hinder the very thing we long to see, which is the glorious return of our exalted Saviour to **wipe away all tears** from the eyes of those who suffer for His sake? We must watch and pray that the situation may soon be changed to an extent that the Islamic backlash triggered by evangelical support for political Zionism may subside. Then, by God's grace, His people may get on with the unfinished task of preaching the gospel and planting new churches among unreached peoples within Islamic countries, and so hasten the day of our Lord's return.

When He comes again the King of all kings will reap the final harvest mentioned in Revelation 14:19. He will **gather the vine of the earth, and cast it into the great winepress of the wrath of God**. This climactic event is described in the following chapter.

Chapter 15

The Glorious Appearing

Looking for that blessed hope, and the glorious appearing of our Great God and Saviour, Jesus Christ (Titus 2:13)

During my early years as a born again Christian, one of the big mistakes I made was to teach that the second coming of our Saviour would be in two stages. But I didn't get it from the Scriptures; I was repeating what I had heard from my teachers, and read in books on prophecy. Further study of the New Testament is what showed me my mistake and guided me into an understanding of the truth, which I happily repeat here.

The traditional teaching which I erroneously followed was that the first stage of our Lord's return would be His coming FOR HIS SAINTS, when believers who are alive on earth at that time would suddenly and secretly be "caught up" into the heavens to be with the Lord. This is what's called "the rapture," after which, I thought, the "tribulation period" would take place. Seven years later, the teaching goes, our Lord would come back WITH HIS SAINTS to fight the "battle of Armageddon."

A primary Scripture reference regarding "the rapture" is I Thessalonians 4:16-17: **The Lord Himself shall descend from heaven with a shout, with the voice of the archangel, and with the trump of God: and the dead in Christ shall rise first; then we which are alive and remain shall be caught up together with them in the clouds, to meet the Lord in the air: and so shall**

we ever be with the Lord. It was presumed that only born again believers would hear the **shout, the voice of the archangel and the trump of God.**

Several verses were used to justify the concept of a second stage of our Lord's return WITH HIS SAINTS. **The Lord my God shall come, and all the saints with thee** (Zechariah 14:5). **Behold the Lord cometh with ten thousand of His saints** (Jude 14). **At the coming of our Lord Jesus Christ with all His saints** (I Thessalonians 3:13).

But the teachers who contrived this dichotomy overlooked an important statement. At His coming FOR HIS SAINTS our Lord will **BRING WITH HIM** those whose bodies shall rise from the dust of the earth and the depths of the seas. Their eternal spirits have already been with Him since the death of their bodies. **While we are at home in the body, we are absent from the Lord . . . we are willing rather to be absent from the body, and to be present with the Lord** (II Corinthians 5:6, 8). **To me to live is Christ, and to die is gain . . . I am in a strait betwixt two, having a desire to depart, and to be with Christ; which is far better** (Philippians 1:21, 23). **Concerning them which are asleep, that ye sorrow not, even as others which have no hope. For if we believe that Jesus died and rose again, even so them also which sleep in Jesus WILL GOD BRING WITH HIM** (I Thessalonians 4:13-14).

When will He BRING THEM WITH HIM? When He comes again FOR HIS SAINTS who are still alive on earth. As He comes, He will BRING WITH HIM the eternal spirits of **the dead in Christ**, and each one will then **be clothed upon with [His new] house . . . that mortality might be swallowed up of life** (II Corinthians 5:2, 4). Our bodies are called our houses in that chapter: the **earthy house** must be **dissolved** so that it can be replaced by one of heavenly origin when our spirits are **clothed upon** with our new, eternal bodies.

In a moment, in the twinkling of an eye, at the last trump: for the trumpet shall sound, and the dead shall be raised incorruptible, and we shall be changed (I Corinthians 15:52). **We**

look for our Saviour, the Lord Jesus Christ, who shall change our vile body, that it may be fashioned like unto His glorious body (Philippians 3:20-21). **When He shall appear, we shall be like Him** (I John 3:2). All of us together, then, will be **caught up in the clouds, to meet the Lord in the air** (I Thessalonians 4:17).

The erroneous teaching which I once followed says that after we are **caught up to MEET the Lord in the air** He will turn around and go back into the heavens for seven years. But the Scripture says that we will be **CAUGHT UP TO MEET HIM AS HE COMES**. If I go to the airport to MEET a friend, he doesn't turn around, take me with him, get back on the plane and fly away. Nowhere does the Scripture indicate that there are two stages to the second coming of our Saviour.

The first premonition that the appearance of our Lord is about to take place will be disturbances in the heavens. **The powers of the heavens shall be shaken** (Matthew 24:29, Luke 21:29). **There shall be signs in the sun, and in the moon, and in the stars; and upon the earth distress of nations, with perplexity; the sea and the waves roaring; men's hearts failing them for fear, and looking after those things which are coming on the earth** (Luke 21:25-26). Movies and television programs have been anticipating these events in recent years with productions that show the earth being invaded by extraterrestrial forces. Undoubtedly, when our Lord begins to shake the heavens, top scientists of the world will begin to speculate that some super-intelligent beings from another planet have a means by which they can manipulate gravitational forces. So a cry of alarm will spread quickly throughout the earth. **And then shall appear the sign of the Son of Man in the sky: and then all the tribes of the earth shall wail** (Matthew 24:30). The Greek word usually translated "sign" is *semeion*, which means "something supernatural" or "out of the ordinary." What people see in the sky in that day will be an event never seen before. Our Lord compared it to a flash of lightening so great that **coming out of the east it would shine even unto the west** (Matthew 24:27). It will be seen completely around the entire world.

Following those lightening flashes in outer space that are seen around the globe, there will be a great blast of sound, as of a trumpet, that will also reverberate throughout the heavens. At that signal **He will send His angels and they will gather together His elect from the four winds** (Matthew 24:31). That great ingathering is what we call the "rapture" of born again believers, with the resurrected bodies of those whose spirits our Lord will bring with Him as He comes.

The **trump of God** was first heard in the time of Moses at Mount Sinai: **there were thunders and lightnings, and a thick cloud upon the mount, and the voice of the trumpet exceeding loud, so that all of the people in the camp trembled . . . and the whole mount quaked greatly. And when the voice of the trumpet sounded long, and waxed louder and louder, Moses spake, and God answered him by a voice** (Exodus 19:16, 19). When our Lord returns it will be **at the last trump: for the trumpet shall sound, and the dead** [in Christ] **shall be raised incorruptible, and we** [which are still alive on earth] **shall be changed. For this corruptible must put on incorruption, and this mortal must put on immortality** (I Corinthians 15:52-53). This verse most surely speaks of the time of the rapture, when our Lord comes both WITH (the spirits of) HIS SAINTS whose bodies have died, and also FOR HIS SAINTS who are still alive on earth. And if it is **AT THE LAST TRUMP**, there is no way that there can be another stage to His return with yet another blast from **the trump of God**.

I have often wondered as to whether every person on earth will, in addition to hearing the great blast of the trumpet, also hear Him **SHOUT, and the VOICE OF THE ARCHANGEL** when these sounds also reverberate throughout the heavens. One thing I'm sure of, and that is that it won't be done in secret, as I ignorantly taught when I followed the "secret rapture" theory.

After we are caught up to meet the Lord somewhere above the planet, there will be a brief lull in the doomsday events as far as the people "left behind" on earth are concerned. That's because the Mighty Conqueror, before He proceeds further to take over our planet, is going to celebrate His wedding. How long it will take we are not told, but it will probably be long enough for leaders of major countries to call an emergency conclave of all heads of state. Earthly differences will be laid aside, as every country will join forces within the framework of the United Nations to defend the planet. I saw a film on TV once called *Independence Day* which portrayed a similar scenario. No doubt, news media all over the earth will say that "aliens are invading" when they report how millions of people have been "abducted" and suddenly transported into the skies.

Let us be glad and rejoice, and give honor to Him: for the marriage of the Lamb is come, and His wife hath made herself ready . . . Blessed are they which are called to the marriage supper of the Lamb (Revelation 19:7, 9). That wedding celebration will be a glorious event, as every believer since Adam and Eve and Abel and Enoch will celebrate with the Lamb of God who **loved us and washed us from our sins in His own blood, and made us kings and priests unto His God and Father, to whom be glory and dominion forever and ever** (Revelation 1:5-6). Since we will all be in our resurrected bodies, which will be like our Lord's body after He arose, no doubt there will be some kind of a great banquet hall in which we are gathered orbiting the earth. There being no gravity in space, it could be a sphere, with all of us weightless inside, yet all standing on the inside floor of the sphere. That way, millions of us would all be able to see everyone else. And the weightless Bridegroom could be in the very center of the sphere, clearly visible to every person. Anyway, let's wait and see. I look forward joyfully to being part of the bride on that glorious wedding day.

One big mistake that many teachers have made is to say that **the Bride, the Lamb's wife**, is a city. They have thus failed to comprehend that the Apocalypse is a book of symbols, metaphors and word pictures. The angel said, **Come hither, I will show thee the bride, the Lamb's wife. And I John saw the holy city, new Jerusalem, coming down from God out of Heaven, prepared as a bride adorned for her husband** (Revelation 21:9, 2). That "city" is made up of living stones. It is not where we are going to live, but rather it is we ourselves, who are going to live forever.

Many such metaphors and symbols are used in the New Testament. Our Lord calls us the **sheep** of His pasture; the **branches** of His vine, the **members** and **parts** of His body, the **living stones** of His building. The **Lamb's wife, the new Jerusalem** is made up of resurrected saints, not of inanimate materials such as gold or pearls. **A book of remembrance was written before Him for them that feared the Lord . . . and they shall be mine, saith the Lord, in that day when I MAKE UP MY JEWELS** (Malachi 3:16-17). The Apostle Paul spoke of true believers as being **gold, silver** and **precious stones**, in contrast to **wood, hay, and stubble** (I Corinthians 3:12) which is representative of carnal church members who defile His body.

The **twelve apostles of the Lamb** (Revelation 21:14) are pictured as being twelve **precious stones** (Revelation 21:19), **jasper, sapphire, chalcedony, emerald, etc.** And Old Testament saints from **the twelve tribes of Israel** are pictured as pearls, but we know from Scripture that this number includes only those who were **circumcised in heart.** If not, as Moses warned, **that soul shall be cut off from Israel** (Exodus 12:15, 19). **And the Lord said unto Moses, Whosoever hath sinned against me, him will I blot out of my book** (Exodus 32:33). **That soul shall be cut off from his people** (Leviticus 7:20, 21, 25, 27). **The same soul will I destroy from among his people** (Leviticus 23:30). **The soul that sinneth, it shall die** (Ezekiel 18:4).

Gleaming brightly among the Old Testament pearls will be the 144,000 Hebrews whom God elected between 30 and 70 A.D. to give His gospel to other nations. As I mentioned earlier, these were **the first fruits unto God and to the Lamb** (Revelation 14:4) who for their witness paid a terrible price of persecution and suffering at the hands of their fellow Judaeans at that time. Our Lord warned of what the remnant [144,000] of true believers would have to suffer. **They shall put you out of the synagogues, yea, the time cometh when whosoever killeth you will think that he doeth God service** (John 16:2). **They will scourge you in their synagogues** (Matthew

10:17). **In the synagogues ye shall be beaten** (Mark 13:9). **They shall lay hands on you, and persecute you, delivering you up to the synagogues** (Luke 21:12). These martyrs will be shining pearls in the New Jerusalem.

At the **marriage supper of the Lamb**, however, there will be no distinction between those He redeemed under the Old Covenant and we who came into His family under the New Covenant. We will all be **one body in Christ**. The focus will not be on us, but rather on our Redeemer, who **first loved us** and died for us **while we were yet sinners**. Those of us who are now awaiting that glorious celebration should remember His concern that **the bride hath made herself ready**, and then **they shall see His face**. At **the appearing of our Lord Jesus Christ, He shall show who is that Blessed and only Potentate, King of Kings and Lord of Lords, Who only hath immortality, dwelling in the light . . . to whom be honor and power everlasting. Amen.** (I Timothy 6:15-16).

When the marriage supper is ended, the King of all Kings will mount a **white horse** and ride off to battle. But remember, the Apocalypse is filled with word pictures and symbols. In Bible times the cavalry won battles on horseback. Today they ride tanks and armored vehicles and jet airplanes. So what will **the Lord from heaven** be riding when He comes to reign as **king over all the earth**? First, let's read some statements about His coming.

This same Jesus, which is taken up from you into heaven, shall so come in like manner, as ye have seen Him go into heaven (Acts 1:11). **The Lord Jesus shall be revealed from heaven with His mighty angels, in flaming fire taking vengeance on them that know not God and obey not the gospel . . . when He shall come to be glorified in His saints, and to be admired in all them that believe** (II Thessalonians 1:7-10). **And I saw heaven opened, and behold a white horse; and He that sat upon it was called Faithful and True, and in righteousness He doth judge and make war . . . and the armies which were in heaven followed Him on white horses . . . and He treadeth the winepress of the fierceness and wrath of Almighty God** (Revelation 19:11-15).

When our Lord was assaulted by the mob which had been sent by the temple priests for His abduction, He told His disciples, **Thinkest thou that I cannot now pray to my Father, and He shall presently give me more than twelve legions of angels?** (Matthew 26:53). When He comes again He will have them, and probably many more, **on white horses**. But what are those horses? Horses that we ride on earth would explode in the vacuum of outer space, and the bits and pieces would freeze instantly as they were scattered in all directions. So obviously the term **horse** is a symbol or picture of something else. Could it be similar to whatever it was that took Elijah bodily into the heavens? **As they went on behold there appeared a chariot of fire, and horses of fire . . . and Elijah went up by a whirlwind into the heavens** (II Kings 2:11). In today's terminology, we would call that event a "blast off." Obviously, Elijah was transported into another dimension in a spaceship. So why should we not expect that when this planet is invaded by forces from above, they will be in spaceships?

And I saw the beast, and the kings of the earth, and their armies, gathered together to make war against Him that sat on the horse [or, rode in the spaceship] **and against His army** [also on white horses, or in spaceships] (Revelation 19:19). Obviously, the term **beast** is used here in reference to the United Nations, as it was used earlier to connote the Roman Empire. This battle was mentioned previously in Revelation 16:14-16: **Behold I come as a thief. Blessed is he that watcheth . . . And He gathered them together in a place called in the Hebrew tongue Armageddon . . . the kings of the whole world, to the battle of that great day of God Almighty.** No battle is further mentioned in the context of those verses, so obviously it refers to what was to be described later. *Mount Megiddo* was to the Hebrews what *Waterloo* (the place of Napoleon's final defeat) is to the French, or *Gettysburg* was to the Confederate states after the Civil War. Numerous decisive battles had been fought at Mount Megiddo in Old Testament times. But the use of the term should in no sense be taken to mean that the final battle of history will be fought in Palestine. On the contrary, it will be fought in the skies with rockets and missiles and atomic bombs.

Movies and television programs have been preparing the human race for what's coming, with productions such as *Star Trek, Star Wars, Independence Day* and many others. So when the invasion from outer space actually comes, it will not be a complete surprise. With so much imagery having already been seen on the subject, people all over the earth will realize that it has finally become a reality.

Foolishly, most world leaders will immediately feel threatened, and will conspire to SAVE THE PLANET at any cost. If our King were received peacefully, **and every knee should bow** to acknowledge His Lordship, war would not be necessary. Instead, world forces allied within the United Nations will start firing missiles armed with atomic bombs as the space ships from heaven come within range. All will be harmless to the invading forces of Him whose **sharp sword** shall **smite the nations** as He **treadeth the winepress of the fierceness and wrath of Almighty God** (Revelation 19:15).

Remember, "grapes in the winepress" is the meaning of the Greek word *thlipsis*, which is usually translated "tribulation" in the New Testament. This is the tribulation which our Lord will bring upon the earth at His second coming, as mentioned in Matthew 24:29 and II Thessalonians 1:6. The great number of military forces which will perish during the invasion are symbolically depicted as food for vultures in both Matthew 24:28 and Revelation 19:17-18. This metaphorical imagery is borrowed from the Old Testament (Ezekiel 39:17-20) where it is used to denote the dead bodies of 185,000 Assyrians slain by an angel of God when the armies of Senacherib attempted to take Jerusalem during the reign of King Hezekiah. It signifies that the number of the dead is so great that there would be no way for their bodies to receive traditional burial.

A great deal of mystery remains as to events that will take place after our Lord has conquered the planet. We do know that **every knee shall bow and every tongue shall confess, "Lord Jesus"** (Philippians 2:11). His terms with the surviving population will be unconditional surrender, **and He shall rule them with a rod of iron** (Revelation 19:15). There are verses which suggest that our Lord will bring His **bride** (resurrected and transfigured believers) back to the earth, **and they lived and reigned with Christ a thousand years. But the rest of the dead lived not again until the thousand years were finished. This is the first resurrection. Blessed and holy is he that hath part in the first resurrection: on such the second death hath no power, but they shall be priests of God and of Christ, and shall reign with Him a thousand years** (Revelation 20:6). This period is generally called "the millennium," but there is mention elsewhere (Matthew 24:29, Mark 13:24) that **the sun shall be darkened**, which means that our planet may be taken out of its present orbit in the solar system. If so, the millennium period would not be in solar years like those we have now.

Another mistake which Scofield and numerous other teachers have made is a concept they call JUDGMENT OF THE NATIONS. In Old Testament times God dealt with nations collectively, but there is no mention of His dealing with an entire nation at once after the Messiah came, other than his terminal judgment upon the apostate Israelites during **the days of vengeance** 66-70 A.D. Rather, God deals with each individual according to that person's faith and works. So shall it be when Christ comes again. **When the Son of Man shall come in His glory, and all the holy angels with Him, then shall He sit upon the throne of His glory: and before Him shall be gathered all nations: and He shall separate them one from another, as a shepherd divideth his sheep from the goats** (Matthew 25:31-32). Sheep and goats graze together, and at the end of the day must be divided one by one. So shall our Lord divide human beings individually when He comes again. To the sheep He will say: **Come, ye blessed of my Father, inherit the kingdom prepared for you from the foundation of the world;** but to the goats: **Depart from me, ye cursed, into everlasting fire** (Matthew 25:34, 41).

The basis of the division may appear to some as being salvation by works, but rather it is evidence that FAITH PRODUCES WORKS, because once we are justified by faith in the finished work of Christ,

God will work within us: **For by grace are ye saved through faith; and that not of yourselves; it is the gift of God: not of works, lest any man should boast. For we are His workmanship, created in Christ Jesus unto good works** (Ephesians 2:8-10). And one of the first works God produces within us is a loving concern for our brothers in Christ: **We know we have passed from death unto life because we love the brethren** [in Christ]. **He that loveth not his brother** [in Christ] **abideth in death** (I John 3:14). So when our Lord divides the human race, He will identify His own by saying, **I was hungry, and you gave me food; I was thirsty, and you gave me drink; I was a stranger, and you took me in; naked, and you clothed me; I was sick, and you visited me: I was in prison, and you came unto me . . . inasmuch as you have done it unto the least of these my brethren, you have done it unto me** (Matthew 25:35-36,40).

Some Bible teachers have erred in saying that our Lord used the term "brethren" to mean the Israelites collectively, even though He called most of them a **generation of vipers**. The only ones He ever called His "brethren" were the true believers. **Who are my brethren? Whosoever shall do the will of God, the same is my brother** (Mark 3:33, 35). **Go tell my brethren to go into Galilee, and there shall they see me** (Matthew 28:10). After He rose from the dead, our Lord said to Mary Magdalene, **Go to my brethren**, by which He meant His disciples. In the Book of Acts the term **brethren** is used more than forty times to mean those who were believers in Christ.

When our Lord said that upon His return **Before Him shall be gathered all nations**, He knew it would be 2000 years later and that by then His gospel would have been **preached in all the world for a witness unto all nations**. So people from every nation will be called upon to give an account of how they treated His **ambassadors who in Christ's stead beseech them to be reconciled to God** (II Corinthians 5:20).

It should be obvious to us that this judgment will not include all the people on the earth, but only some of those who are still alive after the MIGHTY CONQUEROR has taken over the planet. The ones who will face this tribunal will be persons who have been personally involved with **Christ's ambassadors** in every nation. No doubt theirs will be public trials to take place at the same time our Lord publicly rewards His resurrected and transformed servants before them. **Behold I come quickly; and my reward is with me, to give to every man according as his works shall be** (Revelation 22:12). **We must all appear before the judgment seat of Christ; that every one may receive the things done in his body; according to that he hath done, whether it be good or bad** (II Corinthians 5:10). Before people of all the nations, **Christ's ambassadors** will be publicly rewarded, and those who have mistreated them will be cast into the outer darkness.

But, as I said, this judgment will not include all people who are still alive after the **King of all kings** takes control over all the earth. It will include only those who were in some way personally involved with **His brethren.** Those who have not been involved with **His brethren, servants** and **ambassadors** will be left alive to experience the **thousand years** when these resurrected believers will **reign with Christ on the earth** (Revelation 20:4-6).

Whatever lies beyond the glorious return of our Lord is shrouded in mystery. To fathom those mysteries is beyond our understanding. My major concern at this present time is to hasten our Lord's return by completing the unfinished task of **taking out a people for His name** from among **every kindred, tongue, tribe and nation.** It's the completion of the reaping of the first harvest mentioned in Revelation 14:14-15. When **His body, His bride** has been completed (**made herself ready**), He will **come again and receive us unto Himself,** and **wipe away all tears from the eyes of those who suffer for His sake.**

Then will occur the second reaping (Revelation 14:17-20) as He comes **in flaming fire taking vengeance on those that know not God and obey not the gospel** (II Thessalonians 1:7-8). **Thrust in thy sharp sickle, and gather the clusters of the vine of the earth, for her grapes are fully ripe. And the angel thrust in his** sickle and gathered the vine of the earth, and cast it into the great winepress of the wrath of God (Revelation 14:18-19). The expression, "grapes in the winepress," is equivalent to the word **tribulation**. As I said above, when our Lord comes again He will bring **tribulation** (Matthew 24:29) on those who have rebelled against Him.

I strongly disagree with those who teach that the **Great God our Saviour** will restore the Old Testament order when He comes again. Some even say there will be a reconstruction of the original temple in Jerusalem, with the resumption of animal sacrifices. Such teachers have apparently never read Paul's **Epistle to the Hebrews** (and, yes, I do believe Paul wrote it). To even suggest such a thing is an insult to the **Lamb of God** whose sacrifice for our sins **once for all** forever ended God's recognition of an earthly temple with its sinful priests and the offering of the blood of animals **which can never take away sins** (Hebrews 10:11).

Clifton L. Fowler, my first teacher, said that our Lord offered to set up an earthly kingdom for the Israelites at His first coming; but that since they said **We will not have this man to reign over us** (Luke 19:14) the kingdom was postponed and the church age inserted instead. However, Fowler continued, after the church age is finished the Messiah would come back and then set up the kingdom of Israel. Lewis Sperry Chafer said the same in his 1915 book, *The Kingdom in History and Prophecy*. But I cannot find any hint or suggestion of such a concept anywhere in the New Testament. Our Lord came and began His kingdom on the day of Pentecost, not for unsaved Israelites, but for born again believers from **all nations**, including Hebrews who believed in Him. As Daniel had foretold, the kingdoms of Babylon, Persia, Greece and Rome would be **broken to pieces, and become like the chaff of the summer threshingfloors; and the wind carried them away, that no place was found for them** [after which] **shall the God of heaven set up a kingdom** [which] **shall stand forever** [and] **never be destroyed** (Daniel 2:44). Earthly empires of Bible times have long since faded away, but the **kingdom of Christ** has spread to thousands of nations, includes millions of believers, and is stronger today that ever before. Its influence over the lives of men is many times greater than those ancient empires ever were.

When the Messiah came He never mentioned or suggested setting up a political kingdom of Israel. The first proclamation of His forerunner, John the Baptizer, was **Repent, for the kingdom of the heavens is at hand** (Matthew 3:2). Then **Jesus came into Galilee, preaching the gospel of the kingdom of God, saying, The time is fulfilled, the kingdom of God is at hand: repent ye, and believe the gospel** (Mark 1:14-15). **The law and the prophets were until John: since that time the kingdom of God is preached** (Luke 16:16). Those who have taught that the "kingdom" was POSTPONED have failed to understand what it really is. Their minds were locked into the Old Testament, from which they could not turn loose.

The **kingdom of God** includes a remnant from **all nations**, of which the Israelites were one nation among six thousand. And each Israelite had to enter the **kingdom of God** in exactly the same way as people from other nations: each individual **must be born again** (John 3:3). There is no mention, hint or suggestion in the New Testament that when our Lord returns the Jewish people will be given some sort of preferential treatment above people from other nations. So we can be sure that when He comes in power and great glory He will have no special interest whatsoever in Jerusalem or any other part of Palestine. **The God of the whole earth shall He be called** (Isaiah 54:5).

The New Testament does not give any details regarding the **thousand years** during which true believers will reign with Christ on the earth. Hundreds of books have been written on the subject that draw inferences from Old Testament symbols and metaphors, but they all refer to Old Testament times. The one thing we do know is that in the Apocalypse John says that an angel **laid hold on the dragon, that old snake, which is the Devil, and Satan, and bound him a thousand years . . . that he should deceive the nations no more, till the thousand years should be fulfilled: and after that he**

must be loosed a little season (Revelation 20:1-3). **And I saw the souls of them that were beheaded for the witness of Jesus, and for the word of God . . . and they lived and reigned with Christ a thousand years** (Revelation 20:4). This is the period which we Christians call **THE MILLENNIUM**. The only specific information we are given about it can be picked up from references to **THE NEW JERUSALEM**, also called **the camp of the saints, and the beloved city** (Revelation 20:9). That city is not made of bricks and mortar or gold and pearls: it is a figurative term for **that great multitude which no man can number of all nations and kindreds and people and tongues . . . who have washed their robes and made them white in the blood of the Lamb** (Revelation 7:9, 14). In our resurrected bodies we shall reign with the **King of all kings** as He causes God's **will to be done on earth as it is in heaven**.

One other thing about which we can be sure is that there will be no millennium of peace and tranquility on this earth until our Lord Jesus comes to impose it. Rather, **evil men and seducers shall wax worse and worse, deceiving and being deceived** (II Timothy 3:13) because Satan, **the god of this world, has blinded the minds of them that believe not** (II Corinthians 4:4). A century ago some overly optimistic simpletons entertained the silly idea that people were evolving toward better things and that as more and more became Christians humanity would enjoy a millennium of peace and tranquility, after which Christ would come again to congratulate us for our accomplishments. This was called "post-millennial" teaching. Two world wars, hundreds of smaller wars, and an increase in crime, violence and immorality throughout the world have shattered this unrealistic way of thinking for all but a few misguided souls who live in sheltered environments and are out of touch with the real world.

Those of us who honestly face the reality of this present evil world know full well that there will be no crime-free, war-free period of peace on this planet until Christ comes to reign in power. That's why we say that His coming must necessarily be PREMILLENNIAL.

Chapter 16

Does the State of Israel have any Prophetic Significance?

None whatsoever.
If it did, there would be some mention of it in the New Testament. But there is no hint or suggestion anywhere in the New Testament regarding a restoration of the Old Covenant, resumed recognition of natural generation, or of an earthly political kingdom approved by God prior to the personal return of the **King of all kings**.

When He said to Nicodemus, **That which is born of the flesh is flesh** (John 3:6), He meant what He said. Only those who are **born again** and **made alive** by the Holy Spirit have any inheritance, share or participation in the plans of God. All others, whether Baptist, Methodist, Muslim or Jewish are **condemned already** (John 3:18) and **shall not see life but the wrath of God abides on them** (John 3:36).

It is true, as I have explained already, that our Lord did call out **an elect remnant (144,000)** of His generation of Israelites (Romans 11:5) to give the gospel to other nations. But nowhere did He say that anyone else would be included in the family of God by natural generation. Each individual must repent and believe for himself, because all are born in sin, dead to God (Romans 5:12), and must be **made alive** by His Spirit (Ephesians 2:1-9) in order to be included in God's New Covenant, as foretold by Old Testament prophets (Jeremiah 31:31-34). And the Old Covenant was **broken off and discontinued** (Hebrews 8:7-13).

The Apostle Paul wrote, **They are not ALL ISRAEL which are of Israel, neither because they are the seed of Abraham are they all children . . . they which are the children of the flesh, these are not the children of God . . . though the number of the children of Israel be as the sand of the sea** [only] **a remnant shall be saved . . . even so then at this present time there is a remnant according to the election of grace** (Romans 9:6-8, 27, 11:5). That remnant, 144,000 of that generation, constituted **ALL ISRAEL** in the sight of God. That's why Paul continued, **Israel hath not obtained that which he seeketh for; but the election** [144,000] **hath obtained it, and the rest were blinded . . . so then ALL ISRAEL shall be saved** (Romans 11:7, 26).

I say then, Hath God cast away His people? God forbid. For I also am an Israelite, of the seed of Abraham, of the tribe of Benjamin. God hath not cast away His people whom He foreknew (Romans 11:1-2). Here the Apostle explains what had happened. God foreknew that He would call out for salvation a **remnant of that generation** of the Israelites, and **whom He did foreknow, He also did predestinate to be conformed to the image of His Son, that He might be the firstborn among many brethren** (Romans 8:29). Our Lord spoke of the Hebrews who were saved as being His **BRETHREN.** Concerning other Israelites, the Apostle says in Romans Chapter Eleven: **The rest were blinded . . . God hath given them . . . eyes that they should not see and ears that they should not hear . . . let their eyes be darkened that they may not see . . . some of the branches were broken off . . . the olive tree . . . because of unbelief they were broken off . . . God spared not the natural branches . . . Behold therefore the goodness and severity of God: on them which fell, severity; but toward thee, goodness, if thou continue in His goodness; otherwise thou also shalt be cut off. And they also, if they abide not still in unbelief, shall be grafted in: for God is able to graft them in again . . . as concerning the gospel, they are enemies for your sakes . . . for God hath concluded them all in unbelief, that He might have mercy upon all** [who believe].

What we can conclude from this great chapter, and many other portions of the New Testament, is that the Israelites, other than the **elect remnant (144,000** OF THAT GENERATION), were **broken off the olive tree** of **Abraham's seed** and those grafted in were the ones who had been reconciled to God through faith in the sacrificial death of Christ for their sins. **THERE IS NO DIFFERENCE, FOR ALL HAVE SINNED** (Romans 3:22-23). A person's ethnic origin had no further significance in the sight of God. **Except a man be born again he cannot see the kingdom of God** (John 3:3). A person of Hebrew ancestry had no priority over Greeks or Romans. All were lost sinners, and **whosoever believed** could be saved and included in God's family; all others were left out on an equal basis.

Failure to acknowledge this fact is a denial of the New Covenant. Those who say that "the Jewish people" hold some special place in the sight of God do so in denial of His revelation in the New Testament. **There is no difference between the Judaean and the Greek: for the same Lord over all is rich unto all that call upon Him** (Romans 10:12). That's why there is no mention or prophecy regarding "Israel" collectively in the New Testament beyond the calling out of the **remnant (144,000)** and the conclusive judgment which took place 66-70 A.D. After that the Israelites were the same as all other nations in the sight of God. They were lost sinners in need of salvation and all who believed in Christ could be reconciled to God. Those who did not believe were the same as all other people, regardless of their ethnic origin or religious affiliation. An unsaved Baptist or Roman Catholic is the same in the sight of God as an unsaved Jew or Muslim, Lutheran or Buddhist, atheist or agnostic. And once we are reconciled to God by faith in Christ, our nationality still has no meaning in His sight. **There is neither Greek nor Judaean, circumcision nor uncircumcision, Barbarian, Scythian, bond nor free: but Christ is all and in all** (Colossians 3:11).

That's why there is no mention, hint or suggestion in the New Testament regarding "Jews going back to Palestine" or "restoration of Israel as a nation." It has no relevance as far as New Testament prophecy is concerned. Both of these events had already happened. They were foretold through Old Testament prophets while many Israelites were held captive in Assyria, and during the seventy years that some Judaeans were captives in Babylon. Accordingly, most Judaeans returned during the days of Ezra, Nehemiah and Zechariah. The other ten tribes also began returning at that time, and their complete return reached fulfillment during the CENTURY OF RESTORATION which was begun by the Maccabee brothers in 165 B.C. During that century the temple was restored, traditional ceremonies resumed, the twelve tribes were again in the land (though still divided culturally if not politically), and the way was prepared for the coming of the Messiah. However, as in previous centuries, the Israelites began killing each other again until the Roman general Pompey came in around 63 B.C. to put an end to the fighting by force of arms and to impose peace under Roman occupation.

There was a century of peace under Roman domination, and religious freedom was allowed to the Judaeans. Then, **when the fullness of time was come, God sent forth His Son . . . to redeem them that were under the law, that we might receive the ADOPTION of sons** (Galatians 4:4-5). God picked just the right time in history to send His Son into the world. And we will never truly comprehend what happened regarding the Israelites until we understand the meaning of the **ADOPTION**. Speaking of his earthly relatives, Paul wrote, **My kinsmen according to the flesh: who are Israelites, to whom pertaineth the ADOPTION** (Romans 9:3-4). The English word, "adoption," comes from the Latin *adoptio*, and we use it today mainly to mean that a married couple takes someone else's child and makes it their own. But the New Testament word has an entirely different meaning.

In a prominent family at that time the *adoptio* was a public ceremony whereby a father would signify that his son had made a transition from childhood to adulthood. Before that ceremony took place, the son was no different than one of the family slaves. In fact, the slaves managed the son rather than the other way around. They

212

told him what to do, when to do it, and how to do it. The young son could not own property or make his own decisions. But once the *adoptio* took place, he became a responsible adult and could act on his own, including giving orders to the slaves and having them obey him. **The heir, as long as he is a child, differs nothing from a slave, though he be lord of all; but is under tutors and governors UNTIL THE TIME APOINTED BY HIS FATHER . . . when the fullness of time was come, God sent forth His Son . . . to redeem them that were under the law** [of Moses] **that we might receive THE ADOPTIO** (Galatians 4:1-2, 4-5).

The illustration of an **ADOPTIO** was used by Paul to portray the transition of the Israelites from the Old Covenant to the New Covenant. Under the old they were like little children, under the rules and regulations of the Mosaic law. But when Christ came, He brought a transition for Hebrew believers from spiritual childhood to responsible adulthood. **Wherefore the law was our schoolmaster to bring us unto Christ, that we might be justified by faith. But after that faith is come, we are no longer under a schoolmaster** (Galatians 3:24-25). And included in that transition was revelation of the fact that God would no longer recognize natural generation. **O generation of vipers . . . think not to say within yourselves, We have Abraham as our father: for I say unto you, that God is able of these stones to raise up children unto Abraham** (Matthew 3:7, 9).

Paul went on to explain that the transition from the Old Covenant to the New Covenant was like Abraham's transition from Hagar's son to Sarah's. **Abraham had two sons, one by a bondmaid, the other by a freewoman. He who was of the bondwoman was born after the flesh . . . which things are an allegory: for these are the two covenants; one from mount Sinai, which genders to bondage, which is Hagar . . . mount Sinai in Arabia answers to Jerusalem which now is and is in bondage with her children. But Jerusalem which is above is free, which is the mother of us all . . . cast out the bondwoman and her son: for the son of the bondwoman shall not be heir with the son of the**

freewoman (Galatians 4:22-26, 30). What he is saying here is that the old covenant has been cast out and the new covenant has been ushered in.

There is no promise or suggestion anywhere in the New Testament of a restoration of figurative Ishmael, Hagar's son, meaning ethnic Israelites (other than the **144,000 elect remnant**), to any place in God's plan for His people on this earth. Only those who are part of the heavenly Jerusalem are included, and their ethnic origin makes no difference whatsoever. Those Israelites whose ancestors were **broken off the olive tree** of God's heritage can be grafted in again if they repent and make peace with God by faith in Christ; otherwise there is no promise regarding them to be found anywhere in the New Testament. The New Covenant superseded the old.

The only verse in the New Testament that even remotely suggested a future place for ethnic Israelites occurred when the Risen Christ met with His disciples, and they asked Him, **Lord, wilt thou at this time restore again the kingdom to Israel?** (Acts 1:6). His answer can only be understood in the light of John 16:12-13: **I have yet many things to say unto you, but ye cannot bear them now. Howbeit, when He, the Spirit of Truth is come, He will guide you into all truth.** Our Lord knew that His disciples were not yet ready to hear about what was coming. If He had told them at that juncture that there would be no "kingdom of Israel" anymore, they would probably have been so fearful and insecure that they may have scattered in all directions rather than coming together in prayer to receive the outpouring of God's Holy Spirit on the day of Pentecost.

So He wisely said, **It is not for you to know** [as yet] **the times or the seasons** (Acts 1:7). Contrast that word with what Paul wrote a few years later: **Of the times and seasons, brethren, ye have no need that I write unto you, for you know perfectly that the day of the Lord so cometh as a thief in the night** (I Thessalonians 5:1-2). In his second epistle Paul wrote, **When I was yet with you I told you these things** (II Thessalonians 2:5). By the time Paul wrote this the **times and the seasons** had been made clear to all believers, including those who asked that original question before they had received the **Spirit of Truth** to guide them. Then they knew that the "kingdom of Israel" had been enlarged to become **the kingdom of God**, and that it was no longer limited to one nation but would include some from every nation, as God had promised Abraham.

They would have learned also the meaning of the Messiah's words, **My kingdom is not of this world: if my kingdom were of this world, then would my servants fight** (John 18:36). As far as God was concerned, there would be no more "kingdom of Israel" with fighting and killing and competition for power over others. In the **kingdom of God** the citizens would not resist, even when attacked. They would love one another, even as Christ **loved us and gave Himself for us.**

It was not until three hundred years later, when the **falling away** occurred, that the kingdom of God was destroyed by merging with the pagan religion of the Greeks and Romans, and killing began again in the name of God. This was a return to the Old Testament, just as the new religion of Islam in the Seventh Century was a return to the Old Testament in many ways.

Sad to say, during the past century many evangelical Christians have also returned to Old Testament ways in their endorsement of and support for political Zionism, which has included the killing of thousands of people. No justification whatsoever for such an association, now being endorsed by certain evangelicals, can be found anywhere in the New Testament.

There was no prophetic significance to the establishment of "the Judaean Kingdom of Khazaria" in southern Russia twelve hundred years ago, when the population of that empire converted to Judaism and made it the state religion there. Or when Yiddish was the official language of Biro-Bidjan, a Jewish region of the Soviet Union. I think it's fine that Jewish people now again have their own small country, although I wish it could have been settled peacefully. I also wish the Kurdish people could have their own country if it could be done peacefully. Now they are divided among

215

the adjoining countries of Iran, Iraq, and Turkey. And what about the Basque provinces of Spain? The Basques have wanted their own independent country for centuries. Likewise the Pushtu people of Pushtunistan, whose territory lies half in Pakistan and the other half in Afghanistan. And the Sikhs of India and Pakistan have long wanted Punjab state to be their own independent country. Then there are the poor Gypsies, who are said to outnumber the Jewish people, and have been persecuted in every country wherever they have wandered. Wouldn't it be wonderful if they had their own country? Wouldn't it be nice if we could give them some of the parts of Florida which we took away from the Seminoles.

When British forces were taking Palestine away from the Ottoman Turks in 1917, the Foreign Secretary, Arthur James Balfour, issued a declaration designating Palestine as a future "national home" for Jewish people. However, he stipulated that "nothing may be done which may prejudice the civil and religious rights of existing non-Jewish communities in Palestine." What a tragedy that this provision was not followed by Jewish immigrants since 1933. Endorsement by evangelicals of events since that time has had a definite influence on the promised second coming of our Lord Jesus Christ, in that they have caused many Islamic nations to close their doors to the spread of the gospel. Our Saviour said He wanted to have a witness for Himself, a people for His name, among every tongue, tribe and nation. Once that goal is achieved, He will come again and wipe away all tears from the eyes of those who suffer for His sake. We need to understand how involvement in political Zionism by certain evangelical Christians, and their unconditional support of the Zionists with hostility toward the Palestinians, has hindered the spread of the gospel among unreached people.

So if there is any prophetic significance to the present-day state of Israel, it is this: endorsement by evangelicals has caused Islamic people to become opposed to Christian missionaries and the spread of the gospel. These events have thus delayed our Lord's return.

Chapter 17

Then what about
"The Times of the Gentiles"?

Use of the word "gentile" in Bible translation has been one of those unfortunate mistakes that have confused evangelical Christians for centuries. In the original Greek language of the New Testament the word is *ETHNOS*, from which we get the word *ETHNIC*. It means a people group having a distinct culture and language, and should always be translated as *NATION*. The devout men who translated the King James Version of the Bible in 1611 did an excellent job on the whole, but sometimes they tended to use the Latin rather than the Greek text. So in translating *ETHNOS* they often used the Latin *GENTILIS* rather than *NATION*. Much confusion has resulted, causing some Christians to divide human beings into "Jew and Gentile" categories. But the New Testament does not do so. It speaks of "Judaeans" and "other nations."

The translators of the King James Version did sometimes translate *ETHNOS* as *NATION*, but only occasionally. In Mark 13:10 they got it right: **The gospel must first be published among all NATIONS.** Also in Matthew 24:9, **Ye shall be hated of all NATIONS**; and Matthew 28:19, **Go ye therefore and teach all NATIONS.** But then in Luke 21:24 they revert back to the Latin: **Jerusalem shall be trodden down of the GENTILES until the times of the GENTILES be fulfilled.** Yet it's the same Greek word *ETHNOS* which is elsewhere translated *NATIONS*. In the original

Greek that verse reads, **Jerusalem shall be trodden down by NATIONS until times of NATIONS be completed**. The point is that after 70 A.D. Jerusalem would have no further significance for either the Israelites or for any other nations.

Fourteen times in the New Testament the Greek word *ETHNOS* is used in reference to the Israelites. Why haven't the translators used *GENTILES* for these passages? If they did, then Acts 10:22 would read that Cornelius had a good report among **all the GENTILES of the Judaeans [Jews]**. Or Luke 7:5 would be translated **The centurion loves us GENTILES and has built us a synagogue**. Or Paul would be quoted as saying, **My manner of life among my own GENTILES at Jerusalem** (Acts 26:4).

The term *GENTILES* should never have been used in translating *ETHNOS*, which means **NATIONS**. The Israelites were one among many nations. Under the old covenant they were the one NATION that God used, to the extent that they would let Him, to bear witness for Him to other nations. But when he started that one nation with Abram, God let him know that it was temporary. ALL NATIONS were to be included eventually in the family of God. That's why the name "Abram" was enlarged to "Abraham," meaning "father of nations." And that promise was fulfilled in Christ, **the promised seed** through whom **all nations would be blessed**.

The TIMES OF THE NATIONS were foretold after God created the nations by confounding their languages at the tower of Babel. Soon thereafter he called out one man, Abram, and gave him two promises. First, He said, Abraham's descendants would be greatly multiplied, and would become a great nation. The times of that ONE NATION lasted for almost two thousand years. Secondly, God told Abraham that through one of his descendants ALL NATIONS would be blessed. Thus THE TIMES OF THE NATIONS would come after the ONE NATION had served its purpose and was discontinued as a separate entity.

And the Scripture, foreseeing that God would justify the NATIONS through faith, preached before the gospel unto Abraham, saying, in thee shall all NATIONS be blessed . . . that

the blessing of Abraham might come on the NATIONS by Jesus Christ . . . there is neither Judaean nor Greek [nations] **. . . for ye are all one in Christ Jesus, and if ye be Christ's then are ye Abraham's seed and heirs according to the promise** (Galatians 3:8, 14, 28-29).

The TIMES OF THE NATIONS began when our Lord died on the cross and reconciled sinful men from every nation to the Living God. Being a natural descendant of Abraham had no further significance (other than the **elect remnant** of **144,000** from that generation of Israelites) in God's sight. Likewise, the city of Jerusalem would have no further significance after the terminal judgment upon it was poured out forty years later by the **wrath of the Lamb** (Revelation 6:17).

So when will the TIMES OF THE NATIONS be completed? Obviously, when the King of all Kings comes back again to take over this planet. Meanwhile, many nations have occupied Jerusalem since the Romans destroyed it in 70 A.D. A peaceful take-over by Muslims took place when the spreading Islamic revival reached Jerusalem around 630. I remember reading in Robert Ripley's *Believe it or Not* about 60 years ago how the city was delivered to Omar Al-Khattab in 637 without a struggle. That's because so many of the Hebrew rabbis in Palestine had come to believe that Muhammad was **that prophet** foretold by Moses in Deuteronomy 18:18-19. They were astounded to see thousands of new converts to Islam from their own synagogues kneeling in prayer to worship God five times daily. Eventually, virtually all the synagogues in Palestine became mosques. Omar is credited with building the gold domed shrine that still stands on the site of Solomon's temple in Jerusalem, although it was more likely completed in 688 by Caliph Abdul Malik.

Hardly any of the Bible prophecy writers of the past century have recognized the ethnic origins of the people who have been living in Palestine for the past two thousand years. A majority have been Muslims who are descendants of Abraham, Isaac and Jacob. One-fourth, or possibly even one-third, of the population was killed or died of starvation during the civil wars and Roman subjugation 66-70 A.D., but they came right back. By the time of their conversion to Islam in the Seventh Century, there were probably three or four million Israelites again living in Palestine. And they have been there ever since, although they were called "Muslims" after 630-650 A.D. Also, they have mixed and inter-married with many other people groups throughout the intervening centuries. Still, those who are today called native "Palestinians" are much more likely to be related to the biblical Jacob than are Ashkenazi Jewish immigrants, originally from Khazaria, but more recently from Europe, Russia, America and elsewhere.

The most horrible period of bloodshed since the **days of vengeance** (66-70 A.D.) took place in Jerusalem in the year 1099 when so-called "Christian" crusaders from Europe took the city and reportedly chopped off the heads of 100,000 native people. Raymond of Toulouse and other European knights boasted that the blood flowed up to the horses' bridles in the streets of Jerusalem. Muslims under Saladin reconquered Jerusalem in 1187. The Ottoman Turks ruled there for four hundred years. Then there was the British mandate from 1917 until 1948. But all the while, Jerusalem was occupied by people from many nations, and still is to this day. There are native Palestinians, most of whose ancestors were Hebrews who converted to Islam in the Seventh Century. The Zionist immigrants who are now in control represent many NATIONS. The largest bloc are the Ashkenazi Yiddish people whose ancestors originally lived in the empire of Khazaria, situated in what is now called Russia and Ukraine. Then there are the Sephardim Jews from Spain, Portugal and Morocco, some of whose ancestors may have been the ancient Israelites of Bible times. As mentioned earlier, those we call "the Jewish people" today originally came from many NATIONS. The fact that their ancestors converted to Judaism does not change their ethnic origins. When actress Elizabeth Taylor became Jewish, it did not change her English ancestry. Nor did it change the African ancestry of entertainer Sammy Davis, Jr. when he became a Jewish man. Evangelicals who seek the conversion to Christ of diverse Jewish people today seldom realize that in so doing they are helping to carry out our Lord's command to go and teach ALL NATIONS. Jewish people come from at least fifty different nations. And according to God's promise in Matthew 24:14, when He has a witness for His gospel, a people for His name, within each of the six thousand or so NATIONS on this planet, He will come again and the TIMES OF THE NATIONS will be completed.

Way back in 1940, when I first came to understand the truth of the gospel, I was greatly helped by a little book by C. I. Scofield called RIGHTLY DIVIDING THE WORD OF TRUTH. Many things were made clearer to me in that booklet, but as I grew in the Lord I later came to realize that Scofield had oversimplified things in one chapter. Based on I Corinthians 10:32 he divided the human race into three groups: "The Jew, The Gentile, and the Church of God." Actually, when Paul wrote that verse to the saints at Corinth, he didn't use the word *ethnos* (nations), but rather *Hellenes*, meaning Greeks. Paul was telling Corinthian believers some of the ways in which they could be good witnesses for Christ, one of which was getting along with other people. So what he really said was, **Don't offend the Judaeans, or the Greeks or the assembly of God, even as I please all men, not seeking my own benefit but the benefit of many that they may be saved.** He could have added many other ethnic groups to the list, but he wasn't trying to explain all the different kinds of people in the world.

If he did so, the list would be long. Living in Palestine at that time, in addition to the Judaeans, were the Samaritans, who were also of Hebrew ancestry. Among them there were those who were **the synagogue of Satan** in contrast to the few who were **circumcised in heart**. There was **Anna, of the tribe of Asher who served God with fastings and prayers day and night** (Luke 2:37) and then there were the scribes and Pharisees who were called **snakes, a generation of vipers, children of their father, the devil**. In the church at Corinth there were perhaps a few who were spiritual, but most were carnal babes in Christ. Some were like **gold, silver and precious stones;** others were **wood, hay and stubble** [I

Corinthians 3:12]. If Paul were writing today he might say that there are some Baptists who are born again and others who are still dead in sins. There are Roman Catholics who are Mafia criminals of the underworld and others who are selfless humanitarians. There may be some true **sheep**, but more likely many **goats** in every church.

Whether or not a person is Jewish, or Catholic, or Presbyterian, or Orthodox, or Muslim or Methodist makes absolutely no difference in the sight of God. All are lost sinners in need of salvation until they claim cleansing for their sins by the blood of Christ, and thus being reconciled to God are eligible to receive His Holy Spirit. Only then can they be made spiritually alive and become new creatures in Christ. And before that happens, their ancestry makes no difference whatsoever in the sight of God.

So I am afraid Scofield had it wrong in that otherwise helpful little book. Our God **is no respecter of persons**. Not since the generation when He began the **New Covenant** has there been any such distinction as **Judaeans and other nations**, much less the distinction of **JEW AND GENTILE**. There are just lost sinners divided up among six thousand tribes and nations, out of which our Lord is taking **a people for His name**. Regarding the lost, their nationality, religion, citizenship or whatever makes no difference in the sight of God. Each must come to Him in repentance and faith in Christ before he or she will be recognized as being any different from other human beings who are still alienated from Him. **He that believeth on the Son has everlasting life: and he that believeth not the Son shall not see life; but the wrath of God abideth on him** (John 3:36).

When a person accepts Christ by faith, receives remission for sins that are past, and is born again by the Spirit of God, he or she starts life anew as a newborn babe in Christ. And that's where the distinctions begin. As explained in the second and third chapters of First Corinthians (and many other places in the New Testament), there will be a struggle between **the old man** and **the new man,** between **the flesh and the spirit,** between **the things of God** and **the things of this present evil world.**

In the First Epistle of John, four kinds of Christians are mentioned in the original Greek text; or four stages of development in the Christian life. They are: **infants, little children, young men and fathers**. Every believer must go through the infant stage, but it is a tragedy to remain there, as the Corinthians did, because of their carnality (I Corinthians 3:1-3). Their growth was blocked by the works of the flesh. **If ye live after the flesh, ye shall die: but if ye through the Spirit do put to death the deeds of the body, ye shall live** (Romans 8:13). Another hindrance to growth is materialism, when **the cares of this world and the deceitfulness of riches choke the Word** (Matthew 13:22). Feeding upon God's Word is essential to growth, as Peter wrote to the new believers who were driven out of Jerusalem by the chief priests, scribes and Pharisees: **As newborn babes, desire the sincere milk of the Word, that ye may grow thereby** (I Peter 2:2).

But most of those who stayed in Jerusalem never grew up, because they failed to turn loose of legalistic traditions of the Old Covenant, including the **Jew-Gentile** dichotomy. Hanging on to Old Testament traditions blocked their growth. Sadly, the Apostle Paul had to write: **When for the time ye ought to be teachers, ye have need that one teach you again which be the first principles of the oracles of God; and are become such as have need of milk, and not of strong meat. For every one that useth milk is unskillful in the word . . . for he is a babe. But strong meat belongeth to them that are of full age** (Hebrews 5:12-14).

New believers in Galatia likewise returned to the Old Testament and lost out spiritually. **O foolish Galatians**, the Apostle wrote, **who hath bewitched you . . . I am afraid of you, lest I have bestowed upon you labor in vain** (Galatians 3:1, 4:11). It was to these wayward children that the Apostle explained, by using the examples of the two sons of Abraham, that returning to the Old Testament was like choosing the son of Hagar over the son of Sarah. **Which things are an allegory: for these are the two covenants; the one from Mount Sinai, which gendereth to bondage, which is Hagar and answereth to Jerusalem which now is, and is in**

223

bondage with her children. But Jerusalem which is above is free, which is the mother of us all . . . cast out the bondwoman and her son (Galatians 4:24-26, 30).

Christians today who abandon the New Testament **saved-unsaved** dichotomy, then return to the Old Testament and keep alive the **Jew-gentile** dichotomy, will lose out spiritually. What they are doing is a denial of the New Covenant and is also contradictory to God's clear revelation in the New Testament. There is no "chosen nation" or "chosen people" any more, and has not been since **all Israel (the remnant, 144,000)** was saved during the Messiah's generation. To say that unsaved people from any ethnic background, Jewish or otherwise, are "covenant people of God" is in direct opposition to all the major truths of the New Testament. We must pray that our fellow Christians who promote this heresy may see the error of their ways and return to the truth of God.

Chapter 18

Gog, Magog, Meshech and Tubal

Son of Man, set thy face against Gog, the land of Magog, the **chief prince of Meshech and Tubal, and prophesy against him** (Ezekiel 38:2). Hundreds of Bible teachers have said that this passage applies to Russia, and that, rather than being concerned with Ezekiel's day, its fulfillment would come 2600 years later. The Scofield Reference Bible of 1909 put it this way: *That the primary reference is to the northern (European) powers, headed up by Russia, all agree. The reference to Meshech and Tubal (Moscow and Tobolsk) is a clear indication . . . The whole prophecy belongs to the future . . . battle of Armageddon.*

When I moved to Washington in 1955 to set up the headquarters of International Students, Inc., I found precious fellowship in Christ at the Fourth Presbyterian Church. I was blessed by the ministry of the pastor, Dr. James H. Miers, *except when he got off on Bible prophecy.* One Sunday he expounded the 38th Chapter of Ezekiel by saying that the Russians had more horses than any other country, and that the Cossacks were going to ride their horses down to Palestine very soon to invade the [then] newly formed state of Israel. He didn't mention tanks or planes, helicopters, armored vehicles or guided missiles, presumably since there is no reference to them in Ezekiel 38. I have heard many other prophecy teachers say more or less the same thing, and it makes no sense. But that's what happens when our dear brothers and sisters in Christ try to apply

Old Testament teachings to the present day. Such interpretations are pitifully erroneous.

After studying Ezekiel, I began to wonder if Dr. Scofield and his disciples such as Dr. Miers had ever read the entire book. **Meshech and Tubal** are mentioned twice in earlier chapters. First, in a prophecy against **Tyrus** (the seaport city of Tyre): **Javan, Tubal and Meshech were thy merchants** (Ezekiel 27:13). Did those merchants come all the way from Russia, by any chance? And then go back to give their tribal names to Moscow and Tobolsk? Then there is a lamentation for some of those that fought against Egypt, including **Meshech and Tubal** (Ezekiel 32:26). Obviously, these didn't come from Russia either, and the lamentation was for that time period, not 2600 years later.

To understand Ezekiel we must recognize several things. One is that he was among the Judaean captives who had been taken to Babylon, and he had been there at least twenty-five years (Ezekiel 40:1). He mentions another captive, **Daniel**, more than once. Ezekiel speaks primarily about God's judgments upon the Israelites and the Judaeans. The first twenty-four chapters are devoted almost entirely to these judgments. BUT EZEKIEL WRITES OF PAST HAPPENINGS IN FUTURE TENSE. THE EVENTS HAD ALREADY HAPPENED BEFORE EZEKIEL WROTE ABOUT THEM.

They shall remove and go into captivity . . . I will bring him to Babylon (12:11,13) was written long after many inhabitants of both Israel and Judah had been taken to Assyria and Babylon respectively. **Because thy filthiness was poured out through thy whoredoms . . . I will judge thee as women that break wedlock are judged** (16:36,38). But the judgment had already taken place. **I will give thee into their hand . . . they shall burn thine houses with fire** (16:39,41) was written as though it were future when it had already taken place. **I will bring him to Babylon** (17:20) is repeated even though it had already happened. The entire Twenty-third Chapter of Ezekiel is written as though it were future, but it had already taken place. BECAUSE YOU DID THAT, I WILL DO

THIS is what God was saying through the prophet.

I say these things because Chapters Thirty-eight and Thirty-nine of Ezekiel HAVE TO DO WITH EVENTS THAT HAD ALREADY HAPPENED.

Who, then, is **Gog, the chief prince of Meshech and Tubal**? Obviously, these people are some nation that existed at that time because, as I said, they had been mentioned by Ezekiel twice already. They were some nearby nation, descendents of Japeth, as opposed to the Israelites who were descendents of his brother Shem: **The sons of Japeth were Gomer, Magog, Madai, Javan, Tubal, Meshech and Tiras** (Genesis 10:2). I have an idea that **Meshech and Tubal** were twins, because they are usually mentioned together. I believe we can determine which nation they were by a process of elimination.

As I said, the first 24 chapters of Ezekiel are devoted to the denunciation of the Judaeans and Israelites for their sins, and to the judgments which God had brought upon them for their evil ways. Sixteen succeeding chapters are then devoted to God's judgments on other nations, especially those which had fought against the Israelites and Judaeans. These include the Ammonites, Moab, Edom, the Philistines, Tyrus, Zidon, Egypt and Mount Seir (Idumea). But the greatest offender of all is identified by its ethnic origin **(Meshech and Tubal)**, not by its political title. That country was the mighty empire of **ASSYRIA**, which had taken ten tribes of the Israelites away as captives some years earlier. **Then the king of Assyria went up to Samaria and besieged it three years . . . and carried Israel away into Assyria . . . the Lord was very angry with Israel and removed them out of His sight: there was none left but the tribe of Judah only** (II Kings 17:18). Here we should note that in addition to the ethnic Judaeans, the Levites and the tribe of Benjamin were also part of Judah. Those taken to Assyria were from the other ten tribes, counting the sons of Joseph as two. We should note also that the Assyrians took mainly the soldiers, rulers and upper classes away as captives. Most of the farmers and poorer classes were left behind, as we shall see.

The defeat and captivity of the Israelites by Assyria brought merciful relief to the Judaeans (Jews), because it ended the terrible civil war that had been going on for more than 200 years. Just a few years earlier, **Pekah, the son of Remaliah, king of Israel, slew in Judah an hundred and twenty thousand** [Judaeans] **in one day . . . and the children of Israel carried away captive two hundred thousand women, sons and daughters** (II Chronicles 28:6,8). These Israelis were planning to keep those 200,000 Judaeans (Jews) as their slaves, but a prophet of God persuaded them to return the prisoners to Judaea.

With the war ended, and the ten tribes of Israel no longer a threat, the Judaeans entered into a period of peace and prosperity which had not been seen since the days of King Solomon over 200 years earlier. King Hezekiah was faithful to God, and **there was great joy in Jerusalem: for since the time of Solomon . . . there was not the like in Jerusalem** (II Chronicles 30:26). One of the greatest wonders during Hezekiah's reign was a coming together of the Judaeans with the other tribes of Israel, for the first time in two hundred years. Hezekiah called for a great Passover celebration, and invited all the tribes of Israel. **And there assembled at Jerusalem much people to keep the feast of unleavened bread, a very great congregation . . . many of Asher and Manasseh and of Zebulun humbled themselves and came to Jerusalem . . . a multitude of people of Ephraim and Issachar . . . and the priests and the Levites praised the Lord day by day** (II Chronicles 30:13,18,21). All the tribes of Israel had been **brought back from the sword** (Ezekiel 38:8).

During those years of peace and prosperity, **King Hezekiah had exceeding much riches and honor: and he made himself treasuries for silver, and for gold, and for precious stones, and for spices, and for all manner of pleasant jewels; storehouses also for increase of corn, and wine, and oil; and stalls for all manner of animals, and flocks and herds in abundance: for God had given him very much substance** (II Chronicles 32:27-29). Except for the forty year period of Solomon's reign, there had never been such a time of prosperity in Judaea before, nor was there afterwards. And, as might be expected, this storehouse of plenty became an increasingly attractive temptation to Senacherib, the King of Assyria, who was called **Gog** by Ezekiel. His armies had already plundered the Israelites in Samaria some years earlier. **After many days thou shalt come into the land that is brought back from the sword, [which] has gathered many people . . . and it shall come to pass that thou shalt think an evil thought: and thou shalt say . . . I will go to them that are at rest, and dwell safely . . . to take a spoil, to take a prey . . . and all shall say unto thee . . . hast thou gathered thy company to carry away silver and gold, to take away cattle and goods, to take a great spoil? Therefore, son of man, prophesy unto Gog, thus saith the Lord God, In that day when my people of Israel dwell safely thou shalt come from thy place out of the north parts, thou and many people with thee, all of them riding upon horses, a great company, and a mighty army** (Ezekiel 38:8-15).

If we compare this account of the invasion by **Gog**, written by Ezekiel, with records of the invasion of Judah by the king of Assyria in II Kings, II Chronicles and Isaiah, it becomes obvious that they are all speaking of the same event. For example, in II Kings 19:28, regarding the armies of Assyria, Isaiah is quoted as saying, **I will put my hook in thy nose, and my bridle in thy lips, and I will turn thee back by the way which thou camest.** Ezekiel puts it this way, **I will turn thee back, and put hooks into thy jaws, and I will bring thee forth, and all thine army, horses and horsemen** (Ezekiel 38:4). Regarding the defeat of the forces of Gog, Ezekiel writes: **Thou shalt fall upon the mountains of Israel, thou and all thy bands, and the people that is with thee: I will give thee unto ravenous birds of every sort, and to the beasts of the field to be devoured . . . and they that dwell in the cities of Israel shall go forth and burn the weapons and rob those that robbed them . . . and seven months shall the house of Israel be burying them** (Ezekiel 39:4,9,12). Now compare: **It came to pass that night that the angel of the Lord went out, and smote in the camp of the**

Assyrians an hundred fourscore and five thousand: and when they arose early in the morning, behold, they were all dead corpses. So Sennacherib king of Assyria departed, and returned to Nineveh (II Chronicles 19:35-36). Obviously, what Ezekiel has written about **Gog and Magog** is a description of the Assyrian invasion of Judaea when, in answer to the prayers of Isaiah and King Hezekiah, an angel of the Lord by supernatural intervention killed 185,000 Assyrian soldiers and caused the rest to flee.

It might be noted that when he wrote his prophecies, Ezekiel was being held as a captive in Babylon, and tensions between that empire and neighboring Assyria were such that it would not have been wise for him to write anything that might portray Assyria in a negative way. That's why, instead of naming Assyria, he used the code words **Gog and Magog.** Also, it's possible that Gog and Magog were used at that time the way we use VANDAL today. The original Vandals were a Germanic tribe that plundered the city of Rome in 455 A.D. Thereafter, their name became part of several languages; in English we speak of vandals and vandalism without any thought of the barbarians who sacked Rome so long ago. The **Gog and Magog** designation was used in Revelation 20:8 to denote **the nations which are in the four quarters of the earth.** Centuries later Muhammad used it in the Qur'an in the same way.

Another thing that leads me to believe that its usage by Ezekiel denotes Assyria is the mention of allied bands from other countries: **A great company with bucklers and shields, all of them handling swords: Persia, Ethiopia, and Libya with them; Gomer and all his bands; the house of Togarmah of the north quarters, and all his bands: and many people with thee** (Ezekiel 38:4-6). In Genesis 10:2-3 it is recorded that **Gomer, Magog, Meshech and Tubal** were all sons of Japeth, the son of Noah. And **Togarmah** was a son of **Gomer.** Apparently these relatives remained somewhat associated by language after the confusion of tongues at the tower of Babel. But no doubt the king of Assyria also hired large bands of mercenary soldiers from other cultures, such as Persia, Ethiopia and Libya, just as Britain hired thousands of Hessian mercenaries from Germany to fight against the American colonies during the Revolutionary War.

Sixty years ago I taught that Ezekiel was writing about things in the far distant future, rather than events that were relevant at that time. In my ignorance I said that Ezekiel was foretelling events that would occur in the Twentieth Century. Eventually I noticed that after saying, **I will send fire on Magog**, God said through Ezekiel, **Behold, it is come, it is done, saith the Lord God; this is the day whereof I have spoken** (Ezekiel 39:6,.8). Then I came to realize that we are being told here that these things had already happened.

However, there is a promise regarding the near future: **Thus saith the Lord God, Now will I bring again the captivity of Jacob, and have mercy upon the whole house of Israel** (Ezekiel 39:25). **And I will make them one nation in the land upon the mountains of Israel; and one king shall be king to them all: and they shall be no more two nations; neither shall they be divided into two kingdoms any more** (Ezekiel 37:22). But like all of God's promises to the Israelites, beginning with Moses, this one was conditional upon them being **circumcised in heart** (Ezekiel 44:9). All of the Old Testament prophets, from Moses onward, offer glowing promises to the Judaeans and Israelites if they would only obey God's laws and keep His commandments. But unfaithfulness would cancel the promises. **The Lord shall bless thee in the land which [He] giveth thee . . . and shall make thee plenteous in goods . . . and bless all the work of thine hand: thou shalt lend unto many nations, and thou shalt not borrow. The Lord shall make thee the head, and not the tail; thou shalt be above only, and not beneath** (Deuteronomy 28:8-13). **But if thou wilt not to do all His commandments and His statutes which I command thee this day; then all these curses shall come upon thee . . . and as the Lord rejoiced over you to do you good, so the Lord will rejoice over you to destroy you, and to bring you to nought** (Deuteronomy 28:15,63).

When the Judaeans returned from Babylon, and the other ten tribes returned from Assyria, they failed to please God and continued their sinful ways. One failure was their continued separation into **Judaea** and **Samaria**. During a thirty-three year period, 198-165 B.C., God allowed the Greek Seleucid empire to conquer Palestine and disrupt the spiritual and economic life of all Israel. It is reported that in 168 B.C. Antiochus Epiphanes dedicated the temple in Jerusalem to a pagan idol and sacrificed a pig on the altar. Once again God had judged the Hebrews for their unfaithfulness. Regarding their return from captivity, God had told the Israelites: **I do not this for your sakes, O house of Israel, but for my holy name's sake, which ye have profaned** (Ezekiel 36:22). Bible teachers make a great mistake when they say that God's promises regarding the return of the Hebrews to Jerusalem was because He regarded them as being special above other people. Not true! Rather, it was because He wanted them to be a witness for His name there.

There was a CENTURY OF RESTORATION beginning 165 B.C. when the Maccabee brothers led in defeating the Greeks and restoring the temple along with traditional rituals. The eight-day *Festival of Lights* or *Feast of Dedication* known as *Hanukkah* is still celebrated by Jewish people to commemorate those glory days. At that time, many of them must have thought that prophecies had been fulfilled regarding the restoration of Israel as one united nation, as foretold by Ezekiel and other prophets. But then they started killing each other again, and the civil wars resumed until the Romans moved in and restored order by force of arms.

It was not until the Messiah came that the heart of the prophecies were fulfilled, not to the glory of "Israel," but rather to the glory of God. **I will sanctify my great name which ye have profaned, saith the Lord God . . . Then will I sprinkle clean water upon you, and ye shall be clean from all filthiness. A new heart also will I give you, and a new spirit will I put within you, and cause you to walk in my statutes, and ye shall be my people and I shall be your God** (Ezekiel 36:23-28). Old Testament prophecies such as these could never be fulfilled by Israelites walking in the flesh. It was not until Christ came and reconciled them to God by His death on the cross that the Holy Spirit could be given. And **the**

righteousness of law might be fulfilled in us, who walk not after the flesh but after the Spirit (Romans 8:4). Among the Judaeans and other Israelites, it was only the elect remnant (144,000) who inherited God's promised blessings. Those who teach that there is any other restoration of Old Testament Israel by God are in grievous error.

Like all other Old Testament books, Ezekiel foretells **WHAT MIGHT HAVE BEEN** if the Israelites were able to keep the law of God in their own strength. But that they could not do because of their inherent sinfulness. Thus Ezekiel's prophecies, like all the rest of the Old Testament, serve to show us that all men are sinners, including the Israelites, and need a Saviour to reconcile them to God. That's why all of the prophetic books in the Old Testament point to the first coming of our Lord Jesus Christ.

WHAT MIGHT HAVE BEEN can never be, apart from Christ. But once Christ came, the old passed away and the new began. There would be no more "chosen nation" or "chosen people," but rather the great company of the redeemed from among all nations, kindreds, tongues, tribes and peoples as God had promised through the prophets from Abraham onward. There would be **neither Greek nor Judaean, Barbarian, Scythians, bond nor free; but all one in Christ Jesus. Amen.**

Chapter 19

Is Zechariah Similar to Ezekiel?

Very much so. He portrays what might be, if the Israelites are faithful to God. But, of course, they never were, so they could not inherit the promised blessings. His book is also similar in some ways to Daniel and Revelation

Zechariah the son of Berechiah the son of Iddo was among the Judaean captives who returned to Jerusalem from Babylon during the reign of Cyrus, also of Darius and Artaxerxes. Leaders among those who returned were **Zerubbabel, Ezra and Nehemiah**. As they repaired the temple and restored traditional ceremonies, there was great optimism. Perhaps now, finally, the Hebrews would begin to serve God faithfully and make further judgments unnecessary. The prophecies of Zechariah, written largely in allegorical form, express this optimism, but upon the condition that the Israelites be faithful to God.

At that time many Israelites from the other ten tribes who had been taken captive to Assyria also returned, and there was great hope for a restoration of "all Israel" as in the days of Solomon, and, to a lesser extent, of Hezekiah. **And the children of Israel, which were come again out of captivity . . . the Lord made them joyful, and turned the heart of the king of Assyria unto them** (Ezra 6:21-22). This prompted the prophecy that all would return eventually: **I will bring them again also out of the land of Egypt, and gather them out of Assyria** (Zechariah 10:10). Many from Judaea had fled to Egypt to escape being taken captive to Babylon, as upper classes of the other ten tribes had been taken to Assyria.

Zechariah makes many predictions and promises regarding WHAT MIGHT BE in the future, usually presenting it as IN THAT DAY, THERE SHALL BE. But Bible teachers have made a great mistake when they have presented these prophecies as being unconditional. At the very beginning Zechariah said, **The Lord hath been sore displeased with your fathers** (Chapter 1:2), and later added, **They made their hearts as an adamant stone, lest they should hear the law: therefore came great wrath from the Lord of hosts, and scattered them as a whirlwind among all the nations, and the land was desolate** (Chapter 7:14). So now that they were beginning to return from captivity, Zechariah begs them: **Be not as your fathers. Turn unto me and I will turn unto you, saith the Lord** (Chapter 1:3-4). So when he makes predictions saying, IN THAT DAY this or that good thing will happen, we must remember that all of these promises are conditional. **THIS SHALL COME TO PASS, IF YE WILL DILIGENTLY OBEY THE VOICE OF THE LORD YOUR GOD** (Zechariah 6:15).

The futuristic prophecies of Zechariah were given to inspire the Israelites to be faithful to God's law, and to give them hope for better things to come if they were obedient to God. Instead of being punished as their forefathers were, they might enjoy great blessings in the future. But, as Moses said, if they failed to do so, they would receive God's curses instead.

Having said these things, we should note that the prophecy of Zechariah is a book of great mysteries, in many ways like Daniel and the Apocalypse. There are **four horses: red, black, white and bay** (6:1-8), that have symbolic meaning, as in Revelation 6:2-8. There are **two olive trees** and a **candlestick with seven lamps** and **two anointed ones** (4:2-14) that parallel the same images in Revelation 1:12-20; 11:3-12.

But the most significant thing about Zechariah is how God used him to include many prophecies of the coming Messiah as picture images within his writings. **Sing and rejoice, O daughter** of Zion: **for, lo, I come, and I will dwell in the midst of thee, saith the Lord. And many nations shall be joined to the Lord in that day, and shall be my people: and I will dwell in the midst** (2:10-11). I have heard Bible teachers say, "The CHURCH is not mentioned in the Old Testament." But here it is as plain as can be in Zechariah. The inclusion of **MANY NATIONS** into the family of God began when our Lord started to build His church to eventually include **ALL NATIONS**, as God promised Abraham.

Behold I will bring forth my servant the BRANCH . . . and I will remove the iniquity of the land in one day (3:8-9). Only the blood of Christ shed for our sins could accomplish that miracle. **Behold the man whose name is the BRANCH . . . he shall build the temple of the Lord, and he shall bear the glory, and shall sit upon his throne, and he shall be a priest upon his throne** (6:12-13). Only the Lord Jesus is both king and priest, and His temple was His physical body while He was on earth, and local bodies of believers ever since (I Corinthians 3:16-17). His temple is made of **living stones**. Here is a clear revelation of how our Lord would be exalted after His resurrection and sit upon the throne of God as both ruler and advocate (I John 2:1). **A high priest forever after the order of Melchisedec** (Hebrews 5:6).

Some teachers have said that certain passages in Zechariah look forward to the second coming of the Messiah, but I disagree. All of his Messianic prophecies relate to the first coming of our Saviour. Some are clearly obvious, others are given as symbols, metaphors and word pictures; BUT ALL RELATE TO HIS FIRST COMING ONLY.

Rejoice greatly, O daughter of Zion; shout, O daughter of Jerusalem: behold thy king cometh unto thee: He is just, and having salvation; lowly, and riding upon an ass, upon a colt the foal of an ass . . . and He shall speak peace unto the NATIONS: and His dominion shall be from sea to sea, even to the ends of the earth (9:9-10). This is the great prophecy concerning what we call "Palm Sunday," when our Lord rode from the Mount of Olives into Jerusalem to be rejected and crucified. Because **mountains** signify

nations in the symbolism of Scripture, that was the day when **His feet stood upon the Mount of Olives** (Zechariah 14:4) and caused it to **cleave in the midst thereof**. It signified that the mountain (nation) of Israel would be divided, with one part going into the kingdom of God and the remainder going into the outer darkness. **The kingdom of God shall be taken from you, and given to a nation bringing forth the fruits thereof** (Matthew 21:43). The nation (mountain) that became the kingdom of God was the true Israel, composed of the **elect remnant (144,000)** whom God called out of the twelve tribes and which Peter called **a chosen generation, a royal priesthood, an holy nation, a peculiar people** (I Peter 2:9). And some see the valley between the two sections of the Mount of Olives as being **Multitudes, multitudes in the valley of decision** (Joel 3:14), as when Peter urged the Israelites to **Repent and be converted** (Acts 3:19). In any case, **it shall be in that day that LIVING WATERS shall go out from Jerusalem; half of them toward the former sea, and half of them toward the hinder sea** (Zechariah 14:8). We know for sure that these verses refer to Messiah's first coming because: **In the last day, that great day of the feast, Jesus stood and cried, saying, If any man thirst, let him come unto me and drink. He that believeth on me, AS THE SCRIPTURE HATH SAID, out of his heart shall flow LIVING WATER** (John 7:37-38). Surely the scripture to which our Lord made reference was Zechariah 14:8.

It should be obvious to us that Zechariah reveals how the coming Messiah will cause a division among the Israelites, with one part being the true Israel and the other being those who condemned Him to death. One part would be known as the heavenly Jerusalem as defined by the Apostle Paul in Galatians 4:26, and the other part would be **the great city, which spiritually is called Sodom and Egypt, where also our Lord was crucified** (Revelation 11:8). And for the first forty years after Pentecost the worldly Jerusalem was the chief persecutor of the heavenly. Paul compares the heavenly Jerusalem to Isaac, and the earthly to Ishmael: and **he that was born after the flesh persecuted him that was born after the spirit, even**

so it is now (Galatians 4:29). Then, after God's final judgment (67-70 A.D.) upon those He called **the synagogue of Satan** (Revelation 2:9,3:9), persecution against true believers came from other nations as well: **Then shall they deliver you up to tribulation, and shall kill you: and ye shall be hated of all nations for my name's sake** (Matthew 24:9).

As part of his prophecies regarding the coming Messiah, Zechariah speaks of what will happen to the new Jerusalem, which will be the body and bride of Christ: **I will gather all nations against [the new] Jerusalem to battle; and the city shall be taken, and the houses rifled, and the women ravished; and half of the city shall go forth into captivity . . . then shall the Lord go forth and fight against those nations, as when He fought in the day of battle. And His feet shall stand in that day upon the mount of olives which . . . shall cleave in the midst thereof toward the east and toward the west, and there shall be a very great valley; and half of the mountain shall remove toward the north, and half of it toward the south. And ye shall flee to the valley of the mountains** (Zechariah 14:2-5). Some teach that this passage refers to the second coming of our Saviour, but there is no way that such an interpretation could apply. When our Lord comes again **with power and great glory**, none of His people **shall flee, like as ye fled before the earthquake in the days of Uzziah** (Zechariah 14:5). Rather, when God divided Israel into two factions (mountains) by separating out the **remnant (144,000)** beginning on the **Day of Pentecost** (Acts 2:1-41), the true believers had to **flee to the valley** [between the] **mountains** (Zechariah 14:5).

It is important to note that God says through Zechariah **I WILL GATHER ALL NATIONS AGAINST JERUSALEM TO BATTLE** (Zechariah 14:2). That battle began when God gathered the nations on the day of Pentecost. **There were visiting in Jerusalem Judaeans, devout men, OUT OF EVERY NATION UNDER HEAVEN** (Acts 2:5). While those thousands of pilgrims from every area of the Roman Empire were visiting in Jerusalem God poured out His Holy Spirit upon **three thousand** of them the first day. Shortly thereafter the number had grown to **five thousand** (Acts 4:4). And the battle royal began.

When Peter described it he quoted the Second Psalm rather than Zechariah, but the subject matter is the same: **Lord, thou art God, who by the mouth of thy servant David hast said, Why do the nations rage, and the people imagine vain things? The kings of the earth stood up, and the rulers were gathered together against the Lord, and against His Christ. For of a truth against thy holy son Jesus both Herod and Pontius Pilate, with other nations, and the people of Israel were gathered together . . . and now, Lord, behold their threatening: and grant unto thy servants that with all boldness they may speak thy word** (Acts 4:24-29).

It should be remembered that when the Romans joined the battle against Christ and His followers, they represented ALL NATIONS, because the empire was said to include **every nation under heaven** (Acts 2:5).

At that time there was a great persecution against the church which was at Jerusalem [Acts 8:1]. **After ye were illuminated ye endured a great fight of afflictions** [tribulations] Paul reminded the Hebrew remnant, **both by reproaches and by tribulations, and ye became companions of them that were so abused . . . and took joyfully the stealing of your possessions** (Hebrews 10:32-34). This was in fulfillment of two things Zechariah had said would happen when the true Jerusalem was attacked by unbelievers: the first being **the houses rifled.** Those **144,000** Hebrews who accepted Christ as Messiah, Lord and Saviour had all their property taken away by unbelievers. The second was that their wives were taken away and sold into prostitution by heads of families from which they originally came. The **144,000** Israelites whom God selected to be included in the new Jerusalem were the first to suffer, but then when a great multitude from other nations began to be included in that heavenly body, they also suffered in ways similar to the Hebrew believers.

Then shall the Lord go forth and fight against those nations. The means whereby He would fight had been mentioned earlier by the prophet: **This is the word of the Lord unto Zerubbabel, saying, Not by might, nor by power, but by my spirit, saith the Lord of hosts. Who art thou, O great mountain? Before Zerubbabel thou shalt become a plain: and he shall bring forth the headstone** [chief cornerstone] **thereof crying, Grace, grace unto it** (Zechariah 4:6-7). These verses foretell how the Messiah would fight **with the sword of His mouth, the Word of God** [which is] **quick and powerful and sharper than any two-edged sword** (Hebrews 4:12); by the gospel of grace which superseded the law; and by the power of His Holy Spirit. **MANY NATIONS shall be joined to the Lord in that day, and shall be my people: and I will dwell in the midst** (Zechariah 2:11).

My Christian brothers who want to make a literal application of our Lord dividing the Mount of Olives, rather than it being figurative, will turn right around and say that the mountain being flattened by Zerubbabel is, of course, figurative and not literal. They are so inconsistent! And they also agree that the many times that Israel, Judaea and Jerusalem are called **Mount Zion**, the **mountain of the Lord**, or some other **mount** or **mountain,** such usages are figurative, not literal. **Thus saith the Lord, Jerusalem shall be called . . . the mountain of the Lord of hosts, the holy mountain** (Zechariah 8:3). Obviously, this prophecy refers to the **elect remnant** who were to be redeemed out of the twelve tribes after the Messiah was exalted and glorified. It is **the new Jerusalem, the Lamb's wife**, and does not include the unsaved Judaeans of the earthly Jerusalem that was destined to be destroyed after their rejection and condemnation of the Son of God who was sent to save them.

The Mount of Olives . . . shall cleave in the midst thereof toward the east and toward the west (Zechariah 14:4). This is a picture of how our Lord would divide the Israelites into two factions. The division of Israel **toward the east** [the sun rising] corresponds to another prophecy, **Behold the day cometh that shall burn as an oven, and all that do wickedly shall be as stubble, and the day that cometh shall burn them up. But unto you that fear my name shall the Sun of righteousness arise with healing in His**

wings [Malachi 4:1-2]. When the Messiah was born some wise men came and said **we have seen His star in the east** [the sun rising] [Matthew 2:2].

All of these things are presented as metaphorical pictures to help us visualize how our Lord would come into the world to divide the Judaeans into the unfaithful majority who condemned Him, and the **elect remnant** who **received Him** and were thenceforth called **sons of God** [John 1:12]. **Think not that I am come to bring peace to the land** [of Israel] the Messiah said; **I came not to bring peace, but a sword. I am come to set a son at variance against his father, and the daughter against her mother, and a man's foes shall be they of his own household** [Matthew 10:34-36].

Many other verses in Zechariah also foreshadow the coming of the Messiah, such as **They weighed for my price thirty pieces of silver. And the Lord said unto me, cast it unto the potter . . . and I took the thirty pieces of silver and cast them to the potter in the house of the Lord** (Zechariah 11:12-13). Compare: **Judas went unto the chief priests and said, What will ye give me, and I will deliver him unto you? And they bargained with him for thirty pieces of silver . . . then Judas repented himself and brought again the thirty pieces of silver and cast them down in the temple . . . the chief priests took the silver pieces . . . and bought with them the potter's field to bury strangers in** (Matthew 26:14-15, 27:3,5,7). These verses provide a good example of how metaphors, symbols and other images are used to give prophetic insight to future events.

Here is another: **Smite the shepherd, and the sheep shall be scattered** (Zechariah 14:7). On His last night with His disciples, our Lord **went out into the mount of Olives** and said to them **All ye shall be offended because of me this night: for it is written, I will smite the shepherd and the sheep of his flock shall be scattered abroad** (Matthew 26:30-31). Obviously He was quoting Zechariah again. And here is still another reference to the coming Messiah, buried in the text: **And one shall say unto him, What are these wounds in thine hands? Then he shall answer, Those** with which I was wounded in the house of my friends (Zechariah 13:6). We remember how the disciple Thomas said, **Except I see in His hands the print of the nails . . . I will not believe** (John 20:25). And regarding the spear in His side, John wrote: **Another scripture saith, They shall look on Him whom they pierced** (John 19:37). This is a direct quote from Zechariah 12:10, **They shall look upon me whom they have pierced.**

One passage seems to foreshadow the actual day when our Lord was sacrificed upon the cross: **It shall come to pass in that day that the light shall not be clear, [but] dark: it shall be one day which shall be known unto the Lord, not day, nor night: but at evening time it shall be light** (Zechariah 14:6-7). The next verse identifies the day as the one when **living waters shall go out from Jerusalem.** So it has to be the same as when **it was about the sixth hour, and there was darkness over all the earth until the ninth hour. And the sun was darkened** (Luke 23:44-45). And the prophecy regarding **living waters** leads us to when our Lord said **He that believeth on me, as the scripture hath said, out of his heart shall flow LIVING WATER** (John 7:38). Obviously, His reference to Scripture has to be to Zechariah 14:8 because we are told, regarding the **living water: This spake He of the Spirit, which they that believe on Him should receive: for the Holy Ghost was not yet given; because that Jesus was not yet glorified** (John 7:39). The Messiah gave the same promise to the woman at Jacob's well in Samaria: **If you knew the gift of God, and who it is that saith unto thee, Give me a drink, you would have asked of Him and He would have given you living water . . . whosoever drinketh of the water that I shall give him shall never thirst; but the water that I shall give him shall be in him a well of water springing up to everlasting life** (John 4:10,14). These verses demonstrate conclusively that the subject matter of Zechariah Chapters 13 and 14 had its fulfillment at the first coming of our Lord and Saviour.

Here is another verse that has to relate to Messiah's first coming: **And it shall come to pass, that in all the land [of Israel], saith the Lord, two parts therein shall be cut off and die; but** the third shall be left therein. **And I will bring the third part through the fire, and will refine them as silver is refined, and will try them as gold is tried: they shall call on my name, and I will say, It is my people; and they shall say, The Lord is my God** (Zechariah 14:8-9). After our Lord's atoning death, resurrection and exaltation, two parts of the Israelites, the Judaeans and the Samaritans, were **cut off** from God, except that a third part, a **remnant (144,000)** drawn from both groups, was preserved by God to be His people. We know this application is correct because after that **remnant** was **scattered abroad** by persecution from other Judaeans, Peter wrote to them almost immediately, saying, **Think it not strange concerning the fiery trial which is to try you . . . that the trial of your faith, being much more precious than of gold that perisheth, though it be tried with fire, might be found unto praise and honor and glory at the appearing of Jesus Christ** (I Peter 1:7,4;12). My liberal professors at the University of Chicago tried to discredit Peter's authorship of this epistle by saying it was written decades later. Nonsense! For sure it was no later than 32 A.D. when Peter wrote this letter.

And here is still another verse that corresponds to the New Testament, immediately following the one about **living waters: The Lord shall be king over all the earth: in that day there shall be one Lord, and His name one** (Zechariah 14:9). After His resurrection our Lord said: **All authority is given unto me in heaven and in earth: go ye therefore and teach ALL NATIONS** (Matthew 28:18-19). To this we should add His earlier words: **This gospel of the kingdom shall be preached in all the world for a witness unto all nations** (Matthew 24:14). Today, millions of people, some in every major nation on earth, join their voices in singing, as George Frederick Handel wrote in his magnificent oratorio more than two centuries ago: KING OF KINGS, FOREVER: AND LORD OF LORDS, FOREVER: AND HE SHALL REIGN FOR EVER AND EVER! HALLELUJAH! HALLELUJAH! HALLELUJAH! In the year 2001 it was even sung before 1000 people in a public auditorium located in the heart of Beijing, capital city of Communist

China, with many government officials present.

In that day I will pour upon the house of David [remember: King Jesus, **the son of David**, is King David's successor] **and upon the inhabitants of** [the new] **Jerusalem, the spirit of grace and supplications . . . and there shall be upon the bells of the horses HOLINESS UNTO THE LORD** (Zechariah 12:10, 14:20). Except for the few prophets among them, a life of personal holiness was virtually unknown among the Israelites in Old Testament times. It was not until our Lord was glorified and poured out His Spirit upon the true believers that multiplied thousands began to live holy lives by His grace and power. During the past 250 years several entire denominations of Christians have been identified as HOLINESS groups.

The very last verse of Zechariah says, **In that day there shall be no more the Canaanite in the house of the Lord.** Obviously, this foretells the time when God's house will be made up of born again believers only. All others, even though they may be Israelites, or priests, or church members, will not be recognized as being within **the house of the Lord. Except a man be born again he cannot see the kingdom of God . . . but is condemned already . . . and the wrath of God abides on him** (John 3:3, 18, 36).

Like Daniel and Revelation, Zechariah uses many allegorical and metaphorical pictures to portray forthcoming events. I am inclined to believe that all of these are related to our Lord's first coming, or to things THAT MIGHT HAVE BEEN IF THE ISRAELITES COULD HAVE MEASURED UP TO GOD'S REQUIREMENTS. I see no clear indication that the prophecies of Zechariah foretell any event beyond the generation that lived as the time of the first coming of the Son of God, our Saviour.

Chapter 20

Are the Jews God's Chosen People?

Which Jews? The Yiddish-speaking Ashkenazim majority, originally from Khazaria? Or the Ladino-speaking Sephardim, originally from Spain and Portugal? Are the "chosen people" American Jews with blond hair and blue eyes, or black African Jews, or brown-skinned Jews among the indigenous tribes of India, or the oriental Jews of China? The ethnic origins of Jewish people of today represent at least fifty different nations of Europe, Asia and Africa. And a majority of the descendants of the twelve original tribes converted to either Christianity or Islam between 30 and 700 A.D.

One of the colossal errors that has been widely taught has to do with the supposed "ten lost tribes" of the Israelites. Only one tribe, the northern-most clan of Dan, had no representation among the **elect remnant (144,000)** who were called out by God to give the gospel to other nations between 30 and 66 A.D. But **the sons of Joseph, Manasses and Ephraim**, were counted as separate tribes. I have mentioned in previous chapters how all of the twelve tribes returned to Palestine from Babylon, Assyria, Egypt and other places beginning during the days of Ezra and concluding during the CENTURY OF RESTORATION started by the Maccabees in 165 B.C.

The fact that all of the twelve tribes were present in Palestine or other known areas of the Roman Empire is confirmed in the New

Testament. **James** addressed his epistle to **the TWELVE TRIBES** (James 1:1). Before King Agrippa, the Apostle Paul said, **Unto which promise our TWELVE TRIBES presently serving God day and night, hope to come** (Acts 26:7). Even if he hadn't told us, we would know that **Saul of Tarsus** was of **the tribe of Benjamin** (Romans 11:1) because he was named after a king from that tribe. Likewise, Peter was of the tribe of **Simeon** (Acts 15:14) and the prophetess **Anna, the daughter of Phanuel, was of the tribe of Asher** (Luke 2:36). Other tribes named elsewhere in the New Testament are **Zabulon** and **Naphtali** (Matthew 4:13, 15), as well as **Judah and Levi**. Then all twelve tribes are listed specifically in Revelation 7:6-8.

I mention these things because so often we hear prophecy teachers speaking of black African Jews or dark brown tribal Jews of India being from the "ten lost tribes." There were no ten lost tribes. Only one tribe, that of **Dan**, disappeared from the records of the twelve tribes up until the time of the New Covenant. It was not until the Seventh Century that the twelve tribes lost their identity, and that was because a majority of the Hebrews in Palestine converted to Islam. A few who did not convert emigrated to Khazaria, where the whole Ashkenazim nation converted to Judaism in the Eighth Century. It is a great mistake to say that because a person is Jewish that they must be biologically related to the original Hebrew tribes. That's like saying that because anyone is a Christian he must be descended from the twelve Apostles of Christ.

About sixty years ago I heard an ignorant fundamentalist preacher say, "Moslems are the descendants of Ishmael and Esau." The half-a-billion or more Muslims in Bangladesh, India, Malaysia and Indonesia have no biological tie whatsoever to any biblical character. And the ancestors of millions of Jewish people living in Europe, Asia, Africa, Latin America and North America became Jews by choice, just as others became Christians, Muslims, Hindus or Buddhists by choice. I remember reading how when King Bulan was choosing a religion for the Ashkenazim people of Khazaria, one reason he preferred Judaism was because it was the original monotheistic religion, before Christianity and Islam.

It is unfortunate that the original term "Judaean" became shortened to "Jew" in English, as William Shakespeare did four hundred years ago, and his usage was not always complimentary. In any case, the translators of the King James version of the Bible (in 1611) followed Shakespeare's usage, and "Jew" became the term that would identify Judaeans in the English language. In recent centuries the many people groups from other nations who came to be identified as Jews have collectively been called "the Jewish people."

So today individuals from many nations identify themselves as being "Jewish." But it is not generally a religious designation any longer, or that of a specific ethnic group. I have known a large number of Jewish people personally during the past seventy years, and only a small minority would be regarded as being religious. A majority have been agnostics or atheists. Quite a few of my Jewish friends accepted Christ as Saviour under my ministry, and thereafter they were known as "Christians." A Christian of Jewish ancestry is no different spiritually than a Christian of Nepalese or Chinese ancestry.

Of the many Jewish persons I have known over the years, I do not recall ever hearing one of them refer to himself or his family as being part of "God's chosen people." No doubt many of them have unhappy memories of Adolph Hitler's propaganda agents speaking of the "Aryan Master Race," and do not want to be guilty of the same attitude. However, some other Jews who have become evangelical Christians have joined ministries that are trying to win their fellow Jews to Christ and, sad to say, I fear that some of them may have used the "chosen people" concept as a fund raising tool to gain financial support from fellow Christians.

Who, then, are "God's chosen people" today?

There aren't any, and haven't been since God segregated a **remnant (144,000)** to be **the firstfruits unto the Lamb** and the rest were **broken off the olive tree** and not counted as the seed of Abraham any more. That **remnant** (Romans 11:5), called **ALL ISRAEL** (Romans 9:6, 11:26), was the last of the "chosen people."

From that time forth Judaeans were no different in God's sight than any other ethnic group. The only people of God are those who are born anew of His Spirit (John 3:3). Regarding all others, God says, **That which is born of the flesh is flesh**, and until they are born again they have no part in matters pertaining to God, but **the wrath of God abides on them** (John 3:36), regardless of their ancestry.

After God created the nations at the tower of Babel, He chose one man, Abram, to be His witness on earth, and wanted to continue that witness through Abram's descendants. Eventually, God promised, that witness would include some from all other nations. That's why He changed Abram's name to Abraham, meaning "father of nations." So God's recognition of Abraham's biological descendants as a special people was temporary. And the mark of identification, circumcision, for them also included Ishmael and sons of Abraham's concubines. More than a billion Muslims have been circumcised during the past 13 centuries, but that didn't make them "a chosen people."

But not all of Abraham's descendants were included in the promise, even though they were circumcised. Eight sons of Abraham are named in the Bible (I Chronicles 1:28-32), but he must have had many more because he had other concubines besides Keturah, the only one that is named: **Unto the sons of the concubines which Abraham had, Abraham gave gifts and sent them away, eastward** (Genesis 25:6). So the original "chosen people" designation passed on to only one person, Abraham's son Isaac. Then Isaac had two sons, but only one was chosen: Jacob, later named Israel. Jacob's twelve sons became fathers of the twelve tribes of Israel, later increased to thirteen when descendants of two sons of Joseph were recognized as two separate tribes.

Then came Moses about four hundred years later with the giving of the Law, and a new development was introduced: if any person failed to keep the law, **that soul shall be cut off from Israel** (Exodus 12:15). Over and over it is repeated in Moses: **that soul shall be cut off from His** [God's] **people**. From that time forth there were repeated statements from God, through His prophets, that those who failed to keep His law would no longer be under His covenant. **I will no more have mercy on the house of Israel; but I will utterly take them away . . . for ye are not my people, and I will not be your God** (Hosea 1:6, 9). But there are also conditional promises of reconciliation and restoration, and these two alternating messages continued throughout the Old Testament period.

Something entirely new happened when Esther became queen of Babylon. While they were held captive in Babylon, many Judaeans rose to prominent positions. Daniel became the equivalent of prime minister under King Nebuchadnezzar (Daniel 2:48), as did Mordecai under King Ahasuerus while his cousin (and adopted daughter) Esther was the queen. And actually it is Queen Esther who should be regarded as the original mother of those whom today we call "the Jewish people."

The Book of Esther records how Mordecai refused to offer required reverence to Haman, the son of Hammedatha, who was **above all the princes of Babylon**. In revenge, Haman hatched a plot to exterminate the Judaeans in Babylon, but through the intervention of Queen Esther their lives were saved and Haman was hanged. Then Queen Esther and Mordacai, the new prime minister, went on a retaliation campaign of their own, and set about to exterminate everyone who had threatened their fellow Judaeans. Not content with hanging Haman and his ten sons, they killed five hundred other men in the king's palace (called Shushan, Esther 9:6) and then began wholesale slaughter of other "anti-Semites" elsewhere. After they had killed over seventy-five thousand people, including women and children (Esther 8:11, 9:16), the terrified residents **in every province, and in every city, withersoever the king's commandment** [being carried out by Mordecai] **and his decree came . . . MANY OF THE PEOPLE OF THE LAND BECAME JUDAEANS; for the fear of the Judaeans fell upon them** (Esther 8:17). We are not told how many from other nations converted to Judaism at that time, but it must have been hundreds of thousands because **no man could withstand** [the Judaeans]**; for fear of them fell upon all people; and all the rulers of the provinces, and the lieutenants, and** the deputies, and officers of the king helped the Judaeans; for the fear of Mordecai fell upon them. For Mordecai was great in the king's house, and his fame went out throughout all the provinces: for this man Mordecai waxed greater and greater. Thus the Judaeans smote all their [presumed] enemies with the stroke of the sword, and slaughter, and destruction, and did what they would to those that opposed them (Esther 9:2-5). I inserted "presumed" above because the "anti-Semites" had not actually started killing the Judaeans. They had only threatened to do so.

Here, for the first time, we learn of large numbers of persons becoming identified as Judaeans who were not descendants of Abraham. How, then, could they come under God's covenant? They were not even Semitic people, since they came mostly from the descendants of Japeth.

The Persian empire ruled by King Ahasuerus and Queen Esther extended **from India to Ethiopia** and included **over 127 provinces** (Esther 1:1). Since most of the inhabitants of those provinces (nations) such as India and Ethiopia had very little organized religion in those days, it is easy to see how Judaism could have been readily adopted by many as their major religion. This also explains why millions of ethnic peoples in countries like India and Ethiopia profess to be Jews unto this day.

I have read reports of how that during the past century zealous rabbis from both Ashkenazi and Sephardi Jewish sects have been engaged in friendly competition trying to persuade various ethnic Jewish tribes in the Northeastern states of India to adopt their respective traditions. No doubt, in Esther's day possibly hundreds of Hebrew teachers went to the provinces **from India to Ethiopia** to teach Hebrew traditions to many thousands of new converts.

An Associated Press article published April 4, 2009 made interesting comments concerning African-American Jewish congregations in the USA today. As many Christians of African ancestry prefer to meet separately in their churches, even so, the article stated, hundreds of "Black synagogues" may be found in America. The AP article states that of six million or so U.S. Jews, about 600,000 identify themselves as nonwhite. This assertion is further confirmation of my earlier statement that those we now refer to as "the Jewish people" have originally come from at least 50 different nationalities. Of course, that's a conservative estimate; the true figure is more likely to be more than 100 nationalities.

Some teachers have promoted the idea that hundreds of thousands of black Jews in Ethiopia were descendants of King Solomon. They speculate that when the Queen of Sheba visited Jerusalem, Solomon fathered a child with her which eventually became the father of Jews in Ethiopia. But I maintain that it is far more likely that they came from the mass conversions that occurred during the reign of Queen Esther. The Media-Persia empire at that time was made up of **127 provinces, from India even unto Ethiopia** (Esther 1:1) and through fear of Mordecai and Queen Esther great numbers converted to Judaism in every province. There is little doubt in my mind that the origin of millions of natives who call themselves Jews in countries like India and Ethiopia dates back to the time of Esther.

Judaism came to be further recognized as a truly international religion during the CENTURY OF RESTORATION which began with the Maccabees around 165 B.C. Since the days of Ezra, Nehemiah and the prophet Zechariah (520-430 B.C.) when exiled Judaeans returned to Palestine from Babylon, and the other ten tribes came back from Assyria, Egypt and elsewhere, they were joined by a mixed multitude of other nationalities who had become identified with them. Some called themselves "Judaeans," but those identified with the other tribes returning from Assyria tended to call themselves "Samaritans." The glory days began when the Brothers Maccabee led military conquests that won independence for the Israelites in almost all of Palestine. The temple was restored, ceremonial traditions resumed, and, as foretold by the Old Testament prophets, **the Judaeans** (and all other Israelites) **had gone back to Palestine**. The 1951 edition of Encyclopedia Britannica (Volume 14, page 549) called this era "the most stirring chapter in Israelitish history." To celebrate their return to Palestine, the Judaeans began to set aside an annual week of feasting, mentioned in the New Testament as **the Feast of Dedication** (John 10:22). Still today Jewish people commemorate it in December as *Hanukkah*.

It was during this century (165-63 B.C.) that the Judaeans became aggressive missionaries seeking to win proselytes within all the surrounding countries, as well as among the numerous minority nationalities in Palestine. And the first generation of converts they won tended to maintain separate identities because they were not the seed of Abraham. There was no such term as "the Jewish people" at that time. There were, rather, the **Judaeans**, which included members of the tribes of Judah, Benjamin and Levi; members of the other ten tribes who preferred to be called **Samaritans;** and **proselytes**. Children of proselytes generally merged into the Hebrew community and were no longer segregated.

Through the Old Testament prophets, God revealed His desire that when the Israelites returned from captivity in Babylon and Assyria, and from exile in other countries, they would no longer be divided, but would be one nation. But it failed to happen. The northern tribes tended to settle in the land of their ancestors, and as one of them said to the Lord Jesus, **The Judaeans have no dealings with the Samaritans** (John 4:9). Some have said that the Samaritans were not full-blooded Israelites, but that idea is not true. The woman just mentioned asked the Lord, **Are you greater than our father Jacob** [Israel]? Then after she believed in Him, she bore witness of Him as the Messiah **and many of the Samaritans believed on Him . . . and said to the woman, now we believe . . . and know that this is indeed the Christ, the Saviour of the world** (John 4:39,42).

After the day of Pentecost, **Philip went down to the city of Samaria and preached Christ unto them**, and a great multitude came to faith in Christ (Acts 8:5-8). Not a word was said about them not being Hebrews, whereas when Peter went to the house of Cornelius, a Roman centurion (Acts 10:1-48), it became a big issue because the centurion was not an Israelite. It was only in Christ that the barriers were broken down and all the Hebrew tribes came together again in one body, no longer called Judaeans or Samaritans, but Christians. And when our Lord called out the **elect remnant (144,000)** to give the gospel to other nations, He chose 12,000 from each of the Hebrew tribes.

So in New Testament times there were still no "Jewish people." There were **Judaeans, Samaritans, proselytes and Christians**. The total number in Palestine was at least four million (of which 144,000 became Christians), but about a million more were scattered throughout the Roman Empire. On the **Day of Pentecost there were Judaeans and proselytes from every nation under heaven visiting** [as pilgrims] **at Jerusalem . . . Parthians, Medes, Elamites, dwellers in Mesopotamia, Cappadocia, Pontus, Asia, Phrygia, Pamphylia, Egypt, Libya, Rome, Cretes and Arabians** (Acts 2:5,9-11). The proselytes tended to have their own segregated synagogues (Acts 6:9), and when one was chosen as a deacon by the Jerusalem church, he was identified as being a proselyte (Acts 6:5). When Paul preached in the synagogue at Antioch in Pisidia, **many of the Judaeans and proselytes followed Paul and Barnabas** (Acts 13:43). Regarding missionaries sent out by the chief priests, scribes and Pharisees, however, our Lord said, **Ye compass sea and land to make one proselyte, and when he is made, ye make him twofold more the child of hell than yourselves** (Matthew 23:15).

The question is, were the hundreds of thousands (or possibly millions) of proselytes after the time of Esther included in God's promise to Abraham, **I will bless them that bless thee**? And the 144,000 who believed in Christ, were they and their children still included? And how about those who were murderers? Surely they could no longer be regarded as being God's people. Our Lord said, **If ye were Abraham's children, ye would do the works of Abraham; but now ye seek to kill me . . . ye are of your father the devil, and the lusts of your father ye will do** (John 8:39-40,44).

The greatest numerical change among those who were called **the seed of Abraham** came in the Seventh Century. Peace prevailed in Palestine at that time, because in the Fourth Century emperors of Rome had professed faith in nominal Christianity and granted toleration to Hebrews and Christians. So the Hebrew population of

Palestine grew steadily until it once again reached three million or more. Then around 630 Islam arrived as a great religious revival, and probably two million Hebrews converted to Islam, changing their synagogues to mosques. The question is, were these converts to Islam and their children still heirs to God's promise to Abraham, **I will bless them that bless thee**? Today, the descendants of these former Hebrews are called Palestinians. They still believe in and worship the God of the Old Testament, still revere Moses and *Isa Masih* (Jesus the Messiah) as the greatest of prophets next to Muhammad, still practice universal circumcision and eat only "kosher" foods. If God's promise to Abraham is still valid, are native Palestinians entitled to the benefits of these promises, including possession of their ancestral homeland? Or rather, did not God's second promise to Abraham regarding his being the father of many nations supersede the first promise regarding the one nation? When the Messiah came and died to reconcile some from every nation unto the God of Abraham, the idea of one special nation was no longer relevant.

The next great development came in the Eighth Century when the Ashkenaz empire of Khazaria (in southern Russia) was Judaized. I have mentioned earlier how the Khazars had no religion, hence no defense against Muslims coming from their east and Roman Catholic pressures from the west. An excellent history of what happened was written by the renowned European author, Arthur Koestler, and published in 1976. He called it THE THIRTEENTH TRIBE. He maintains that the Ashkenazi Jewish people originally came from Khazaria, where Judaism was the official state religion in the Ninth Century. And although many Judaeans of Palestine who resisted conversion to Islam had emigrated to Khazaria in the Eighth Century, they were a small minority there. Occasional traces of their DNA might possibly be found in some Ashkenazim Jews today, however.

Actually, almost all of the Ashkenazi Khazar Yiddish people should show traces of Levant or Near East ancestry in their DNA because they originally came from some region south of the Caucasus mountains, not far from Babylon. Speaking of coming judgment against Babylon, God said through His prophet, **Prepare the nations against her, call together against her the kingdoms of Ararat, Minni and ASHKENAZ** (Jeremiah 51:27). So the **ASHKENAZ** nation was a strong and formidable kingdom even in Old Testament times.

That Ashkenazi Jews are not a Semitic people should be obvious to everyone who has studied the Old Testament. **Ashkenaz** was **the son of Gomer** and grandson of **Japeth**, as well as being the nephew of **Magog, Meshech and Tubal** (Genesis 10:2-3, I Chronicles 1:6). When **Magog, Meshech, Tubal, Gomer and Togarmah** are mentioned in the 38th Chapter of Ezekiel, it should be remembered that all of these men were immediate family members of **Ashkenaz**. So the Ashkenazi people must have lived near the tribes of those other Japhethites somewhere northwest of Babylon.

Presumably, in later centuries the Ashkenazim people migrated over the Caucasus mountains to settle in Khazaria, the rich and fertile region between the Black Sea and Caspian Sea, which is now part of Southern Russia and Southeastern Ukraine. There they grew into a strong and powerful empire which, when the entire population converted to Judaism in the Eighth Century, was greater than the previous kingdom of Israel which had existed in Palestine during the reign of King Solomon. We might have expected that they would have called their new location Ashkenaz, but what is now the Caspian Sea was called the Sea of Khazaria before they settled there. So they retained Khazaria, the original name of the region, as the name of their new homeland. But they also continued to be identified as the Ashkenazim people.

In later centuries the Khazars were gradually driven out of their homeland and migrated northward into Europe, especially Russia, Poland and Germany. When rabbis originally came to Khazaria from Spain, Constantinople and other places to teach Judaism to the population, they used the Hebrew alphabet to provide literature for their purposes. The written language of Khazaria was thenceforth reproduced in Hebrew letters, even though it had hardly any Hebrew words in it. When the Ashkenazim people migrated, or were forced to migrate, northward into other countries, they took their language with them. And that, together with their adopted Hebrew religion, helped to identify them as a separate and distinct ethnic people group. The language came to be called Yiddish, and they were known in Europe as "the Yiddish people." Yiddish was the official language of Biro-Bidjan, a predominantly Jewish region of the Soviet Union, which became a third "national homeland" for Jewish people. The first was Palestine and the second was Khazaria. Yiddish was spoken by all of the Jewish people living in Russia and every other country of Eastern Europe, and by most of those living in Western Europe.

When Ashkenazi Yiddish people settled within the eastern part of what is now Germany, they were the business and intellectual leaders of the region. Through their educational influence, many Yiddish words were incorporated into the language of eastern Germany, but not that of what is now western Germany. Because of this, some Europeans thought Yiddish might have developed in Germany, but it was the other way around in that Yiddish teachers exerted a marked influence on the language of eastern Germany 800 years ago. Most of the four or five million Jews who migrated to the USA and other countries from Europe were the Ashkenazim, or Yiddish-speaking people.

Another interesting nationality group are the totally black Lemba Jews of Zimbabwe, South Africa and other areas in that general region. They number hundreds of thousands and are in stark contrast to the white Ashkenazim Jews of South Africa. The two groups do not generally associate together, even though traces of Levant DNA have been found in some of the Lemba people. The obvious reason is the same as why traces of European DNA can be found among black tribespeople of Liberia. When the forefathers of these Liberians were slaves in America, some were illegitimate children of their owners on Southern plantations. No doubt some ancestors of the Lemba tribes were once slaves in the Middle East, as were some of the forefathers of black Ethiopian Jews.

The point of all this is that those whom we now call "the

Jewish people" originally came from many nations, and few if any are related to Abraham and the original Israelites of Bible times. Since the days of Queen Esther, the Maccabees and the Khazars, the promises God made to Abraham regarding his biological descendants had no bearing on the millions of proselytes who came to be called Judaeans. In addition to the Yiddish people from Khazaria, there are today the Sephardim, originally from Spain, Portugal and Morocco (who may possibly be partially related to the original Hebrews), and also Chinese Jews, Indian Jews, Ethiopian Jews and residents of many other countries who are included among those we now call "the Jewish people." I have heard estimates that nearly a million ethnic tribespeople of India call themselves "Jews." A large number are natives of Assam and Manipur in the Northeast, but indigenous people identified as Jews can be found in other parts of India as well.

When actress Elizabeth Taylor, of English ancestry, chose to become a Jewish person, that did not suddenly make her an heir to God's promises to Abraham. Nor did it change the status of entertainer Sammy Davis, Jr. (of African ancestry) when he decided to become a Jewish man. The Jewish people today are a polyglot of many nations, and should not in any way be compared to the twelve tribes of Israel before the days of Esther in Old Testament times.

So there are no "chosen people" any more, and haven't been in God's sight since the original Hebrews were **broken off the olive tree** when the New Covenant period began. Rather, there are today those whom we call "the Jewish people" whose ancestors came from at least fifty different nations. None of them have a clearly defined blood relationship to Abraham, Isaac and Jacob who lived four thousand years ago. And there are millions more, such as the Palestinians, whose Hebrew ancestors converted to Christianity or Islam, who would therefore be eligible for inclusion among the "chosen people" if the designation was based on the fact that their ancestors were Hebrews.

Chapter 21

Is the Fig Tree a Symbol
of the Israelites?

Yes, it is so used on two occasions in the New Testament. But the olive tree is used several times to symbolize the Hebrew tribes.

In chronological order, the first usage occurs in Luke 13:6-9: **A certain man** [who] **had a fig tree sought fruit thereon and found none. So he said, "Three years I seek fruit on this fig tree and find none: so cut it down."**

But his servant said, "Let it alone this year also until I cultivate and fertilize it. If it bears fruit, well: if not, then thou shalt cut it down."

Which is exactly what Christ did with unfruitful Israel after He and His disciples had ministered to the nation in vain: **The kingdom of God shall be taken from you, and given to people bringing forth the fruits thereof** (Matthew 21:43).

In the Apocalypse our Lord revealed that **THE TIME WAS AT HAND** for the unfruitful fig tree to be cut down and cast out of His garden.

The second time when a fig tree was mentioned as a parable of the Israelites was when our Lord spent a night in Bethany during His final week. Returning to Jerusalem next morning he was hungry, but when he approached a fig tree, He found no fruit on it, but leaves only. So He said, **Let no fruit grow on you henceforward for ever. And the fig tree withered away** (Matthew 21:19)

It should be obvious to us that the Messiah did this act to illustrate what He was experiencing during His visit to Jerusalem. He had come to His temple but found no spiritual fruit there. Rather, He called it **a house of merchandise** and **a den of thieves**. So He let it be known that He was finished with that unfruitful tree. He was not going to leave one stone upon another of that earthly temple. With regard to its relationship to God, Israel as a nation was going to **wither away** and be **dried up from the roots** (Mark 11:20).

The word used most frequently to indicate that terminal judgment is **DESOLATE**. It occurs more than one hundred times in **Isaiah, Jeremiah** and **Ezekiel** to foretell the eventual destiny of both Judah and Israel. Then, in His final denunciation of His own people, the Messiah said, **Behold, your house is left unto you DESOLATE** (Matthew 23:38). The fig tree will be **dried up from the roots** and **NO** [spiritual] **FRUIT WILL GROW ON THEE HENCEFORWARD FOREVER.** The term **DESOLATE** was also used by Daniel to foretell how God would eventually discard the Israelites as a nation because of their abominations.

The Lord Jesus used a fig tree in a different way also. Regarding His second coming, **He spoke to them a parable, Behold the fig tree, and all other trees; when they shoot forth their leaves you know that summer is near at hand. So likewise, when you see these things come to pass you know that the kingdom of God is near at hand** (Luke 21:29-31).

The point of this parable is that the second coming of our Saviour will be like the budding of all different trees in springtime. The preliminary buds will be **signs in the sun, and in the moon, and in the stars; and upon the earth distress of nations, with perplexity; the sea and the waves roaring, men's hearts failing them for fear, and for looking after those things which are coming on the earth: for the powers of heaven shall be shaken** (Luke 21:25-26).

There is no way that the parable of the budding of the trees can be logically applied to the Israelites. No such association is made in the New Testament in any way whatsoever. Those who have attempted to make such applications are trying to read into the biblical record something that simply isn't there.

The olive tree is the one that is symbolic of "Israel" in Scripture. Under the Old Covenant God wanted the seed of Abraham to be His olive tree bearing witness for Him to other nations. But He was continually breaking off the dead branches. All of Abraham's many sons were broken off except one, Isaac. Then his grandson, Esau, was broken off, along with his posterity.

At one point God threatened to break off the entire twelve Hebrew tribes and start over again with one person. It was while Moses was on Mount Sinai receiving the law, and the whole company of Israelites down below went into idolatry. **And the Lord said unto Moses, Your people which you brought out of Egypt have corrupted themselves . . . they have made them a molten calf and have worshipped it . . . I have seen this people and behold, it is a stiffnecked people: now therefore let me alone, that my wrath may wax hot against them, and that I may consume them: and I will make of thee a great nation** (Exodus 32:7-9).

At this point God's word gives us a striking example of the efficacy of intercessory prayer, as Moses pleaded with God to spare those wicked sinners. But it was not for their sakes that the Lord God Almighty spared them, but rather to protect the honor of His name. His purpose for the Hebrew nation was to have a people for His name on this earth. If they failed to fulfill that purpose, then He needed them no longer.

Through Moses God listed dozens of offenses for which souls would be **cut off from Israel**. Likewise the prophets repeatedly stated how God had rejected all Hebrews who committed spiritual whoredom. The Messiah said to the Israelites, **The kingdom of God shall be taken away from you and given to people bringing forth the fruits thereof** (Matthew 21:43).

But it was through the Apostle Paul that the Holy Spirit revealed the parable of God's family olive tree. **Because of unbelief** [disobedience] **the original branches** [the Israelites] **were broken off and believers from other nations were grafted in instead**

(Romans 11:17, 19). Thereafter, in order for any Hebrew person to be included in God's covenant he had to be **grafted into the olive tree** by repentance and faith in Christ the same as non-Hebrews (Romans 11:23). Thus the **olive tree** is a picture of God's people on this earth. Each individual must be **grafted in** by faith in Christ. This expression is identical in meaning to **being born again**. These metaphors help us visualize how we become **children of God** by faith in Christ.

The point of the **fig tree** incident in Matthew 21:19 and Mark 11:14 was to let us know that God would not recognize natural generation any longer. All men are **born in sin, dead to God** (Romans 5:12) and there was no way that the Israelites could be any different. Their 2000 year history up until the coming of the Messiah demonstrated that fact. To introduce the transition, our Lord chose **a man of the Pharisees named Nicodemus, a ruler of the Judaeans, a teacher of Israel** (John 3:1,10) and told him **That which is born of the flesh is flesh**, and **Except a man be born again he cannot see the kingdom of God**. The Israelites who refused to accept Christ **were condemned already** and **shall not see life, but the wrath of God abides on them** (John 3:18, 36).

Bibles teachers who want to extend God's recognition of the Israelites as a special people beyond the Messiah's generation are in grievous error; what they are doing is in denial and contradiction of God's clear revelation in the New Testament. Those who say that the formation of the State of Israel by political Zionists is "the budding of the fig tree" have no basis whatsoever in the New Testament for such conclusions.

Our Lord also gave us several other parables to teach how the Israelites, other than **the elect remnant** (12,000 from each tribe), would be terminated as "God's earthly people."

One example is the parable of the vineyard in Matthew 21:33-41 and Luke 20:9-16). **When the chief priests and the Pharisees heard it, they perceived that He spake of them.** The **householder who planted the vineyard** is God. The **vineyard** is His witness on earth. The **husbandmen** to whom He entrusted it were the Israelites. When God **sent His servants** [the Old Testament prophets] **that they might receive the fruits of it, they** [Judaeans] **took His servants and beat one and killed another and stoned another. Again He sent other servants more than the first: and they did unto them likewise. Last of all He sent unto them His Son, saying, They will reverence my Son. But the husbandmen** [the Israelites] **said, This is the heir; come, let us kill Him and seize His inheritance. And they caught Him, and cast Him out of the vineyard and slew Him. Therefore the Lord of the vineyard will miserably destroy those wicked men, and will let out His vineyard to other husbandmen which will render Him the fruits in their seasons. Therefore I say unto you, the kingdom of God shall be taken from you and given to people bringing forth the fruits thereof.**

What could be more obvious to anyone than that in this parable our Lord is saying that God will no longer rely on natural generation for His witness on earth. Rather, **His vineyard** will be in the hands of people who have been **born again** and have become **new creatures in Christ Jesus.**

Another parable which teaches likewise is that of **a certain king who made a marriage for his son** (Matthew 22:2). Obviously, the king is God and His Son is the Messiah **who came unto His own and His own received Him not** (John 1:11). The **marriage** is that which was announced by John the Baptizer: **Repent, for the kingdom of the heavens is at hand. John was a voice crying, Prepare ye the way of the Lord. I baptize you with water but He shall baptize you with the Holy Spirit.** John was the first of many **servants which the king sent forth to call them that were bidden to the wedding. But they would not come. They** [unregenerate Judaeans] **took His servants and entreated them spitefully and slew them.** This looks forward to the time when the gospel of salvation was preached **to the Judaeans first** after the **day of Pentecost.** Then the king **sent forth His armies and destroyed those murderers and burned up their city.** This prophecy was literally fulfilled during **the days of vengeance, 66-70 A.D.**

265

Still another parable on this subject begins in Luke 19:12. **A certain nobleman went into a far country to receive for Himself a kingdom, and to return.** This is the Messiah after His **resurrection** and exaltation as **King of all Kings.** His **ten servants** are the apostles and others **who would believe on Him through their word.** It was to them that He said, **Occupy till I come.** But the Judaeans (other than the **elect remnant of 144,000 from the twelve tribes**) who should have proclaimed Him as their Messiah, rejected Him. They are pictured as **His citizens** [who] **hated Him and sent a message after Him, saying, We will not have this man to reign over us.** Forty years later there was a literal fulfillment of the prophecy in the parable: **Those mine enemies, which would not that I should reign over them, bring hither and slay them before me** (Luke 19:27).

But the compassionate Christ spoke those fateful words with deep sorrow. **When He was come near** [to Jerusalem] **He beheld the city, and wept over it, saying, If you had known, at least in this thy day, the things which belong unto thy peace! But now they are hidden from thine eyes. For the days shall come when your enemies shall cast a trench about you, and compass you around, and keep you in on every side, and lay you even with the ground, and your children within, because you knew not the time of your visitation** (Luke 19:41-44). Those fateful words were literally fulfilled during the three-and-a-half years of **great tribulation** that began thirty-six years later.

From that time forth all of the Israelites were **broken off the olive tree** of God's inheritance except for **the elect remnant (144,000)** from the twelve tribes who alone were recognized as God's inheritance. Collectively, they were called **ALL ISRAEL** (Romans 9:6-8, 11:5-7, 26). This **remnant** is pictured as **a woman who had on her head a crown of twelve stars** (Revelation 12:1). But none of the biological descendants of those **144,000** Hebrews were counted as being children of God as a result of having Christian parents. Each one had to be individually **justified by faith** in order to **have peace with God** (Romans 5:1). Concerning the **144,000** represented by the woman in Revelation 12, **the remnant of her seed** are they **which have the testimony of Jesus Christ** (verse 17).

So there is no way that **the fig tree** in the New Testament can be said to typify present-day Jewish people, or the state of Israel, or any other unsaved, unregenerate people. Those who so teach are spiritual babies who need to **grow in knowledge** to a point where they comprehend that **God is no respecter of persons.** There are only two kinds of people in His sight: saved and unsaved; or those who are eternally separated and cut off from Him and those who have made peace with Him through faith in Christ and are now members of His family and heirs to His promises.

Chapter 22

Was the Holocaust Foretold in Scripture?

Numerous forthcoming holocausts were foretold in the New Testament. Three of them identify the specific people group which would suffer. But all three pertained to that period in history, not to the present time.

The term HOLOCAUST does not appear in the Bible. It is a combination of two Greek words: *holos*, meaning "whole," and *kaustos*, meaning "burnt." The ancient Hebrews are believed to have associated the Greek word with the concept of a **whole burnt sacrifice** mentioned in Deuteronomy 33:10. The 1951 edition of ENCYCLOPEDIA BRITANNICA used it this way: *The 1918 influenza epidemic was the most destructive in history; in fact it ranks with the plague of Justinian and the Black Death as one of the most severe HOLOCAUSTS of disease ever encountered.* I have seen estimates as high as 100 million for the number of people who died from the 1918 epidemic. That's more than triple the number who were killed in the World War which was just ending. The Sixth Century plague during the reign of Justinian wiped out half the population of the Byzantine Roman Empire. During the Fourteenth Century bubonic plague, or "black death," killed half the population of Europe and western Asia.

So the most destructive of all "holocausts" have been caused by microscopic microbes that have taken the lives of billions of human beings throughout the centuries. Malaria alone has killed over a billion people, including my grandparents when they were only 37 years old. That such plagues would be forthcoming is mentioned frequently in the Apocalypse, as are holocausts implemented by men. Our Lord foretold how **nation would rise against nation and kingdom against kingdom** (Matthew 24:7). But none of these things signify the end of the age. **Ye shall hear of wars and rumors of wars: see that ye be not troubled: for all these things must come to pass, but the end is not yet. There shall be famines and pestilences and earthquakes. All these are only the beginning of sorrows** [suffering] **that shall come** (Matthew 24:6-8).

Many of the most horrible holocausts have occurred during terrible wars that have caused untold suffering for billions of people throughout the centuries. At any given time in history numerous wars were being fought somewhere on our planet, causing widespread death and destruction. These tragic conflicts have been personal holocausts for those who have lost homes and properties, who have been killed or wounded, and have lost members of their families forever.

The most widespread use of the term HOLOCAUST in our day has been by the Jewish people in reference to what they suffered from the Nazi regime in Europe during the World War II period. Surely, as conscientious Christians we share our deepest concern and utmost sympathy with all who were victims of injustice and persecution during that frightful time. The concept of a "whole burnt sacrifice" is indeed appropriate because the entire Jewish community was affected in every country occupied by Germany up until the end of the war.

But even as we offer our condolences to our Jewish friends, we must not ignore other people groups which have also endured terrible periods of suffering at the hands of their fellow human beings.

I experienced firsthand some exposure to the aftermath of a terrible holocaust while traveling through India in 1948. After arrival at the Delhi airport I rode a bus into the city and was horrified to see hundreds of thousands of starving people along the roadsides and sitting helplessly without shelter on sidewalks throughout the city. Mothers sadly clutched their emaciated children, helpless to alleviate the hunger that was slowly killing them one by one. The railway station was packed with families lying on the floor, seeking shelter and begging for food. The main station in Calcutta was totally congested, with an estimated 10,000 refugees crowding all available floor space.

Following independence and the end of British rule in 1947, some Islamic leaders called for partition of the country with East Bengal becoming East Pakistan, and the western region becoming West Pakistan. In Urdu the name "Pakistan" means "Holy Land." But some Muslims must have thought it wouldn't be holy with Hindus living there, so they started killing hundreds of thousands of Hindus and taking their property. Millions had to flee empty handed across the borders into India, but upon arrival they found millions of Muslims living there. So these Hindu refugees began killing thousands of Muslims and taking their property. I have seen reliable estimates that over seven million people were killed or died of starvation, including both Hindus and Muslims. Eye witnesses on both sides told me how they were horrified to see "dead bodies stacked like cordwood." The Hindus had no firewood with which to burn their own, and the Muslims had no laborers left alive who could dig the needed graves. In addition to those killed, the total number of refugees who had to abandon everything and flee across the borders was probably in excess of ten million. The killing was finally stopped when Mahatma Gandhi endured a "fast unto death," refusing to eat until peace was restored. For so doing Gandhi was killed by a fellow Hindu that wanted to continue killing Muslims. That was indeed a terrible HOLOCAUST period for those pitiful victims of political division based on religious segregation.

Some Palestinian Christian refugees have told me that what they suffered from the Zionists is comparable to that experienced by the Hindus who were driven out of Pakistan. But even though the circumstances are somewhat similar, the scope is much smaller. As the British were preparing to leave Palestine, on April 9, 1948 a team of militant Zionists invaded the town of Deir Yassin and brutally murdered about 250 Palestinian residents. Then they spread the word that as soon as the British left they intended to do likewise to the native people of every town in Palestine. An estimated 250,000 indigenous Palestinians fled for refuge to neighboring countries, and Zionist immigrants quickly occupied their houses. Soon thereafter on May 14, 1948, the "State of Israel" was declared. During the wars that followed, two or three million more Palestinian natives were uprooted and displaced, losing everything they owned. At least a million barely stayed alive in the squalor of refugee camps.

So it is easy to see why Palestinians, forty percent of whom were nominal Christians, since 1948 have spoken of the Zionist occupation as being their "holocaust." But even though almost the whole population of native Palestinians have been adversely affected, the loss of life in no way compares with what the Jewish people suffered from the Nazi regime. However, there is one major difference: since 1945 the German government has paid over thirty billion dollars in reparations to Jewish people who lost homes, property or relatives during the World War II era; but as far as I have been able to determine, the government of Israel has paid nothing to the Palestinians who lost everything after April 9, 1948.

Deaths and deprivation suffered by Jewish people in Europe during World War II gained sympathy and compensation for them from millions of non-Jews in many countries. But those who have expressed sympathy and demanded justice for deprived and dislocated Palestinians have often been labeled as being "anti-Semitic." It is blatantly false to say that people are concerned for Palestinian refugees "because they hate Jews." It has nothing to do with a so-called "rising tide of anti-Semitism." Rather, it is a universal expression of belief in fair play and relief of suffering for more than two million Palestinians who were expelled from their homes and deprived of their freedom and property. Hundreds of thousands of conscientious Jews inside and outside of Israel are included among those who demand justice for victims of the Palestinian "holocaust."

Many other terrible "holocausts" have been waged against minority groups during the past century. Armenians say that more than 90% of their people who were living in Turkey were killed or displaced by Muslims during the genocide of 1915-1919. The Japanese inflicted a terrible holocaust upon eastern China from 1937 to 1945. Millions of Japanese women and children were killed or left homeless by incendiary bombs dropped by Americans, climaxed by atomic weapons that obliterated two cities instantly. The British holocaust was caused by Nazi bombs on London and other cities during the war. But civilians in Germany suffered far greater losses, as Allied air raids destroyed every major city, devastating or ending millions of lives. And every American who has faced military combat has had a personal holocaust during one or more of the many wars in which they have served.

An estimated three million Cambodians, more than half the population of their country, were brutally massacred under the mad rule of Pol Pot of the Khmer Rouge. Most were bludgeoned to death with farm tools or clubs. And the entire Tutsi population of Rwanda was decimated by rival Hutus in 1995. Over one million died and three million fled on foot to neighboring countries. Soon thereafter an estimated three million natives died in neighboring Congo. And the list goes on, in one country after another. Hundreds die in "holocausts" somewhere in the world with every passing day.

One of the most disturbing ironies of history is that the most horrible holocausts of all time were perpetrated by the disciples of an Ashkenazi Jewish man named Karl Heinrich Marx, who was born in Germany in 1818. Perhaps even more ironic is the fact that when Karl was six years old his father became a "Messianic Jew" and was baptized as a Protestant. In 1847 Karl Marx, together with his fellow-terrorist Friedrich Engles, published the COMMUNIST MANIFESTO which would be used by their followers as a blueprint for the slaughter, enslavement, imprisonment, deprivation or debilitation of more than a billion victims. With one exception, no other holocaust in history can be compared with that inflicted upon their fellow human beings by Marxists tyrants Trotsky, Lenin, Stalin and their successors in the Soviet Union for seventy years from 1917 to 1987.

And another paradox of history is that one of the evil villains who began this monstrous procession of horrors was a Jewish man named Leib Bronstein. Together with numerous young Marxist atheists which he recruited in New York, he went to Russia in 1917 to lead the Bolshevik revolution, changing his name to Leon Trotsky. Together with Nikolai Lenin he seized upon Marx's concept of "the dictatorship of the proletariat" as an excuse to exercise absolute power over the population, killing anyone and everyone who was not in complete subjection to his rule. Lenin did likewise after he gradually replaced Trotsky as leader of the revolution. Lenin's successor, Joseph Stalin, was probably responsible for the death, displacement and imprisonment of more people than any tyrant in history, except one. And that holocaust was continued by the dictators who followed him, until the collapse of Soviet Communism around 1990.

The only holocaust that possibly exceeded the horrors which occurred in the Soviet Union was the reign of terror exercised in China by Mao Tse-tung from 1949 until his death in 1976. And the communist dictators who followed him in China continued the holocaust for another thirty years, although to a lesser extent. No one knows how many millions died under the dictatorship of Mao and his followers, but some estimates put the figure as high as sixty million. And the number who were dislocated, being deprived of their homes and property, and put to forced labor in prison camps or communes was probably more than two hundred million.

Other Marxist despots who seized ownership and control of wealth and property, while depriving their citizens of life and liberty in their respective countries, would include Kim Il Sung in North Korea from 1946 until 1994 (followed by his son Jong Il), Fidel Castro in Cuba since 1959, Ho Chi Minh in Vietnam (1945-69) and many others in Asia, Africa and Latin America. There can be no doubt that despotic followers of Karl Marx have implemented the most horrible series of holocausts in all of human history.

Were any of these terrible man-against-man holocausts foretold in the New Testament? Or those caused by plagues, earthquakes, asteroids, floods, storms or volcanoes? The answer is "yes" in a general sense, but not specifically. For example, the **myriads of horsemen from the east** (Revelation 9:16) foreshadow the hordes of Asian invaders led by such conquerors as Attila the Hun (450 A.D.) and Genghis Khan (1200) **by whom the third part of men were killed** (Revelation 9:18). The forces led by Genghis alone are said to have killed over five million. Some say that the "Black Death" plague, which wiped out half the population of Europe in the Fourteenth Century, was God's judgment against the Roman Catholic "Inquisition": **I heard a voice saying to the angels, Go your ways and pour out the vials of the wrath of God. And the first went and poured out his vial upon the earth; and there fell a grievous sore upon the men which had the mark of the beast** [Rome]**, and them which worshipped his image** [the Papacy] (Revelation 16:1-2). I am not sure, however, as to whether or not these general predictions refer to specific "holocausts" which were to come.

However, three specific holocausts are foretold in the New Testament. The first concerned the **elect remnant (144,000)** of Hebrew believers who are called **ALL ISRAEL** (Romans 9:6-8, 11:26), and **THE ISRAEL OF GOD** (Galatians 6:16). After 5000 of them were driven out of Jerusalem by **a great persecution** (Acts 8:1) from their fellow (unbelieving) Hebrews, Peter wrote a letter to them saying: **Think it not strange concerning the fiery trial which is to try you . . . that the trial of your faith, being much more precious than of gold which perisheth, though it be tried with fire might be found unto praise and honor and glory at the appearing of Jesus Christ** (I Peter 1:7, 4:12). Here for the first time we have the figure of the **burnt sacrifice** or HOLOCAUST being used to identify suffering. And, appropriately, it had reference to Hebrew believers who, tragically, were being put through the fires of suffering by their fellow Judaeans who did not believe.

The second HOLOCAUST foretold in the New Testament

depicted God's fiery judgment upon the unrighteous Hebrew majority which rejected His Son who had been sent to be their Messiah and Saviour. **He came unto His own, and His own received Him not** (John 1:11). **Him ye have taken and by wicked hands have crucified and slain . . . the Just One, of whom you have been the betrayers and murderers** (Acts 2:23, 7:52). I have already described (in Chapter Nine) the holocaust which came forty years later when God **sent forth His armies and destroyed those murderers and burned up their city** (foretold in Matthew 22:7). Those three and a half years of internal strife and bloodshed while more than three million Judaeans were bottled up inside the walls of Jerusalem without food or water was a time of **great tribulation** that has never been equaled.

The third specific HOLOCAUST period foretold in the New Testament concerned two centuries of suffering which Christians endured from **the beast** to whom **it was given to make war with the saints, and to overcome them** (Revelation 13:7). We know that this beast was the Roman Empire because it alone had **power over all kindreds, and tongues and nations** (Revelation 13:7). I have mentioned this HOLOCAUST period in more detail in previous chapters.

Sometimes we hear Christians ask, "Why does God allow all this suffering on the earth? Why should there be HOLOCAUSTS?"

The answer to this question takes us to the very heart of ultimate reality, to the nature of man and the meaning of life on our planet.

First of all, we must understand that God is an unseen Spirit, and before He created the first man and first woman in His own image He had already created other unseen spirits. Some people have a problem understanding spirits because we don't see them. But there was a great man named Isaac Newton three hundred years ago who believed in spirits and made a special study of them. For this reason, other scientists were critical of his ideas. Then when Newton postulated that a powerful "unseen force" held planets in orbit around the sun, his peers accused him of witchcraft. They said his silly idea was like saying you could twirl a ball around your body with no string to hold it. But now we know that the "invisible force" which Newton called "gravity" is a powerful and deadly reality. Defy its existence by jumping off a building and it will crush every bone in your body.

God is a Spirit (John 4:24). And just as surely as gravity is present as a mighty "unseen force" throughout the universe, so the presence of Almighty God is everywhere.

But God is also a Person. Someday He will show His people how He can be a Person and also occupy an infinite universe. It will help us to understand now, however, if we examine the first man that God made "in His own image." Our bodies are composed of trillions of cells, each one as complex as a galaxy. How can I be a "person" and occupy such an entire universe? If all the cells in my body were enlarged so that all the atoms and molecules and chromosomes and genes and DNA were visible, they would cover the entire continent of North America. Yet each one of those trillions of cells has a direct, living relationship with my brain and with my heart. This fact is hard to believe, but we know it is true.

Likewise, God hasn't told us all the details regarding His relationship to the universe, except that He created it and occupies it. We know also that He created other spirits, called **angels**, and that some of them rebelled against Him. So there was a spiritual warfare going on already before God created the first man **in His own image**. As created, that man was a human body, but then **God breathed upon his face the breath of lives, and mankind became a living soul** (Genesis 2:7). The word "soul" refers to the whole man, both body and spirit combined. And when God made that first man **a living spirit**, He also made the eternal spirits of all men and women who would later become **living souls** at conception.

As created, that first man had no knowledge of good and evil, or the spiritual warfare that existed around him. In due time, however, it would be revealed that God's purpose in creating man and woman in His own image was that four thousand years later **His only begotten Son** would be born as a man, conceived by the Spirit of God in the womb of a virgin woman. So when God made that first man, He didn't manufacture a computer that would read back only what was pre-programmed into it. He made another spiritual being like unto Himself, with power of choice, which would later be exposed to forces of good and evil. That way His **only begotten Son** would grow up in a difficult environment and be tested in every way that might prove the fidelity of His character. And as no doubt God had hoped and planned, after His Son had experienced thirty years of trials and temptations He could proudly say, **This is my beloved Son in whom I am well pleased** (Matthew 3:17).

After the first man and the first woman were exposed to the knowledge of good and evil, and came under the influence of spiritual beings that were alienated from God, bad things began to happen. Their firstborn son killed his younger brother, marking the beginning of man against man violence that would continue from that day forth. After seven generations the people became **corrupt before God, and the earth was filled with violence** (Genesis 6:11). **And God saw that the wickedness of man was great in the earth, and that every imagination of the thoughts of his heart was only evil continually. And the Lord was sorry that He had made man on the earth, and it grieved Him at His heart. And the Lord said, I will destroy mankind whom I have created from the face of the earth . . . for I am sorry that I have made them** (Genesis 6:5-7). So God cleaned His house and started over with the one chosen family of Noah.

People haven't changed much since those evil days, nor will they ever. Our Lord said that until the time of His return human beings would continue to be as they were **in the days of Noah** (Matthew 24:37-39). That's the main reason why we continue to have man against man holocausts. And let's not forget that Satan is called **the god of this world** who continually motivates people to kill one another.

But another reason why holocausts, especially those which occur in nature, are valuable is because life on this earth is temporary. If we are healthy and prosperous, living in peace and serenity, we tend to become materialistic and indifferent toward eternal life with God. But when we lose everything (home, property, business, friends, family), there in only one thing left, which is our hope of being in Heaven forever. Also, the fires of suffering purify and prove our faith. **Concerning the fiery trial which is to try you, rejoice, inasmuch as you are partakers of Christ's sufferings** (I Peter 4:12-13). **The Captain of our salvation was made perfect through His sufferings** (Hebrews 2:10).

Finally, let's not forget, **Vengeance is mine, I will repay, saith the Lord** (Romans 12:19). **To me belongeth vengeance, the Lord shall judge His people** (Deuteronomy 32:35-36). **The wrath of God is revealed from heaven against all ungodliness and unrighteousness of men** (Romans 1:18). His power restrains the forces of darkness most of the time, but there are occasions when He lifts His restraining hand and allows His enemy to unleash evil activities upon rebellious men and women who have sinned against Him.

And I saw seven angels having the seven last plagues; for in them is filled up the wrath of God (Revelation 15:1). **And I heard a great voice saying, Go your ways and pour out the vials of the wrath of God upon the earth** (Revelation 16:1). **And the rest of the men which were not killed by these plagues yet repented not, that they should not worship devils, and idols of gold and silver and stone and of wood: which neither can see nor hear nor walk. Neither repented they of their murders, nor of their sorceries, nor of their fornication, nor of their thefts** (Revelation 9:20-21). **Thou art righteous, O Lord, because thou hast judged thus. Even so, Lord God Almighty, true and righteous are thy judgments** (Revelation 16:5, 7).

Chapter 23

Are We Living in the Last Days?

The term **LAST DAYS** is used two ways in Scripture. There are the **last days** of the Old Covenant period, and the **last days** of the New Covenant period, or "church age," in which we live now.

God, who at sundry times and in divers manners spake in time past unto the fathers by the prophets, hath in these LAST DAYS spoken to us by His Son (Hebrews 1:1-2). The coming of the Lord Jesus marked the beginning of the LAST DAYS of the Old Covenant period. Those **LAST DAYS** continued on for about forty years, and were finalized by **the days of vengeance** from 66 to 70 A.D. when God concluded His dealings with the unfaithful Israelites (other than the **elect remnant, 144,000**, who alone He recognized as being **ALL ISRAEL**) by unleashing His terminal judgment upon them.

A major event foretold to occur at the end of the Old Covenant period was the inclusion of other nations besides the Israelites within the covenant people of God. When the Holy Spirit was poured out upon **devout men from every nation under heaven** (Acts 2:5) on the day of Pentecost, **Peter lifted up his voice and said . . . this is that which was spoken by the prophet Joel: it shall come to pass in the LAST DAYS, saith God, I will pour out my Spirit upon ALL FLESH** [meaning ALL NATIONS, not just Judaeans] . . . **and on my servants and on my handmaidens I will pour out in those [LAST] DAYS of my Spirit** (Acts 2:14-18).

Based upon Peter's quotation, we must conclude that Joel's prophecy speaks of the LAST DAYS of the Old Covenant period; but as we read the entire prophecy we can see that Joel was one of very few Old Testament prophets who spoke also of the second coming of the Messiah: **And I will show wonders in the heavens above, and signs in the earth beneath . . . the sun shall be turned into darkness, and the moon into blood, before that great and notable DAY of the Lord come** (Acts 2:19-20, quoted from Joel 3:28-31).

Another prophet who foretold the end [LAST DAYS] of the Old Covenant period was Jeremiah: **Behold the [LAST] DAYS come, said the Lord, when I will make a new covenant with the house of Israel, and the house of Judah: not according to the covenant with their fathers in the day that I took them out of the land of Egypt; which my covenant they broke . . . but this shall be the covenant that I will make with the house of Israel; after those [LAST] DAYS, saith the Lord, I will put my law in their inward parts, and write it in their hearts . . . and they shall teach no more every man his neighbor, saying, Know the Lord: for they shall all know me, from the least unto the greatest of them** (Jeremiah 31:31-34). This entire passage is quoted in the Epistle to the Hebrews (8:8-11) to explain the transition from the Old Covenant to the New Covenant, which took place during the LAST DAYS (40 years) of the Old Covenant period. After that transition period God did away with the Old Covenant entirely: **In that He saith, A NEW COVENANT, He made the first old. Now that which decayeth and waxeth old is ready to vanish away** (Hebrews 8:13). As far as God was concerned, the Old Covenant did **vanish away** when our Lord said **This is my blood of the New Covenant which is shed for many for the remission of sins** (Matthew 26:28). He thus fulfilled and forever terminated all of the Old Covenant rituals of animal sacrifices and intercessory priests **which can never take away sins** (Hebrews 10:11). By offering His own blood as a sacrifice for our sins, the Son of God became **the mediator of the new covenant** (Hebrews 9:15) and forever abrogated further recognition of the old covenant as having any validity in the sight of God: **He taketh away the first, that He may establish the second** (Hebrews 10:9). And as if to affirm and finalize the transition from the first covenant to the second, God saw to it that the temple in Jerusalem was destroyed at the end of the LAST DAYS of the Old Covenant period in the year 70 A.D.

Now what about the LAST DAYS of the New Covenant period? I have already explained that events mentioned in Matthew 24:5-13 are not unique to the LAST DAYS of the church age. False prophets, false Christs, persecution, Christians going through tribulation, wars, famines, pestilences, earthquakes in divers places: all of these things have been going on for almost 2000 years. None are indicative of our Lord's imminent return, or that the LAST DAYS of this age have arrived. There are, however, several New Testament passages that do refer to the LAST DAYS of this present age.

A panorama of the highlights of history may be found in the Fourteenth Chapter of the Apocalypse. Verses 1-5 speak of the last and final "Israel," the **remnant (144,000)** called "all Israel" which our Lord called out from 30 A.D. to 70 A.D. to give His gospel to other nations (vs. 6-7). Next, the conclusive judgment upon the Israelites which took place 66-70 A.D. is mentioned in verse 8. Then in verses 9-13 there is a jump ahead to the dark ages (400-1600 A.D.) when true believers paid a terrible price for their refusal to conform to idolatrous practices forced upon them by the Vatican. After this terrible period there is a picture of the great evangelistic harvests that began in the Eighteenth Century and are still going on today (verses 14-16). Finally, there is a reference to things that will happen when our Lord Jesus comes again in power and great glory (vs. 17-20).

Today we are in the EVANGELISTIC HARVEST period which was foretold to take place just prior to the second coming of our Saviour. When the harvest has been reaped, He will come again, as He said: **This gospel of the kingdom shall be preached in all the world for a witness unto all nations; and then shall the end come** [Matthew 24:14].

The harvest metaphor is used several places in Scripture: **Lift up your eyes and look on the fields; for they are white already to harvest. He that reapeth . . . gathereth fruit unto life eternal** [John 4:35-36]. **Thrust in thy sickle, and reap: for the time is come for thee to reap; for the harvest of the earth is ripe. And he that sat on the cloud thrust in his sickle on the earth; and the earth was reaped** [Revelation 14:15-16]. This reaping began around 1750 when some European believers called Moravians began to send out missionaries to foreign countries. It was through their witness that John Wesley found salvation in Christ, and became the first preacher to evangelize large crowds in open-air meetings, mainly in England. His disciples, called Methodists, carried on the harvest for more than a century, both in Britain and in the American colonies. Contemporary with Wesley was George Whitefield who was also used of God to reap a great harvest of souls in Britain and America. From that time until now the reapers have brought millions of lost souls into the kingdom of God on every continent.

"**What shall be the sign of thy coming, and of the end of the age?**" the disciples asked. And our Lord gave only one sign: "**The gospel must first be published among all nations**" [Mark 13:10]. So as we look for indications of the approaching time of His coming, there is only one place to look: WATCH THE SPREAD OF HIS GOSPEL AMONG ALL NATIONS. His coming has nothing whatsoever to do with events in Palestine, the state of Israel, the city of Jerusalem, or any other location or people in that part of the world. Rather, as He said to Abraham, and through His apostles, His first concern is to **visit the nations, to take out of them a people for His name** [Acts 15:14]. There are more than 6000 nations in this world, and when our Saviour has received some from all of them into His body (church), He will come again to receive us unto Himself and wipe away all tears from the eyes of those who suffer for His sake.

So are we getting close? Is the time drawing near when His body, His bride will be completed; when **His wife has made herself ready** [Revelation 19:7]? The Eighteenth Century could be called the firstfruits. That period was the beginning of the end. Then, during the Nineteenth Century things really started moving. Missionaries began to go out to China, India, many parts of Africa and other places where hitherto our Lord had no people for His name. And there were great evangelistic campaigns also, such as those conducted by Dwight L. Moody and his team.

Following World War II an evangelism and missionary explosion that was totally without precedent spread throughout the world. Hundreds of new mission boards and evangelistic organizations sprang up and multiplied, and through them millions of new believers were brought into the kingdom of God. Indigenous missions took root and grew in countries that were formerly called "mission fields," and through them more millions of new believers were added unto the Lord. Huge evangelistic meetings were conducted by gifted evangelists such as Billy Graham, Nicholas Bhengu (in Africa) and many others.

On the other hand, **in the LAST DAYS perilous times shall come. For men shall be lovers of their own selves, covetous, boasters, proud, blasphemers, disobedient to parents, unthankful, unholy, without natural affection, trucebreakers, false accusers, incontinent, fierce, despisers of those that are good, traitors, heady, highminded, lovers of pleasures more than lovers of God . . . ever learning, but never able to come to the knowledge of the truth** (II Timothy 3:1-7). What we can learn from this prophecy is that human beings, in general, are basically self-centered and rebellious against God. **The heart is deceitful above all things, and desperately wicked: who can know it** (Jeremiah 17:9). Little has changed since those words were written, except for true believers who have been reconciled to God by faith in the atoning sacrifice of Christ, and have been given a new heart by the indwelling power and presence of His Holy Spirit. **Therefore, if any man be in Christ, he is a new creature: old things are passed away; behold, all things are become new** (II Corinthians 5:17).

While it is true that there are millions of born again Christians in the world today, all of us put together probably make up less than five percent of the total population of this planet. While the figure might be higher in some countries like South Korea, it is much lower (almost zero) in such places as Tibet and Saudi Arabia. And in countries like the USA where evangelical churches flourish, true believers are nevertheless at the mercy of the unsaved majority who control sources of information such as movies, television and public education. Unbelievers, therefore, strongly influence moral standards and human behavior. I have watched the behavioral patterns of the U.S. population for seventy years, and seen how vile and ungodly conduct portrayed in films and television programs is soon followed and imitated by a majority of the population.

As it was in the days of Noah, so shall it be also in the days of the Son of man. They did eat, they drank, they married wives, they were given in marriage, until the day that Noah entered into the ark, and the flood came and destroyed them all. Likewise also as it was in the days of Lot; they did eat, they drank, they bought, they sold, they planted, they builded: but the same day that Lot went out of Sodom it rained fire and brimstone from heaven, and destroyed them all. Even thus shall it be in the day when the Son of man is revealed (Luke 17:26-30).

These verses indicate that the LAST DAYS will be business as usual for the general population of the world. Most people will be preoccupied with the cares of this life, having no time or thought for their Creator. There will be no warning signs to let them know in advance that the planet is about to be invaded by the Supreme Being from outer space. **For yourselves know perfectly that the day of the Lord so cometh as a thief in the night** (I Thessalonians 5:2). Our Lord's return will be completely unexpected by all except true believers who are living in expectation of His coming.

Some prophecy teachers have invented a dramatic scenario of cataclysmic events which they think may be a prelude to the end of the age, but the Scriptures do not say so. In particular, today's would-be prophets predict some political developments or future wars in Israel/Palestine as being the harbinger of the end, similar to the teachings of the Jehovah's Witnesses who warned my mother about the soon coming battle of Armageddon about seventy-five years ago. But what the Scriptures actually teach is that the LAST DAYS will occur during a relatively peaceful period in world history. True, there have been, and always will be, wars going on somewhere on the earth, and no doubt will be as the LAST DAYS burst upon us. But they will not involve the majority of the world's population. Rather, **When they shall say, Peace and safety; then sudden destruction cometh upon them, as travail upon a woman with child, and they shall not escape** (I Thessalonians 5:3). But regarding true believers in Christ, **God hath not appointed us to wrath, but to obtain salvation by our Lord Jesus Christ** (I Thessalonians 5:9). As the LAST DAYS come suddenly upon an unsuspecting planet, we will be **caught up to MEET** our Sovereign Lord AS HE COMES **with His mighty angels, in flaming fire taking vengeance on them that know not God, and that obey not the gospel of our Lord Jesus Christ: who shall be punished with everlasting destruction from the presence of the Lord, and from the glory of His power; when He shall come to be glorified in His saints, and to be admired in all them that believe IN THAT DAY** (II Thessalonians 1:7-10).

One thing we can be sure of: events in Israel/Palestine have no bearing whatsoever on the LAST DAYS before the sudden, unexpected return of our Lord. If so, there would be some mention of it in the New Testament, but there is none. Rather, the one thing we are told to watch is the spread of the gospel among ALL NATIONS. As I have mentioned earlier, our Lord said that when He has a witness IN ALL THE WORLD AMONG ALL NATIONS, **THEN SHALL THE END COME** (Matthew 24:14). I have also discussed the **reaping** metaphors in Revelation 14. Just before the **vine of the earth is cast into the great winepress of the wrath of God** (Revelation 14:19) there will be a great reaping of lost souls throughout the earth (Revelation 14:15-16), as millions from every nation are brought into the kingdom of God. This river of life began as a mere trickle around 1730 and continued to grow throughout the Eighteenth Century. It became a rushing torrent during the Nineteenth

Century when a witness for our Lord was planted in about half the countries of the world. During the Twentieth Century ripe fields were harvested for Christ throughout the world, as churches were planted within almost every country, and multiplied millions were swept into the kingdom of God. This advance of the gospel is the surest indication given to us in the Word of God that we are living in the LAST DAYS immediately preceding the return of our Lord.

Those things which God had showed before by the mouth of all of His prophets, that the Christ should suffer, He hath so fulfilled. Repent ye therefore and be converted, that your sins may be blotted out when the times of refreshing shall come from the presence of the Lord; and He shall send Jesus Christ, who was before preached unto you: whom Heaven must receive until the times of restitution of all things, which God hath spoken by the mouth of all His holy prophets since the world began (Acts 3:18-21).

Chapter 24

Other Issues and Answers

1. <u>WILL THE TEMPLE BE REBUILT IN JERUSALEM?</u>

Which temple? Five different temples are identified in the New Testament.

The term **TEMPLE** is used in Scripture to indicate a place on earth where God dwells, or where He wanted to be present among His people. The most important of all was the body of the Son of God. He said, **Destroy this temple, and in three days I will raise it up. But He spoke of the temple of His body** (John 2:19, 21).

In Old Testament times, God instructed King Solomon to build Him a house so He could come and dwell there in the **Holy of Holies, which was a temporary figure for the time then present** (Hebrews 9:9). **Holy places made with hands are figures of the true** [which is] **Heaven itself** (Hebrews 9:24). So the temples that Solomon built (later destroyed as God's judgment), and which King Herod built a thousand years later, were temporary figures, or illustrations, of true reality. The true **Holy of Holies is Heaven itself. Christ being come an high priest of things to come, by a greater and more perfect temple, not made with hands, not this building; neither by the blood of goats and calves, but with His own blood He entered once for all into the** [true] **holy place, having obtained eternal redemption for us** (Hebrews 9:12-13). The earthly temple in Jerusalem was a temporary picture, awaiting its fulfillment when **the Lamb of God** would be sacrificed **once for all** to atone for the sins of all humanity.

To signify that the building in Jerusalem would serve no further purpose, **the veil of the temple was rent in twain from the top to the bottom** (Matthew 27:51). Thus did God Almighty let it be known once and for all that He would never again recognize an animal sacrifice in that or any other earthly temple made by man. And forty years later He had that temple destroyed, **without one stone left upon another that was not thrown down** (Matthew 24:2). The site was completely cleared in 135, then for the next 500 years it became a rubbish heap until disciples of the Antichrist (Muhammad) came and constructed a gold domed shrine there. But they do not call it a "temple," although a mosque on the site nearby is called "a house of prayer."

In addition to the temporary temple building in Jerusalem, the body of the Lord Jesus and Heaven itself, a fourth temple mentioned in the New Testament is a gathering of believers. As our Lord promised, **Where two or three are gathered together in my name, there am I in the midst of them** (Matthew 18:20). **Ye are the temple of God, and the Spirit of God dwells in your midst**, Paul said to the church at Corinth (I Corinthians 3:16). And the fifth temple is the individual body of a born again believer: **Your body is the temple of the Holy Ghost which is in you, which ye have of God . . . therefore glorify God in your body and in your spirit, which are God's** (I Corinthians 6:19-20).

If present day Zionists, or whoever, should put up a building in Jerusalem which they choose to call a "temple," we can be sure that God in Heaven will have no interest in it whatsoever. The one built by King Herod in Messiah's time soon became **a house of merchandise** (John 2:16) and **a den of thieves** (Matthew 21:13); and as Daniel had foretold: **For the overspreading of their abominations, he shall make it desolate** (Daniel 9:27). The Messiah repeated that prophecy, saying, **Behold, your house is left unto you desolate** (Matthew 23:38). And forty years later the temple building was laid even with the ground, and that was the end of the matter concerning an earthly temple building as far as God was concerned.

2. <u>WHAT IS "THE DAY OF THE LORD"?</u>
The term is used two ways in Scripture. In the Old Testament it refers to God's judgments upon the unfaithful Israelites; while in the New Testament it refers to God's judgment upon unbelievers at the second coming of our Lord. It is equivalent to the contemporary expression: A DAY OF RECKONING.

Alas for the day! For THE DAY OF THE LORD is at hand, and as a destruction from the Almighty shall it come . . . sound the alarm in my holy mountain: let all the inhabitants of the land tremble: for the DAY OF THE LORD cometh, it is nigh at hand; a day of darkness, of clouds and thick darkness . . . for THE DAY OF THE LORD is great and very terrible; who can abide it (Joel 1:15, 2:1-2, 11)?

These verses, and many others in Joel and other Old Testament prophets, relate to the many times when God allowed armies from neighboring kingdoms to plunder the Israelites. In fact, many of the prophets said that God sent those forces to execute judgment upon the unfaithful Hebrews. This was particularly true regarding the Assyrians who conquered Samaria (Israel) and took captive the soldiers and upper classes of people; and of the Babylonians who later did likewise to the Judaeans. THE DAY OF THE LORD refers to times when God allowed these judgments to come.

Joel is one of the very few Old Testament prophets through whom God revealed events related to both the first coming and also the second coming of the Messiah. On the day of Pentecost, Peter told the multitude that the outpouring of the Holy Spirit which they had experienced was **that which was spoken by the prophet Joel: it shall come to pass in the last days** [of the Old Covenant period], **saith God, I will pour out of my Spirit upon all flesh** (Acts 2:17, quoted from Joel 2:28). But then the prophecy leaps ahead to the second coming of the Lord: **I will show wonders in the heavens above and signs in the earth beneath . . . the sun shall be turned into darkness and the moon into blood before that great and terrible DAY OF THE LORD comes** (Acts 2:19-20 quoted from Joel 2:30-31).

In the Old Testament, THE DAY OF THE LORD had to do with God's judgments upon the unfaithful Israelites, while in the New Testament it refers to the time **when the Lord Jesus shall be revealed from heaven with His mighty angels, in flaming fire taking vengeance on them that know not God and obey not the gospel** (II Thessalonians 1:7-8). Paul had already told those saints **that THE DAY OF THE LORD so cometh as a thief in the night; for when they shall say "peace and safety," sudden destruction cometh upon them, as travail upon a women with child** (I Thessalonians 5:2-3).

True believers in Christ will have been caught up to be **with the Lord** before that judgment falls upon unsaved sinners, as the Apostle assured his fellow saints, **But ye, brethren, are not in darkness, that that day should overtake you as a thief** (I Thessalonians 5:4).

In the New Testament **THE DAY OF THE LORD** is also called **THE DAY OF CHRIST** (II Thessalonians 2:2; Philippians 1:10, 2:16), the **DAY OF WRATH** (Romans 2:5) and the **DAY OF JUDGMENT** (I Peter 3:9, 1 John 4:17). Among early Christians it was so important that they often referred to it simply as **THAT DAY** (I Timothy 1:12, 1:18, 4:8).

To summarize: under the Old Covenant **THE DAY OF THE LORD** was a term to denote God's impending judgment upon the Israelites who could not keep His law in their own strength, but under the New Covenant it refers to the second coming of the Messiah to reward His victorious saints who have been triumphant through the power of His Holy Spirit working in them, and to punish unbelievers who have persecuted His servants.

3. <u>WHO ARE THE DESCENDANTS OF ABRAHAM, ISAAC AND JACOB?</u>

There aren't any living today. No pure-blooded natural descendants, that is.

After four thousand years they have all become mixed with people of other nations. And millions of people from other nations have converted to Judaism and are now included among those we call "the Jewish people." Multiplied thousands from many nations became Judaeans when Esther was Queen of Babylon (Esther 8:17). None were related to the "twelve tribes of Israel."

Thousands more from other nations were converted to Judaism through missionary activities begun during the CENTURY OF RESTORATION inaugurated by the Maccabees in 165 B.C. and continued during the century of peace imposed by the Romans 63 B.C. to 66 A.D. Flavius Josephus, the First Century Hebrew historian, wrote of how many thousands of proselytes from all over the Roman Empire would visit Jerusalem each year as pilgrims. He thus confirmed the biblical record: **Visiting in Jerusalem were devout men from every nation under heaven** who asked, **How hear we every man in our own tongue wherein we were born? Parthians, Medes, Elamites, dwellers in Mesopotamia, Cappadocia, Pontus, Asia, Phrygia, Pamphylia, Egypt, Libia, Rome,** also **Cretes and Arabians** (Acts 2:5, 8-11). The fact that the mother tongue of these pilgrims was not Hebrew is convincing evidence that many were from families that had converted to Judaism. The record in Acts 2:10 states only that they were both **Judaeans and proselytes.**

Then in the Seventh Century probably two million Judaeans and Samaritans became Muslims. Today their descendants are called "Palestinians." In the Eighth and Ninth Centuries two or three million Ashkenazim people converted to Judaism in Khazaria, and later migrated to Russia, Europe and America to be known as "the Yiddish people." Their descendants today number about ten million.

It is possible that some, but definitely not all, of the Sephardim (who call themselves "the real Jews"), originally of Spain and Portugal, are distantly related to the original Hebrews. But even they are not pure blooded and make up only about ten percent of all Jewish people. The largest ethnic group who may possibly be descended from Abraham, Isaac and Jacob are the people we call "Palestinians," whose Hebrew ancestors converted to "Christianity" between 30 and 630 A.D., and to Islam in the Seventh Century. But they also have inter-married and comingled with other nationalities during the past 1900 years; so it would be hard to say how many are "the seed of Abraham."

Of the fifty or more nationalities who are called "Jewish people" today, I seriously doubt that even one percent are descendants of Abraham, Isaac and Jacob. No people on earth today can say for sure that they are descended from them in a biological sense. But millions can be counted as **the seed of Abraham**, nevertheless, because they belong to Christ. **Now to Abraham and one of his descendants were the promises made. He saith not, and to descendants (plural) as of many: but to your descendant (singular), which is Christ** (Galatians 3:16). Abraham had many sons, but all of God's promises went through just one: Isaac. But physical generation produced rebellious sinners whom God cast out, just as Abraham's son Ishmael was cast out (Galatians 4:30). So Christ was the new Isaac, through whom God started over to gain a new line of descendants for Abraham who were born not of the flesh but of the Spirit. Among these **There is neither Judaean nor Greek, there are neither slaves nor free, there is neither male nor female: for all are one in Christ Jesus. And if ye be Christ's, then are ye Abraham's seed and heirs according to the promise** (Galatians 3:28-29).

4. <u>THEN WHO OWNS PALESTINE?</u>

First of all we must clarify the meaning of the term. **PALESTINE** is the Bible name for all the land area bordering the eastern end of the Mediterranean Sea. **What have ye to do with me, O Tyre and Zidon, and all the coasts of Palestine?** (Joel 3:4). Following the reign of Solomon, the Hebrews divided their land, which had been consolidated by King David, into two regions: Judaea and Samaria. But the two areas combined were spoken of as **PALESTINE. Sorrow shall take hold of the inhabitants of Palestine** (Exodus 15:14). **Rejoice not thou, whole Palestine, because the rod of him that smote thee is broken . . . thou, whole Palestine, art dissolved** (Isaiah 14:29, 31). The land areas that came to be called Judaea, Samaria and Galilee combined make up what

294

the Bible calls **whole Palestine**.

But when God originally called Abraham to go there, it was called the land of Canaan because it was inhabited mainly by the descendants of Canaan, the son of Ham. Canaan's sons produced numerous tribes: the Jebusites, Amorites, Girgasites, Hivites, and others. Sidon, Canaan's oldest son, settled on the seacoast where the city that bore his name stood for centuries. When, in response to a divine call, Abram migrated from the land of the Chaldees to the land of the Canaanites, God promised him, **Unto thy seed will I give this land** (Genesis 12:7). Later, Abram divided some of the land with his nephew, Lot. He gave the valley of the Jordan river to Lot and retained the hill country west of that valley. Then God spoke to him again, **From the place where you are standing look northward, southward, eastward and westward: all the land that you see I will give to you and to your seed forever** (Genesis 13:14-15). Based on his visibility, that would have been a relatively small area, at most thirty miles square. But later the promise was enlarged to include not only **all the land of Canaan** (Genesis 17:8) but a territory **from the river of Egypt** [the Nile Delta] **unto the great river, the river Euphrates** (Genesis 15:18).

Today that would include part of Egypt, all of Palestine, part of Syria, all of the Hashemite Kingdom of Jordan, part of Saudi Arabia and half of Iraq. Some evangelical Christians who promote political Zionism insist that all of these territories belong to "Israel" and are committed to making it happen, even if it brings on a world war and causes the genocide of millions of indigenous people living in the area between Egypt and the Euphrates river.

The larger question is, however, who are the **seed of Abraham** today? I have already explained that the vast majority of "the Jewish people" are not biologically related to Abraham. Most are the Ashkenazim who are descended from the original residents of Khazaria in southern Russia. Many of the native Palestinians, on the other hand, are descended from the ancient Hebrews who converted to Christianity and Islam. Does not God's promise to Abraham apply to them? And the 144,000 Israelites whom God called during the forty years, 30-70 A.D., are their descendants still heirs to God's promise?

The answer to all these questions was revealed to the Apostle Paul. **All the promises of God in Christ Jesus are yea and amen** (II Corinthians 1:20). The Messiah was the new Isaac. God made a clean break with the past and started over with **JESUS, the son of David, the son of Abraham.** Unregenerate Israelites were **broken off the olive tree** and not counted as the seed of Abraham any more, as Moses had foretold would happen to those who failed to keep God's law. **But Christ has redeemed us from the curse of the law, being made a curse for us . . . that the blessing of Abraham might come on all nations through Jesus Christ . . . and if ye be Christ's, then are ye Abraham's seed and heirs according to the promise** (Galatians 3:13-14, 29). Palestine, and the rest of the world also, belongs to the Messiah, who **in His times will show who is that blessed and only potentate, King of all kings and Lord of all lords** (I Timothy 6:15). And the only people who could make a claim to Palestine today (based on biblical promises) are those who are children of God through faith in Christ.

5. BUT WHAT ABOUT THE "FOREVER" PROMISES IN GENESIS?

They were conditional, as God revealed through Moses in Deuteronomy. The giving of the **LAW** made clear once and for all that God's promises are canceled if His people fail to keep His commandments.

And the Lord said unto Abram, All the land which thou seest, to thee will I give it, and to thy seed forever (Genesis 13:14-15). **I will give unto thee, and to thy seed after thee, the land of Canaan for an everlasting possession** (Genesis 17:8). **I will give this land to thy seed after thee for an everlasting possession** (Genesis 48:4).

Today, 4000 years later, evangelical Zionists foolishly say that these promises still apply to "the Jewish people," 99% of whom are not directly related biologically to Abraham, Isaac and Jacob. In so doing they not only ignore the facts of history but also blatantly disregard the conditions which God laid down when He gave the LAW through Moses. **If thou wilt not observe to do all the words of this law that are written in this book . . . ye shall be plucked from off the land whither thou goest to possess it. And the Lord shall scatter thee among all nations, from one end of the earth even to the other** (Deuteronomy 28:58, 64). **As the Lord rejoiced over you to multiply you, so the Lord will rejoice over you to destroy you, and to bring you to nought** (Exodus 28:63). **Therefore the Lord was very angry with Israel, and removed them out of His sight. And the Lord rejected all the seed of Israel until He had cast them out of His sight . . . so was Israel carried away out of their own land to Assyria unto this day** (II Kings 17:18, 20, 23).

When God told Abraham **To thy seed will I give this land**, not all of his **seed** were included. He had six sons by his wife **Keturah**, but they were **broken off the olive tree** of Abraham's seed. Likewise his son **Ishmael** didn't count, or his grandson **Esau**. The inheritance was narrowed down at that time to **Jacob (Israel) and his twelve sons**, but that also was temporary. God started over again when the promised Messiah, **the son of David, the son of Abraham** came into the world to **redeem them that were under the law**. Christ was the new Isaac, and through Him alone **would the seed be called.** All who accepted Him were included in God's **New Covenant**. Those who rejected Him were **broken off the olive tree** and not counted as the **seed of Abraham** any longer.

God made it very clear through Moses that His promises to Abraham, Isaac and Jacob concerning their inheritance of the land of the Canaanites was conditional. Failure to keep His law forever disqualified their descendants from having any claim to the possession of that land. Those who teach things contrary to this fact do so in contradiction of God's clear revelation through Moses as well as through the Messiah and His apostles.

6. <u>SHOULD WE PREACH THE GOSPEL TO THE JEW FIRST?</u>

That's not what the Scripture says. Rather, **the gospel must**

FIRST be published among ALL NATIONS (Mark 13:10).

What the Apostle Paul said was that **the gospel of Christ is the power of God unto salvation to every one that believeth; unto the Judaeans first, and also to the Greeks** [other nations] (Romans 1:16). Some of the Judaeans, and some other Israelites, had been used by God for 2000 years to receive His message and communicate it to other nations. The **gospel of Christ** was the culmination and conclusion of that message, so quite naturally it should begin with the Judaeans, temporarily. **When the Judaeans saw the multitudes, they were filled with envy, and spake against those things which were spoken by Paul, contradicting and blaspheming. Then Paul waxed bold, and said, It was necessary that the word of God should FIRST have been spoken to you: but seeing ye put it from you, and judge yourselves unworthy of everlasting life, lo, we turn to other nations** (Acts 13:45-46).

Let me repeat: **The gospel must FIRST be published among all nations.** For the past 1978 years, our Lord's number one priority has been that His gospel might be preached among those people (nations) and in those places where as yet He has no people for His name.

7. SHOULD WE PRAY FOR THE PEACE OF JERUSALEM?

Yes. And also for peace in Chicago. And London. And Baghdad. And all other cities. But there is no biblical reason why we should be more concerned about Jerusalem than we are about other places.

King David gave us the Psalm: **Pray for the peace of Jerusalem** (Psalm 122:6) and then abrogated that prayer in Jerusalem by taking Bathsheba into a bed of adultery and killing her husband, Uriah. As judgment for his heinous crime, God told David, **The sword shall never depart from thine house . . . I will raise up evil against thee** (II Samuel 12:10-11). Shortly thereafter David had to flee for his life from Jerusalem to escape being killed by his own son, Absalom; and there has been precious little peace in Jerusalem during the three thousand years since that time. God gave forty years respite until David's son Solomon had completed the temple in Jerusalem, and then all hell broke loose. Ten (counting Joseph as two) tribes revolted against Solomon's son Rehoboam and set up a rival kingdom in Samaria with Jereboam as king. The two kingdoms then fought each other for more than two hundred years. There was no peace in Jerusalem after that time, except for short intervals.

Jerusalem was the place which God chose **to put His name there**. But that was temporary until the Messiah came and began to build God's temple out of **living stones**, not just in Jerusalem but **among all nations**. The temple in Jerusalem served no other purpose after the **Lamb of God** was sacrificed, so God had it destroyed in 70 A.D. In 132 the site of the temple was completely cleared by the Romans and has been vacant ever since except for a big mosque and the Dome of the Rock shrine built there by the Muslims after they won over Jerusalem in 637.

Our Lord and Saviour did not **pray for the peace of Jerusalem**. Rather, He wept over the city, crying, **O Jerusalem, Jerusalem, thou that killest the prophets, and stonest them which are sent unto thee . . . the days shall come that thine enemies shall cast a trench about thee, and keep thee in on every side, and shall lay thee even with the ground, and thy children within thee** (Matthew 23:37, Luke 19:43-44). Jerusalem today is still populated almost entirely by unsaved people, and we should pray for them that they might be saved. But in the sight of God they are no different than unsaved souls in Beijing or Tokyo or Moscow or Los Angeles. All need Christ equally.

8. IS THE COMING OF ISLAM FORETOLD IN REVELATION?

Yes, in several places. One concerns **a great star from heaven burning as it were a lamp, and it fell upon the third part of the rivers, and upon the fountains of waters; and the name of the star is called APSINTHOS** [Greek word], **and a third part of the waters became *apsinthos*; and many men died of the waters, because they were made bitter** (Revelation 8:10-11). *Apsinthos* was an herb that grew around the eastern Mediterranean area in Bible times, and if added to water no one could drink it. The **water of life** (John 4:14, Ephesians 5:26, Revelation 22:17) in the New Testament is the Word of God. The sayings of Muhammad, written down as the Qur'an, changed many things that had been previously written in the Bible.

The Bible says that the Lord Jesus was the Son of God incarnate, that He died for our sins as He bore our sins in His own body upon the cross. The Qur'an speaks often about Jesus the Messiah, virgin-born son of Mary, but denies that He is the Son of God. It also implies that He never died, but that God took Him alive into heaven, and that another was crucified in His place. So in the Qur'an there is no blood atonement offered for sins. The Bible teaches salvation by grace through faith, not by works; the Qur'an teaches salvation by works.

Millions of professing Christians accepted Islam in the Seventh Century, and died spiritually. And a third part of the **rivers** and **fountains** (Christian teachers), and at least one third of all professing Christians were made *Apsinthos* by Islam. So it is easy to see what is meant by the "star" that changed the waters, since much of Christendom was converted to Islam in the Seventh Century.

About seventy years ago one of the most prominent preachers and teachers of Islam in what is now Pakistan was a man named Abdul Haqq. He read the New Testament so he would know how to oppose the Christians, but it spoke to his heart and he became a believer in Christ. When I met him around 1960 he was being greatly used of the Lord to preach Christ among Muslims in Pakistan and India. He told me that God allowed the coming of Islam as His judgment upon the apostate churches that had fallen away from Christ and His Word.

9. WHO ARE THE KINGS OF THE EAST AND HORSEMEN FROM EUPHRATES?

Interspersed throughout the Psalms and Old Testament prophets are short statements or symbols that foretell future events, especially those related to the coming Messiah. Likewise, in Revelation there are frequent short references to future events, usually written in mysterious symbolism. Here is an example: **Loose the four angels that are bound in the great river Euphrates . . . which were prepared for an hour, and a day, and a month, and a year, for to slay the third part of men. And the number of the horsemen were two myriads of myriads** (Revelation 9:14-16). The translators of the King James version translated the Greek word *myriads* as "thousands," but the word for thousand is *chilias*, as in Revelation 20:6. *Myriad* in Greek simply means *innumerable*, as it does in English. This prophecy is repeated later as: **The sixth angel poured out his vial upon the great river Euphrates, and the waters thereof were dried up, that the way of the kings of the east might be prepared** (Revelation 16:12).

Both of these prophecies foretell the migration of hordes of warlike tribes from Asia into Europe and the Mediterranean area over a period of several hundred years. In a Medieval European history class at the University of Virginia in 1943, my textbook was written jointly by J. W. Thompson and E. N. Johnson and published by W. W. Norton Co. of New York in 1937. While reading it I was astounded at the similarity of the language used by historians and that of Revelation. They wrote, *The Huns,* [originally from Mongolia] *fiercer than ferocity itself, a race of men hitherto unknown, suddenly descended like a whirlwind, as if they had risen from some secret recess of the earth, were ravaging and destroying everything that came in their way. They practically lived on horseback; there was not a person in the whole nation who could not live on his horse day and night. They terrorized the Germans by their sudden, fierce, unexpected appearances, led by their great king, Attila.* [Then came the Visigoths who] *poured across the river day and night without ceasing. The man who wished to ascertain their number might as well attempt to count the waves of the African Sea, or the grains of sand tossed about by the zephyrs.*

Another horde of horsemen were the Magyars, who plundered Europe for two centuries. But the greatest of them all was the murderous army of Genghis Khan which conquered most of Asia, Russia and Eastern Europe around the year 1200. The Mongolian horsemen with Genghis were said to have been responsible for the deaths of more than five million people.

Although horrible suffering was caused by these migrations of warriors, they served to open lines of communications between east and west, and some among all these tribes, even the plundering Vandals, eventually professed faith in Christ. Throughout history, most of humanity has tended to rob and kill other human beings who were not part of a given tribe or ethnic group. These ongoing tragedies have served to show that all men are sinners who desperately need the redeeming grace of God in Christ. And the Apocalypse forewarned the churches that great tribulation lay ahead for all men everywhere so those who had heard or read it were prepared when times of killing and destruction were brought upon them by millions of invaders from Asia.

Chapter 25

How Do We Know Who Has It Right?

G od's word says, **We know in part** (I Corinthians 13:9). No one knows it all, and those who say they do probably teach more errors than the rest of us.

As I have mentioned earlier, God has arranged things so that we begin the Christian faith as newborn babes in Christ. All of us are born into this world dead to God because **by one man sin entered into the world and death by sin, so death passed upon all men because all have sinned** (Romans 5:12). That's why our Lord Jesus said, **Ye must be born again** (John 3:7) or **made alive. Even when we were dead in sins, God has made us alive** (Ephesians 2:5). Our former self, our old life, must be crucified, dead and buried. Then we start all over again **being born again . . . as newborn babes** (I Peter 1:23, 2:2).

So, **except ye be converted, and become as little children, ye shall not enter the kingdom of God** (Matthew 18:3). And those who fail to turn loose of the humanistic baggage of their former life are destined to remain as spiritual babies even though they may be members of Phi Beta Kappa and hold Ph.D. degrees. Likewise, any who further indulge their carnal nature are likely to be still born. To **be converted** involves complete repentance: **laying aside all malice and all guile, and hypocrisies and envies and all evil speaking, as newborn babes desire the sincere milk of the word, that you may grow thereby** (I Peter 2:1-2).

Members of the church at Corinth were involved in fighting with each other, committing adultery and fornication, visiting idol temples and other carnal practices that hindered their growth. **I could not speak unto you as unto spiritual, but as unto carnal, even as unto babes in Christ. I have fed you with milk, and not with solid food: for hitherto ye were not able to receive it** (I Corinthians 3:1-2).

Likewise, most of the Hebrew congregation in Jerusalem failed to grow because they would not turn loose of their Old Covenant traditions. The Apostle Paul wanted to explain to them how the temple priesthood practiced by descendants of Aaron had been succeeded by the Messiah, **called of God a high priest forever after the order of Melchisedec. Of whom we have many things to say and hard to be uttered, seeing ye are dull of hearing. For when by this time you ought to be teachers, you need someone to teach you again the first principles of the oracles of God; and are become such as have need of milk, and not of solid food. For everyone that uses milk is unskillful in the word of righteousness, for he is still a baby. Solid food belongs to those who have grown to maturity** (Hebrews 5:10-14).

Today we have a plethora of would-be prophecy teachers who are like those spiritual babies in Jerusalem so long ago. By holding on to Old Covenant traditions which God discarded, they have protracted their spiritual childhood to the point that they are almost blind to things which were revealed under the New Covenant when the Messiah came and started over.

But none of us will ever **grow in grace and knowledge** (I Peter 3:18) to the point where we know it all. The truth of God is infinite and inexhaustible. There is no limit to how much we can grow. One of the most brilliant minds who ever lived was Sir Isaac Newton, who was the first to discern how the planets are held in orbit by an invisible force which he called "gravity." He devoted a great deal of his time late in life trying to understand the book of Revelation. But he didn't get the half of it. Nor has anyone else understood it all. Even the most brilliant of scholars will always have more room to grow.

One reason is because God keeps Himself invisible to us, and our knowledge of Him and His creation is like seeing a reflection. **We behold as in a mirror the glory of the Lord** (II Corinthians 3:18). **Now we see as in a mirror, dimly** (I Corinthians 13:12). Therefore **we know in part** (I Corinthians 13:9). None of us will have all the answers until we are **with the Lord** and see Him **face to face: now I know in part; but then shall I know as well as He knows me** (I Corinthians 13:12). Then we will **put away the childish things** we are teaching now because our Lord will tell all of us what really happened in ages gone by as well as between now and when we see His face.

Let's consider an example of one mystery reflected in the mirror of God's word, and concerning which I have read at least a dozen completely different interpretations. It's found in Revelation 11:3-12.

I will give to my two witnesses [Greek: martyrs]. We are not told what is given. **And they shall prophesy 1260 days, clothed in sackcloth.** If these are literal days they would refer to **the days of vengeance**, the time of **great tribulation** from 66-70 A.D. If they indicate 1260 years, they would refer to the period from the **falling away** to the Reformation.

These are the two olive trees. This relates back to the same image in Zechariah: **Behold a candlestick of gold, with a bowl on top of it . . . and two olive trees by it . . . Knowest thou what these be? This is the word of the Lord saying, Not by might, nor by power, but by my Spirit, saith the Lord** (Zechariah 4:2-6).

If any man hurt them, fire proceeds out of their mouth and devours their enemies. This seems similar to our Lord at His second coming: **Out of His mouth goes a sharp sword that with it He should smite the nations** (Revelation 19:15).

These have power to shut heaven, that it rain not in the days of their prophecy. This is similar to the power of Elijah who **prayed earnestly that it might not rain: and it rained not on the earth for three years and six months** (James 5:17). **And have**

power over waters to turn them to blood [as Moses did the Nile], **and to smite the land with plagues as often as they will** [as Moses did in Egypt]. The parallel to Moses and Elijah seems significant here.

And when they have finished their testimony, the beast that ascends out of the bottomless pit shall make war against them, and shall overcome them, and kill them. If the beast is an empire, it would seem strange to **make war** against only two people, so if the witnesses are human they must represent two groups or bodies of people. This seems especially evident since the conquest is in two stages, first **overcoming** (conquering) and then **killing** them.

And their dead bodies shall lie in the street of the great city, which spiritually is called Sodom and Egypt, where also our Lord was crucified. This can only mean Jerusalem, which both Isaiah and Ezekiel called **Sodom** (Isaiah 1:10, Ezekiel 16:48), and concerning which Paul said **Jerusalem which is now in bondage with her children** (Galatians 4:25). He was comparing it to the time the Hebrews were in bondage in Egypt. So the death of the two witnesses has some relevance to the city of Jerusalem prior to its destruction 66-70 A.D., especially since it was the place **where our Lord was crucified.**

And they of the people and kindreds and tongues and nations shall see their dead bodies three days and a half, and shall not suffer their dead bodies to be put in graves. And they that dwell upon the earth [land] **shall rejoice over them, and make merry, and shall send gifts to one another; because these two prophets tormented them that dwelt upon the earth.** Does this sound like Christmas time? And how could it include so many people in just three and a half days? And what's the point of sending gifts to celebrate someone's death? Can you decipher this?

After three days and a half the Spirit of life from God entered into them, and they stood upon their feet; and great fear fell upon them which saw them. And they heard a great voice from heaven saying unto them, Come up hither. And they ascended up to heaven in a cloud; and their enemies beheld

them.

So who are these two witnesses? As I said, I have books that offer more than a dozen different answers, but not one of them fits the complete text. The easiest solution is to project it all into the future and say, "It hasn't happened yet, but it surely will, just the way it's written." And those who so say insist that it must happen LITERALLY. But does that make sense? If they had flame throwers in their mouths by which they killed others in today's world, they would immediately be shot by police. And what waters would they turn into blood? The Jordan river, perhaps? And dead bodies are all cremated or buried immediately in Israel and Palestine today, unless they are held in a morgue for identification or police investigation. And Jerusalem has not been called "Sodom and Egypt" for almost two thousand years.

Shall I explain what's being communicated by the allegory of the **two witnesses** in Revelation 11, also called the **two olive trees** both in Revelation and in Zechariah? I believe I know the meaning of the mystery, but I prefer not to divulge it here. If I did, then you would want me to explain the meaning of the **seven trumpets** in Chapter 8, the **seven last plagues** in Chapter 15, and the **seven vials of the wrath of God** in chapters 15 and 16. It is not my purpose to attempt an exposition of the entire Apocalypse in this volume. Rather, I have dealt primarily with some popular teachings which I believe are misleading evangelical Christians today, and hurting the cause of Christ.

Multiplied thousands, if not millions, have been diverted from our primary calling, which is to plant a witness for our Saviour in every nation. Now their focus is on unconditional support of political Zionism and political activism on behalf of the state of Israel. To a large extent, evangelical political lobbies were responsible for America launching the unprovoked war against Iraq, and as of this writing they are clamoring for an attack against Iran. The consequences of these actions could be disastrous for the whole world.

Then there is the return to the Old Testament which has

adversely affected the spiritual lives of millions of Christians. And brought dishonor to our exalted Redeemer through the dissemination of teachings which deny the New Covenant. My focus in this book has been an attempt to restore a proper understanding of what happened when **Jesus Christ, the son of David and the son of Abraham** came into this world as the promised **Messiah** and established His kingdom among **ALL NATIONS**, as God has promised through Abraham and the Old Testament prophets.

Nevertheless, in saying these things I wish to emphasize again what I said earlier: **NOW WE KNOW IN PART.** No one has all the answers. Many deep mysteries, symbols and allegories in God's word still remain to be deciphered. No living human being has what the Scripture speaks of as **ALL KNOWLEDGE.** So we need to approach prophecies such as Revelation with deep humility. Likewise, Christians should relate to one another in both love and humility.

Some of the thoughts I have shared in this book were published in an article I wrote for CHRISTIAN MISSION magazine. When one particular Christian leader saw it, he published a vicious attack against me and against Christian Aid Mission in his own magazine. This caused attitudes of hatred and bitterness to be spread around within the evangelical community. Such actions are of the flesh; they are not blessed by the Spirit of God.

In the original Greek, four stages of Christian growth are mentioned in the First Epistle of John: **infants, little children, young men and fathers.** All of us must grow through these stages as we mature in Christ. But what parent would whip one of his children for saying the moon is made out of cheese? All of us go through the baby stage, and each should respect the babies, as well as the level of understanding achieved by others. Rather than spreading hatred toward those who teach differently, we should be compassionate as Paul was toward the Galatians: **My little children, of whom I travail in birth again until Christ be formed in you** (Galatians 4:19). Yet Paul recognized that he also had passed through the baby stage; in fact he was already in it compared to where he would be when he went to be with the Lord: **When I was a child I spoke as a child, I understood as a child, I thought as a child; but when I became a man I put away childish things** (I Corinthians 13:11). **Now we know in part,** but when **He which is perfect** [complete] **is come,** and we see Him **face to face, that which is in part shall be done away** (I Corinthians 13:10).

O the depth of the riches both of the wisdom and knowledge of God! How unsearchable are His judgments and His ways past finding out! For who hath known the mind of the Lord, or who hath been His counselor? For of Him, and through Him, and to Him are all things: to whom be glory forever. Amen. (Romans 11:33-36).

About the Author

Robert Finley is a leading proponent of MISSIONARY ESCHATOLOGY. He says that the key to understanding biblical prophecy is to watch the spread of the gospel to every nation, based on Mark 13:10 **"The gospel must first be published among all nations."** He developed this understanding while traveling for many years as a missionary evangelist throughout North America, then in Europe, Asia, Africa and Latin America. He served with Youth for Christ, InterVarsity Christian Fellowship and the Billy Graham Evangelistic Association until he started his own organizations in 1953 and 1970. He was the founder and first president (for 17 years) of International Students, Inc. (ISI) now based in Colorado Springs. He was also founder and first president of Overseas Students Mission (OSM), and Christian Aid Mission in the U.S. and Canada. His home base is now in Charlottesville where he attended the University of Virginia. In 1944 he was an honor student, president of the student body and undefeated Inter-Collegiate Boxing Champion. He is the author of two other books, *The Future of Foreign Missions* and *Reformation in Foreign Missions.* Christian Aid Mission sends financial support to more than 800 indigenous evangelistic ministries in Asia, Africa, Eastern Europe, and Latin America. They deploy about 80,000 native missionary workers reaching more than 3000 tribes and nations with the gospel of Christ.

Robert Finley
3045 Ivy Road
Charlottesville, VA 22903

rvfinley@gmail.com
www.TheTimeWasAtHand.com